DISCOURSES

WITH

AYATOLLAH ALIRAWANI

THE ROLE OF ISLAM IN OUR LIVES

HAIDAR BAHRELULOOM

THE MAINSTAY FOUNDATION

Author: Haidar Bahreluloom

Printed in the United States.

ISBN: 978-1943393220

In the Name of Allah, the All-beneficent, the All-merciful.

May peace and blessings be upon the Messenger of God,

Muhammad, and his pure family.

To the Master of the Time.

May God hasten his emergence.

Contents

Contents ... *i*

Note on Usage and Spelling ... *iii*

Introduction ... 1

The Search for Truth ... 9

The Noble Quran ... 19

God Almighty ... 41

Divine Leadership ... 75

The Scholars ... 87

The Juristic Process ... 111

The Community ... 153

The Family ... 171

Spiritual Growth ... 185

Mourning Rituals ... 199

Career Choices ... 203

The Twelfth Imam (a) ... 227

Afterword ... 241

Select Bibliography ... *245*

Author Biography ... *247*

Note on Usage and Spelling

We have chosen to standardize usage and spelling in a manner that should be accessible to most readers.

Words that are commonly used in the English language or are defined in a standard English dictionary are used in their common spelling (e.g. Mecca, not Makkah). This applies to some commonly used given names (e.g. Ali, not ʿAli). This is also specifically applied to the word Shia (not Shīʿah).

We have used the IJMES transliteration system, with some notable deviations. The Arabic ta marbutah is rendered *ah* if it is not in the Arabic *iḍāfah* construction. If it is in an *iḍāfah* construction, it is rendered *at* except where it is part of a given name.

All words are rendered in their marfuʿ state where possible.

Elision are rendered only if the elided letter is preceded by a *harf ʿillah* (e.g. *Dhu'l-Hijjah*).

The reader should note that the supplication of ṣalawāt (may God send his peace and blessings upon Muhammad and the household of Muhammad) and salutations (peace be upon them) are usually recited at the mention of the Holy Prophet and his family. This is normally marked in elaborate calligraphy in Arabic text and is marked with (sa) and (a), respectively, in this book. At times, we have dropped the title of some important religious and historical figures. For example, we refer sometimes to Ali rather than Imam Ali. Again, the intent in these instances is to maintain the flow of the book. These decisions in no way are meant to disregard the status and reverence of these individuals.

Finally, we relied on the translation of Ali Quli Qara'i when citing to the verses of the Holy Quran throughout this book, with minor adaptations that allowed us to weave the verses more properly with the rest of the work.

Introduction

We walked out into the narrow allies of the old city.

Leaving the narrow alley, we found ourselves on al-Rasūl Street, bathed in the dazzling glow of the golden dome atop the Shrine of the Commander of the Faithful (a). My companion for the day was none other than my brother in both blood and scholarship, Sayyid Hassan al-Hakeem. With our recent hour-and-a-half conversation with a prominent figure from the Holy City of Najaf fresh in our minds, our destination was clear – we were headed to pay our respects to our beloved Imam (a).

As we strolled along, deep in thought, the Shrine's entrance came into view. Without exchanging a word, we walked in. Facing the sacred resting place of our Imam (a), Sayyid Hassan started the customary supplication, and I followed his lead. Afterward, we found a quiet spot beside the hallowed resting place and settled in.

Sayyid Hassan turned to me, a grin spreading across his face. "That was quite a session, wasn't it? A true blessing from the Commander of the Faithful (a). Our conversation branched into countless discussions. Clear thoughts, profound ideas, and we covered each topic thoroughly. Time flew by."

I couldn't help but return his smile.

"Are you thinking what I'm thinking?" he asked.

"Yes," I replied.

"I'll work on convincing him, and you'll handle the rest," he declared.

"Absolutely! With God's blessings."

Our journey frequently leads us to meetings with the titans of contemporary Shia thought. Each encounter fills us with hope for what lies ahead. As long as luminaries like them continue to guide us, the path remains illuminated.

Yet, a persistent question continues to linger: "How can we share these profound insights with the rest of the world?"

Our recent discussion with one of these remarkable figures provided many answers and left us brimming with inspiration. That particular figure was Ayatollah Baqir al-Irawani.

The Genesis of this Book

This was not our first encounter with the Ayatollah, and it wouldn't be our last. Armed with our questions, we sat down with him once again. His responses were as clear and systematic as ever. This was hardly surprising – his knack for lucid prose and his meticulous approach were widely recognized.

The insights and wisdom of the Ayatollah were too valuable to remain confined to our conversations. It became evident that we had a responsibility to record, translate, and make these enlightening discussions accessible to all who sought to tap into the rich reservoir of knowledge within the Islamic Seminary.

That is the objective of this book: To do just that.

After the Fall

After the fall of the oppressive Saddam regime in 2003, an opportunity

I had long yearned for finally materialized: a visit to the Islamic Seminary in the Holy City of Najaf. For many years, I had maintained correspondence with scholars from this revered institution, benefiting immensely from their wisdom. Now, I stood on hallowed ground, honored to meet them in person.

The dark era of Saddam's rule had cast a shadow over Iraq, particularly the religious and intellectual pursuits in Najaf. During those difficult times, connecting with these scholars was a lifeline for those seeking knowledge and spiritual guidance.

Meeting the Ayatollah for the first time in the Holy City of Najaf was an experience I cherish. I had the privilege of attending one of his seminary courses and witnessed firsthand the dynamic between him and his devoted students. Every educator possesses a distinctive teaching style, and the defining feature of the Ayatollah's approach is the sheer clarity of his prose. With remarkable finesse, he unravels the most intricate and arcane concepts, leaving his audience awestruck by the simplicity and brilliance of his explanations, even in the most complex discussions.

In our frequent visits to the Holy City of Najaf, Sayyid Hassan and I would regularly seek out the Ayatollah to continue drawing from his wellspring of wisdom and insight. His genuine interest in the challenges faced by Shia communities around the world sparked numerous engaging conversations. We would relay the intricacies and nuances of the situations unfolding in our respective communities. With unwavering generosity, he devoted his precious time to provide us with invaluable insight and guidance. His teachings illuminated our path, and his clarity and practical advice served as a compass for our thoughts and questions.

After a particularly enlightening session, an idea began to take shape within us. We were inspired to document these profound conversations, to preserve and share them with a wider audience, enabling others to benefit from the wisdom of this eminent scholar.

Cultivating a strong Shia identity within an individual begins with the nurturing of a robust intellectual foundation. This foundation serves as the launching pad that propels one into the realms of spirituality and emotional connectedness. These, in turn, cast a profound influence on one's actions and behaviors. It is for this very reason that the development of a solid intellectual groundwork is of paramount importance for Shia Muslim individuals. Such a foundation equips them to recognize and confront the challenges of contemporary life, challenges that touch all of us. How we grapple with these challenges hinges on our comprehension and relationship with our faith.

Throughout our interactions with the Ayatollah, his unwavering commitment was to instill in us a profound understanding of our faith. He aimed to ensure that anyone he engaged with comprehended each concept in all of its dimensions. His teaching style emphasized illustrating the interconnectedness of ideas and their deep-seated roots. To him, there are no isolated or disjointed thoughts; everything converges within a holistic and intricately woven system of ideas.

Central to his teachings is the principle of forging a connection with the Almighty through the Noble Quran and the Ahl al-Bayt. He doesn't compartmentalize the intellectual from the spiritual. In his view, a proper understanding and thoughtful approach permeate an individual's spirit, influencing their actions and shaping their relationships with God Almighty, themselves, and their community.

About Ayatollah Shaykh al-Irawani

His Eminence Ayatollah Shaykh Muhammad Baqir al-Irawani is the son of Ayatollah Shaykh Muhammad Taqi al-Irawani. The scion of a scholarly family, his lineage traces back to al-Fāḍil al-Irawani – a nineteenth century scholar, marjiʿ, and a student of Shaykh al-Jawāhirī and Shaykh al-Anṣārī.

Ayatollah Shaykh Muhammad Baqir al-Irawani was born in 1949 in the Holy City of Najaf. He attended school (primary and secondary) at the

Dār al-Nashr Schools, which were led by a group of scholars including Ayatollah Shaykh Muhammad Riḍā al-Muẓaffar.

During his senior year, he began his seminary education and studied under a handful of the esteemed scholars of the Holy City of Najaf. He attended the Advanced Seminars (*al-baḥth al-khārij*) of Grand Ayatollah Sayyid Abulqasim al-Khoei and Shahīd Sayyid Muhammad Baqir al-Sadr. He was one of Shahīd al-Sadr's students at the time of his teacher's assassination at the hands of the Saddam Regime. Ayatollah al-Irawani also attended the advanced seminars in Fundamentals (*uṣūl*) of Grand Ayatollah Sayyid Ali al-Sistani and the advanced seminars in Jurisprudence (*fiqh*), of Grand Ayatollah Sayyid Muhammad Saeed al-Hakeem.

Ayatollah al-Irawani taught Advanced Intermediate Studies (*suṭūḥ ʿulyā*) in the Islamic Seminary of the Holy City of Najaf, including the books of *al-Makāsib*, *al-Rasāʾil*, and *al-Kifāyah*. However, as the Iran-Iraq War drove conditions worse, Ayatollah al-Irawani migrated to the Holy City of Qom. There, he taught Advanced Intermediate Studies for about five years, then began to teach Advanced Seminars in Jurisprudence (fiqh) and Fundamentals (uṣūl).

Many of the seminaries' students in the Holy Cities of Najaf and Qom have attended his seminars. He has also authored several textbooks for seminary students, including:

- *Al-Uslūb al-Thānī li'l-Ḥalaqah al-Thālithah*, a unique commentary on the uṣūl textbook *al-Ḥalaqah al-Thālithah* by Shahīd al-Sadr.
- *Durūs Tamhīdiyyah fi'l-Fiqh al-Istidlālī*, a complete course on applied fiqh, presented in a new and unique way. This book is now studied as a textbook in several seminaries. Ayatollah al-Irawani wrote it to replace a*l-Rawḍah al-Bahiyyah* as a seminary textbook.
- *Durūs Tamhīdiyyah fi'l-Qawāʿid al-Rijāliyyah*, a set of lectures on the principles of authenticating narrators. The Respected

Ayatollah delivered those lectures to the students of the seminary of the Holy City of Qom when he first migrated there.

- *Durūs Tamhīdiyyah fi'l-Qawā'id al-Fiqhiyyah*, a set of lectures on some of the most important and useful principles of fiqh for the seminary student. He delivered those lectures in the Holy City of Qom.
- *Durūs Tamhīdiyyah fī Tafsīr Āyāt al-Aḥkām*, a set of lectures on Quranic commentary to the verses that include divine commands and prohibitions.

In addition to the above textbooks, Ayatollah al-Irawani has also authored the following books for a more general readership:

- *Ḥukm al-Hilāl wa A'māl al-Ḥajj* (The Ruling on the Crescent Moon and the Actions of Ḥajj)
- *Mūjaz Aḥkām al-Ḥajj* (Summary of the Rulings on Ḥajj)
- *Al-Madāris al-Fiqhiyyah wa Marāḥil Taṭawwur Fiqh Ahl al-Bayt (a)* (The Schools of Thought of Fiqh and the Stages of Development of the Fiqh of the Ahl al-Bayt (a))
- *Fiqh al-Bunūk* (The Fiqh of Banks)
- *Al-Imām al-Mahdī (a) bayn al-Tawātur wa Ḥisāb al-Iḥtimāl* (Imam al-Mahdī (a) between Tawātur [of Ḥadīth] and the Calculation of Probabilities)

A Dialogue

This book is the culmination of the extensive series of discussions and sessions we were privileged to have with the esteemed Ayatollah al-Irawani. Throughout our interactions, Ayatollah al-Irawani displayed a remarkable depth of knowledge, offering profound insights into certain subjects and conducting thorough analyses of others. With his gracious consent, we have endeavored to convey his invaluable wisdom and perspectives to English-speaking readers.

In the course of our dialogues, Ayatollah al-Irawani consistently emphasized the importance of referring to the primary sources of

Islamic knowledge when addressing specific issues. His guidance and scholarly expertise have played an instrumental role in shaping the content of this work, ensuring its scholarly rigor and reliability. The meticulous referencing and compilation of the material within these pages are a testament to his commitment to upholding the highest standards of Islamic scholarship and making these insights accessible to a broader audience.

The Search for Truth

Today, Shia Muslims often find themselves in a perpetual intellectual struggle. Amidst the sea of diverse ideas, both beneficial and detrimental, they navigate a challenging course. Some ideas uplift and enrich, while others have the potential to wreak havoc.

Many Shia Muslims look to the Holy City of Najaf[1] and its esteemed Islamic Seminary for guidance and solutions in the midst of this ongoing intellectual conflict.

What guidance would you offer for the personal development of Shia Muslims seeking to strengthen themselves in this enduring struggle?

First and foremost, I want to acknowledge the arduous journey you

---

[1] Najaf, located in modern-day Iraq, is a holy city of paramount importance in Shia Islam. It is renowned as the burial place of Imam Ali (a), the first Imam of Shia Islam and the cousin and son-in-law of Prophet Muhammad (sa). The shrine of Imam Ali (a) in Najaf is a major pilgrimage site and a center of religious scholarship. The city is home to the prestigious Hawza, an Islamic seminary established over a thousand years ago by its founder, Shaykh al-Ṭūsī. This Hawza attracts scholars and students worldwide for the study of Islamic jurisprudence and theology. Najaf, beyond its religious significance, has a rich cultural heritage and historical importance, serving as a hub for scholarly debates during the early Islamic period. Despite facing modern

undertook to stand in the presence of your Imam, the Commander of the Faithful, Ali ibn Abi Ṭālib (a), in the Holy City of Najaf.

I deeply appreciate the profound connection you have forged with this sacred city. Your pilgrimage stands as a testament to the depth of your bond with Najaf and your unwavering determination to nurture it further. This connection is born from your spiritual and emotional affinity with your Imam, which, in itself, reflects your dedication to the intellectual dimension of your faith. It underscores your contemplation of your Imam and the concept of imamate, irrespective of the extent of your understanding of this profound concept.

Am I in Need?

This connection is a tremendous blessing!

It serves as a tangible testament to a profound link with the Almighty. The most paramount connection that any individual must cultivate and nurture is the one with God.

The essence of self-awareness lies in recognizing the depth of your existential connection with the Divine. As you delve deeper and contemplate this connection, you will increasingly comprehend your innate need for God.

رَبِّ إِنِّي لِمَا أَنزَلْتَ إِلَيَّ مِنْ خَيْرٍ فَقِيرٌ

My Lord! I am indeed in need of any good You may send down to me![2]

This realization, "I am in need! I am dependent!" is the foundation of

---

challenges, especially during the era of Saddam, Najaf remains a symbol of resilience, spirituality, and devotion, drawing pilgrims and visitors from diverse backgrounds to experience its religious and historical significance.

[2] The Noble Quran, 28:24.

your success in this life and the next.

True abundance is found in the realization of one's dependence on God. The pinnacle of wisdom is recognizing this fundamental truth. Our journey of personal development commences and culminates with this profound reflection: What is your relationship with God?

Is the Struggle Real?

Intellectual and spiritual battles are omnipresent. A multitude of ideas, often divergent and conflicting, surround you as you embark on your quest for truth. The struggle is real.

You yearn to unravel the essence of your existence. So, ask yourself:

Who are you, truly? Why do you occupy this existence? Which path should you tread in this journey of life to attain the most favorable outcome?

Within the depths of your being, you grapple with profound questions, engaging in an inner struggle of great significance.

In this struggle, you are embodying this verse from The Noble Quran:

وَالَّذِينَ جَاهَدُوا فِينَا لَنَهْدِيَنَّهُمْ سُبُلَنَا - وَإِنَّ اللَّهَ لَمَعَ الْمُحْسِنِينَ

As for those who strive in Us, We shall surely guide them in Our ways, and God is indeed with the virtuous.[3]

You have embarked on a voyage of knowledge and self-discovery, earnestly seeking the truth. This is indeed a genuine "striving towards God." In return, God Almighty has pledged His guidance to you, leading you along His path.

---

[3] The Noble Quran, 29:69.

What is the Divine Promise?

If I were to make a promise to you, there exists a possibility – however minuscule – that I might, for various reasons, fail to honor my commitment. Yet, when it comes to God Almighty making a promise, there is absolutely no room for doubt regarding its fulfillment. It is utterly inconceivable.

Why, you may ask? Because He is God!

He says,

وَالَّذِينَ آمَنُوا وَعَمِلُوا الصَّالِحَاتِ سَنُدْخِلُهُمْ جَنَّاتٍ تَجْرِي مِن تَحْتِهَا الْأَنْهَارُ
خَالِدِينَ فِيهَا أَبَدًا ۖ وَعْدَ اللَّهِ حَقًّا ۚ وَمَنْ أَصْدَقُ مِنَ اللَّهِ قِيلًا

***But those who have faith and do righteous deeds, We will admit them into gardens with streams running in them, to remain in them forever - a true promise of God, and who is truer in speech than God?*[4]**

Pay attention to the last phrase in the verse:

"...who is truer in speech than God?"

God poses this question to humanity, inviting us to contemplate and reflect upon it.

Who could possibly be more truthful than God?

The answer is unequivocal: No one can surpass the absolute truthfulness of God!

Human beings may, at times, falter in keeping their promises due to their limitations, whether it be inability, ignorance, forgetfulness, or dependency on external factors. These deficiencies underlie the breaking of promises.

However, it is inconceivable to attribute any deficiency to the Almighty

---

[4] The Noble Quran, 4:122.

God. This is precisely why it is always...

"a true promise of God."

Read the verse once more. And again. And once more.

With each reading, you'll find yourself drawn closer to it.

Why, you may wonder?

Because it dispels the shadows of ignorance and beckons you towards knowledge and understanding. This verse, among others, guides you from obscurity into the radiance of enlightenment.

In this particular verse, God underscores a fundamental law and principle of creation: the unwavering truthfulness of His promises. In God's promises, there is no room for failure or deficiency.

When God makes a promise, He undoubtedly fulfills it. There is no room for doubt.

Now, what exactly does He promise?

If you do *x*, then *y* will inevitably follow.

Why is it inevitable?

Because the verse says,

"A true promise of God."

His promise is inevitable, certain, and indubitable.

What is the condition precedent to the fulfillment of this promise?

"Those who have faith and do righteous deeds...."

And what inevitably follows the fulfillment of this condition?

"We will admit them into gardens with streams running in them...."

Not only that, but the promise is eternal and everlasting.

"... to remain in them forever."

This is a crucial point.

God's promise is eternal, an unceasing continuum without end.

This perspective should underscore our enduring relationship with the Almighty. It constitutes a genuine, long-term investment.

Each one of us engages with God and seeks to establish a connection while navigating this finite and transient world. Our individual journeys will inevitably conclude at a gravesite.

لَم أُمَهِّدهُ لِرَقدَتي وَلَم أفرُشهُ بِالعَمَلِ الصّالِحِ لِضَجعَتي

[A grave] that I have neither prepared for my long stay nor furnished with righteous deeds for my extended abode.[5]

I must invest in this opportunity while I still can. I must strive to do good and refine my faith in God Almighty. I must strive to be an example of the Quranic verse,

"But those who have faith and do righteous deeds."

Only then will I achieve the inevitable result,

"We will admit them into gardens with streams running in them, to remain in them forever."

A result that is certain without the shadow of doubt because it is

"a true promise of God, and who is truer in speech than God?"

And as the other verse stated,

"As for those who strive in Us, We shall surely guide them in Our ways, and God is indeed with the virtuous."

Strive in the way of God. Seek to know Him and connect with Him. Work towards obeying His commands and fulfilling your obligations towards Him. After all, He is the One who gave and blessed us with

---

[5] Al-Qummī, *Mafātīḥ al-Jinān*, Duʿāʾ Abī Ḥamzah al-Thumālī.

everything we have. With this, speak to God and don't abandon that conversation.

How do we Speak to God?

Speak to God as our Imams have taught us. Stand like Imam al-Ḥusayn (a), as he stood on Mount ʿArafah during Ḥajj. He set a powerful example for his followers in how they should communicate with their Lord. Count all your blessings that God Almighty has graciously bestowed upon you. Say,

وَإِن أَعُدُّ نِعَمَكَ وَمِنَنَكَ وَكَرائِمَ مِنَحِكَ لا أُحصيها، يا مَولايَ

If I count Your bounties, favors, and generous gifts, I will never number them.

O' my Master!

أَنتَ الَّذي مَنَنتَ، أَنتَ الَّذي أَنعَمتَ، أَنتَ الَّذي أَحسَنتَ،

It is You Who bestowed [upon me].

It is You Who conferred favors [upon me].

It is You Who did good [to me].

أَنتَ الَّذي أَجمَلتَ، أَنتَ الَّذي أَفضَلتَ، أَنتَ الَّذي أَكمَلتَ،

It is You Who treated [me] excellently.

It is You Who favored [me].

It is You Who perfected [Your blessings upon me].

أَنتَ الَّذي رَزَقتَ، أَنتَ الَّذي وَفَّقتَ،

It is You Who provided [me] with sustenance.

It is You Who led [me] to success.

أنتَ الَّذي أعطَيتَ، أنتَ الَّذي أغنَيتَ...

It is You Who gave [me].

It is You Who enriched [me]. [...]

تَبارَكتَ وَتَعالَيتَ فَلَكَ الحَمدُ دائِماً وَلَكَ الشُّكرُ واصِباً أبَداً...

Blessed be You and Exalted be You.

So, all praise be to You permanently, and all thanks be to You enduringly and eternally.[6]

This profound connection with God, which we ardently seek to nurture and fortify, forms the bedrock upon which we must construct the entirety of our relationships and the various dimensions of our lives. It is the spiritual anchor that steadies us amid life's storms and guides us through the complexities of existence.

To embark on this journey of deepening our connection with the Divine, we must dedicate ourselves to a rigorous exploration of the Quran, the divine book that serves as a guiding light illuminating our path. We should also delve into the rich treasury of supplications and teachings bestowed upon us by the Ahl al-Bayt, the immaculate household of the Prophet Muhammad (sa). These profound sources offer profound insights into the essence of faith and the means to strengthen our bond with God.

Yet, to navigate the intricate terrain of divine knowledge, we find ourselves in need of the guidance and wisdom of learned scholars. These scholars, who have devoted their lives to the meticulous study of these sacred sources, serve as beacons of understanding and guardians of tradition. By fostering a deep connection with such individuals, we open our minds to a wealth of insight and wisdom.

Through this enriching journey, we not only come to a clearer

---

[6] Al-Qummī, *Mafātīḥ al-Jinān*, Supplication of Imam al-Ḥusayn (a) on Mount ʿArafah.

understanding of our purpose in this world, but also discern our sacred duty to our Creator and His creation. Armed with this knowledge, we are empowered to pursue our life's mission with unwavering determination, striving to fulfill our responsibilities to the highest degree possible.

Our relationship with God, nurtured through study, reflection, and guidance from scholars, serves as the driving force behind our quest for spiritual growth and the fulfillment of our divine purpose. It is the foundation upon which we build our lives, infusing our every action and relationship with the profound sense of purpose that stems from a deep and abiding connection with the Divine.

The Noble Quran

Many of us read and listen to the Noble Quran[7], but for various reasons our relationship with it is weak. What is your advice to someone who may feel this way? Should we continue to read the Noble Quran?

The Noble Quran addresses this matter explicitly. However, before we delve into the intricacies of recitation, let us first contemplate the profound significance of forging a connection with the Quran. God Almighty proclaims,

إِنَّ هَٰذَا الْقُرْآنَ يَهْدِي لِلَّتِي هِيَ أَقْوَمُ

***Indeed this Quran guides to what is most upright.*[8]**

The Noble Quran stands as the fountain of correct thinking, and faith. It imparts the principles of righteous action, ethical behavior, and virtuous conduct. It serves as the comprehensive compendium of law

---

[7] The Noble Quran, also referred to as the Holy Quran or simply the Quran, is the central religious text of Islam and is considered the literal word of God as revealed to the Prophet Muhammad (sa). It holds a unique and sacred position in Islamic faith and practice. The Quran was revealed and is written in the Arabic language. It is composed of 114 chapters, known as Surahs, which vary in length.

[8] The Noble Quran, 17:9.

and knowledge, the ultimate arbiter of right and wrong, the mediator in conflicts and disagreements, and a source of immense pride and strength for the Muslim community.

The Quran's magnificence is such that it is said that merely gazing upon it is an act of worship. Reciting its verses and contemplating their meaning bestow knowledge and insight, while true guidance is found in living according to its teachings. One of God's greatest blessings upon all of humanity is the divine preservation of this sacred book, guarding it against any alteration. The Ahl al-Bayt exerted unwavering efforts and made numerous sacrifices to ensure the preservation of this divine scripture following the passing of the Prophet (sa). Scholars have carried forward this noble legacy, authoring countless volumes on Quranic disciplines, insights, interpretations, recitations, legislation, and history.

What did the Holy Prophet (sa) say about the Noble Quran?

Al-Ḥārith al-Hamadānī, a prominent tābiʿī[9] and a follower of Imam Ali (a), narrates an enlightening interaction he had with the Imam. He entered the mosque and saw people arguing about some Prophetic traditions. He went to Imam Ali (a) and complained, "Do you not see that some people are arguing about [Prophetic] traditions in the mosque?"

Imam Ali (a) responded,

أَمَا إِنِّي قد سَمِعْتُ رَسُولَ الله (ص) يَقُولُ: أَلَا إِنَّهَا سَتَكُونُ فِتَن،

فقلت: مَا المَخْرَجُ مِنْهَا؟

I heard the Messenger of God say, 'There will be calamities [after I pass away].'

[9] A tābiʿī (literally, follower) is an individual who lived in the early days of Islam but did not have any personal interaction with the Prophet (sa). They are therefore not a companion, but a contemporary of the companions.

I said, 'What is the way out of [these calamities]?'

قالَ: كِتابُ الله،

He said, 'The Book of God.

فِيهِ نَبَأُ مَا كان قَبْلَكُمْ، وَخَبَرُ مَا بَعْدَكُمْ، وَحُكْمُ مَا بَيْنَكُمْ، وَهُوَ الفَصْلُ لَيْسَ بِالْهَزْلِ،

In it is news of what was before you, tidings of what will come after you, and judgment amongst you. It is a solemn discourse and not a matter of jest.

مَنْ تَرَكَهُ مِنْ جَبّارٍ قَصَمَهُ الله، وَمَنْ ابْتَغَى الهُدَى فِي غَيْرِهِ أَضَلَّهُ الله، وَهُوَ حَبْلُ الله المَتِينُ،

God will crush any insolent person who abandons it. Whoever seeks guidance from anything else, God will allow them to be misguided. It is God's sturdy rope.

وَهُوَ الذِّكْرُ الْحَكِيمُ، وَهُوَ الصِّرَاطُ الْمُسْتَقِيمُ، هُوَ الَّذِي لاَ تَزِيغُ بِهِ الأَهْوَاءُ، وَلاَ تَلْتَبِسُ بِهِ الأَلْسِنَةُ، وَلاَ يَشْبَعُ مِنْهُ الْعُلَمَاءُ، وَلاَ يَخْلَقُ عَلى كَثْرَةِ الرَّدِّ، وَلاَ تَنْقَضِي عَجَائِبُهُ.

It is the wise reminder. It is the straight path. It is that which hearts do not swerve away from. Neither do tongues confuse its words. Scholars will never tire of it. It is not worn by repetitive reading. Its wonders never cease.

هُوَ الَّذِي لَمْ تَنْتَهِ الْجِنّ إِذْ سَمِعَتْهُ حَتّى قالُوا:

إِنّا سَمِعْنَا قُرْآنا عَجَبًا،

It is that which when the jinn heard it, they said,

"Indeed, we heard a wonderful Quran."[10]

هُوَ الَّذِي مَنْ قالَ بِهِ صَدَقَ، وَمَنْ حَكَمَ بِهِ عَدَلَ، وَمَنْ عَمِلَ بِهِ أُجِرَ، وَمَنْ دَعَا إِلَيْهِ هُدِيَ إِلَى

---

[10] The Noble Quran, 72:1.

صِرَاطٍ مُسْتَقِيمٍ.

It is that which whoever speaks by it is truthful, whoever judges by it is just, whoever acts according to it is rewarded, and whoever calls towards it is guiding towards a straight path.[11]

As believers, we embark on a journey of self-improvement, constantly striving to purify ourselves through self-reflection and inner growth. In this ongoing endeavor, there exists a pivotal key: nurturing and deepening our connection with the Noble Quran. When we do so, the Quran becomes the guiding torch that illuminates our path toward God Almighty and His boundless grace.

To establish a robust and profound connection with the Quran, it's essential to approach this sacred text correctly. Each of us should engage with the Quran with the right mindset and foundational understanding. This means taking deliberate steps to ensure that we approach it with the reverence it deserves and a commitment to learning and understanding its teachings.

Approaching the Quran

But what does it mean to approach the Quran correctly?

It means recognizing that the Quran is not just a book; it's a divine source of wisdom, guidance, and enlightenment. It's a timeless and boundless reservoir of knowledge and spiritual nourishment that has the power to transform our lives.

Approaching the Quran properly also entails humility and an open heart. We must approach it with a sincere desire to learn and grow, setting aside preconceived notions and prejudices. It's about listening with the intent to understand rather than listening just to respond.

---

[11] Al-Dārimī, *Sunan al-Dārimī*, 2:527, Tradition 3332.

Furthermore, seeking guidance from scholars who have dedicated their lives to the study of the Quran can be immensely beneficial. These scholars can provide insights, interpretations, and historical context that can enhance our understanding and appreciation of this sacred scripture.

Building a strong and meaningful connection with the Quran is not just an individual endeavor; it's a lifelong journey that requires the right mindset, humility, and a thirst for knowledge. When we approach the Quran with the proper foundations and understanding, it becomes a profound source of enlightenment, guiding us toward a deeper relationship with God and His eternal blessings.

Numerous Prophetic traditions have provided valuable insights into this vital issue. The Holy Prophet Muhammad (sa) conveyed a profound message when he said:

لَوْلَا أَنَّ الشَّيَاطِينَ يَحُومُونَ عَلَى قُلُوبِ بَنِي آدَمَ لَنَظَرُوا إِلَى مَلَكُوتِ السَّمَاوَاتِ والْأَرْضِ.

> *If it were not for devils surrounding the hearts of the Children of Adam, they would have seen the [unseen] dominions [of God] of the heavens and the earth.*[12]

In this statement, the Holy Prophet (sa) vividly underscores the challenge at hand. He portrays the human heart as susceptible to veiling and sealing, preventing individuals from perceiving the signs and dominions of God. This predicament is exacerbated by the insidious influence of demonic whispers, a force that inhibits the human mind and heart from embracing the divine light.

These whispers, stemming from Satan himself, have the capacity to overpower individuals, thwarting their ability to receive the profound messages embedded within the verses of the Quran. Such interference hinders them from employing these verses in the transformative process

---

[12] Al-Majlisī, *Biḥār al-Anwār*, 60:332.

of self-purification.

Hence, the path to self-purification through the Noble Quran necessitates a fundamental step: the rejection of thoughts and beliefs that shackle the mind and heart. It involves recognizing and repelling the insidious whispers that seek to divert us from the path of enlightenment.

However, it is essential to emphasize that true purification can only be attained when we wholeheartedly embrace the Noble Quran as our guide in life. It is not enough to merely cast aside the impediments to understanding; we must actively incorporate the Quranic teachings into our daily existence.

The Quran is more than just a book of verses; it is a living guide that illuminates our path. It provides the means to navigate the complex journey of self-purification by offering clarity, guidance, and a framework for moral and spiritual development.

Essentially, self-purification through the Noble Quran requires a twofold approach: the rejection of negative influences and the wholehearted acceptance of divine guidance.

By doing so, we embark on a transformative journey, transcending the shackles of doubt and misconception, and emerging as individuals who are truly purified and spiritually enriched by the profound teachings of the Quran.

The Quran as a Guide

What does it mean to take the Quran as a guide?

Embracing the Quran as our guiding light entails wholeheartedly adhering to its every command and embracing its teachings in their entirety. The Prophet Muhammad's (sa) methodology in imparting wisdom to his companions was rooted in instilling the Quranic principles in their lives. They were not only instructed on the Quran's words but also on how to internalize its guidance.

ʿAbdu'l-raḥmān al-Salamī, a narrator of hadith and a reciter of the Noble Quran, born during the lifetime of the Prophet (sa), narrated an enlightening tradition:

حَدَّثَنَا مُحَمَّدُ بْنُ فُضَيْلٍ عَنْ عَطَاءٍ عَنْ أَبِي عَبْدِ الرَّحْمَنِ قَالَ حَدَّثَنَا مَنْ كَانَ يُقْرِئُنَا مِنْ أَصْحَابِ النَّبِيِّ صَلَّى اللَّهُ عَلَيْهِ وَسَلَّمَ أَنَّهُمْ كَانُوا يَقْتَرِئُونَ مِنْ رَسُولِ اللَّهِ صَلَّى اللَّهُ عَلَيْهِ (وآله) وَسَلَّمَ عَشْرَ آيَاتٍ فَلَا يَأْخُذُونَ فِي الْعَشْرِ الْأُخْرَى حَتَّى يَعْلَمُوا مَا فِي هَذِهِ مِنْ الْعِلْمِ وَالْعَمَلِ قَالُوا فَعَلِمْنَا الْعِلْمَ وَالْعَمَلَ.

> *We were told by the companions who taught us that they used to take ten verses from the Messenger of God (sa), but they would not take another ten [verses] until they learn the knowledge and instructions in the former.*[13]

This tradition emphasizes the depth of understanding and practical application that was instilled in the companions by the Prophet himself. It underscores the value of not merely reciting the Quran but internalizing its profound teachings and living by them.

In another tradition, the Prophet (sa) imparted invaluable guidance:

اقْرَأِ الْقُرْآنَ مَا نَهَاكَ، فَإِذَا لَمْ يَنْهَكَ فَلَسْتَ تَقْرَأُهُ.

> *Read the Quran so long as it prevents you [from evil]. If it does not, you are not [really] reading it.*[14]

Here, the Prophet emphasizes the transformative power of the Quran. Reading it should act as a safeguard against sinful behavior and guide us towards righteous conduct. If it is not serving this purpose, our engagement with it requires introspection and recommitment.

Furthermore, the Prophet (sa) emphasized the significance of abiding

---

[13] Ibn Hanbal, *Musnad Ahamd,* Tradition 23482

[14] Al-Rayshahrī, *Mīzān al-Ḥikmah*, 3:2529.

by the Quran's prohibitions when he said:

مَا آمَنَ بِالْقُرْآنِ مَنِ اسْتَحَلَّ مَحَارِمَهُ.

> *One who disregards the prohibitions of the Quran has not [truly] believed in it.*[15]

This profound statement underscores that genuine belief in the Quran goes beyond mere verbal affirmation; it entails a commitment to live in accordance with its moral and ethical guidelines.

In essence, embracing the Quran as our guide means not only reciting its verses, but also internalizing its wisdom, adhering to its commands, and avoiding its prohibitions. By doing so, we honor the profound teachings of the Quran and uphold its transformative power in our lives.

What is a 'Quranic Education'?

Young Muslim men and women need a strong intellectual and spiritual foundation to face the many challenges of contemporary life. How can we build such a foundation based on the teachings of the Noble Quran?

In today's world, there is a significant emphasis on education, often measured by the degrees individuals hold. Knowledge, undoubtedly a virtue, holds the potential to shape and enrich our lives. However, knowledge reaches its pinnacle when it is sharpened by practical insight. Theoretical knowledge serves as a strong foundation, yet its true value emerges when it is transformed into real-world applications. This holds true across the spectrum of learning, and it is especially relevant when we consider the study of the Noble Quran.

To embark on a 'Quranic education' is to embark on a journey of

---

[15] Al-Tirmidhī, *Sunan al-Tirmidhī*, Tradition 2918.

profound transformation. It means constructing one's behaviors, values, and conscience upon the foundation of Quranic principles. Only then can an individual cultivate a Quranic character that permeates their thinking and daily life. In essence, a Quranic education is a commitment to uprightness in conduct, guided by the timeless wisdom and teachings of the Quran.

God Almighty, in His divine wisdom, provides clear guidance in the Quran:

فَاسْتَقِمْ كَمَا أُمِرْتَ وَمَن تَابَ مَعَكَ وَلَا تَطْغَوْا - إِنَّهُ بِمَا تَعْمَلُونَ بَصِيرٌ

So be upright, just as you have been commanded—[you] and whoever has turned [to God] with you—and do not overstep the bounds. Indeed, He watches what you do.[16]

This verse serves as a direct divine command for us to lead lives characterized by uprightness. It calls upon us to stand firm against deviation in all its forms and to uphold the divine values and principles found in the Quran. A Quranic education, therefore, signifies a steadfast commitment to living in accordance with these principles and striving to embody them in every facet of our lives.

In practical terms, a Quranic education equips us with the tools to navigate life's challenges and dilemmas with unwavering moral clarity. It enables us to make decisions that are rooted in righteousness, justice, and compassion, while rejecting any form of deviance or wrongdoing.

Quranic education transcends the acquisition of theoretical knowledge; it embodies the pursuit of a profound transformation in our character and conduct. It is a lifelong commitment to align our actions with the values and principles of the Quran, manifesting God's guidance in our daily lives. This, indeed, is the essence of a Quranic education.

---

[16] The Noble Quran, 11:112.

Making Reading Quran a Habit!

How Do I Make Reading the Quran a Habit?

To foster a profound connection with the Quran, one must make the act of reading it and learning from it a habitual practice. Numerous narrations from our Imams emphasize the paramount importance of this endeavor. Imam al-Ṣādiq[17] (a) conveys this significance with a clear statement:

يَنْبَغِي لِلْمُؤْمِنِ أَنْ لَا يَمُوتَ حَتَّى يَتَعَلَّمَ الْقُرْآنَ أَوْ يَكُونَ فِي تَعَلُّمِهِ.

> *A believer should learn the Quran or be in the process of learning it before they die.*[18]

This directive underscores the critical role of Quranic knowledge in a believer's life and highlights the urgency of acquiring it. The Prophet Muhammad (sa) himself emphasized the value of Quranic learning with the following proclamation:

خَيرُكُم من تعلَّمَ القرآنَ وعلَّمَهُ.

> *The best of you is one who learns the Quran and teaches it.*[19]

This profound statement encourages not only the acquisition of Quranic knowledge but also the sharing of it with others, underscoring

---

[17] Imam Ja'far al-Ṣādiq is a highly important figure in Islamic history, particularly in Shia Islam. He was born in 702 CE (17th of Rabi' al-Awwal in the Islamic calendar) in Medina, Hijaz (present-day Saudi Arabia). He is the sixth Imam of Twelver Shia. Imam al-Ṣādiq was the son of Imam Muhammad al- Bāqir and the great-grandson of Imam Ali ibn Abi Talib and Lady Fatima, the daughter of the Prophet Muhammad (sa). He lived during the Umayyad and early Abbasid caliphates, a period marked by political turmoil and intellectual development in the Muslim world. Imam Ṣādiq played a crucial role in the development of Islamic jurisprudence (fiqh) and theology (ilm al-kalam). He established a prominent school of thought in Medina where he taught a wide range of students, including both Shia and Sunni scholars. Many of his students later became prominent scholars and contributed significantly to the Islamic intellectual tradition.

[18] Al-Majlisī, *Biḥār al-Anwār*, 89:189.

[19] Al-Bukhārī, *Ṣaḥīḥ al-Bukhārī*, Tradition 4739.

its communal and educational dimensions. Imam al-Ṣādiq (a) further illuminates the significance of Quranic engagement:

عَلَيْكُمْ بِتِلَاوَةِ الْقُرْآنِ فَإِنَّ دَرَجَاتِ الْجَنَّةِ عَلَى عَدَدِ آيَاتِ الْقُرْآنِ فَإِذَا كَانَ يَوْمُ الْقِيَامَةِ يُقَالُ لِقَارِئِ الْقُرْآنِ اقْرَأْ وارْقَ فَكُلَّمَا قَرَأَ آيَةً رَقِيَ دَرَجَةً.

You must recite the Quran. Surely, the levels of Paradise are equal to the verses of the Quran. On the Day of Resurrection, the reciter of the Quran will be told, 'Recite and ascend!' For every verse they recite, they will ascend a level.[20]

This vivid metaphor underscores the transformative power of the Quran in elevating the believer's spiritual status.

Additionally, Imam al-Bāqir[21] (a) reports a tradition from the Prophet (sa) that illustrates the profound impact of Quranic recitation:

مَنْ قَرَأَ عَشْرَ آيَاتٍ فِي لَيْلِهِ لَمْ يُكْتَبْ مِنَ الْغَافِلِينَ،

Whoever recites ten verses at night will not be recorded amongst the heedless.

ومَنْ قَرَأَ خَمْسِينَ آيَةً كُتِبَ مِنَ الذَّاكِرِينَ،

Whoever recites fifty verses will be recorded amongst the mindful.

---

[20] Al-Ṣadūq, *al-Amālī*, 441.

[21] Imam Muhammad al-Bāqir, born in 677 CE, is the fifth Imam in Twelver Shia Islam. He was a descendant of the Prophet Muhammad through his father, Imam Ali ibn Husayn. Imam al-Bāqir lived during a tumultuous period in Islamic history when the Umayyad Caliphate ruled, and there was widespread oppression and persecution of the followers of the Ahl al-Bayt (the Prophet's family). History tells that he was present on the Day of Ashura at the Massacre of Karbala, where he witnessed the tragedies befallen while being just shy of four years old. Despite the challenging circumstances, Imam al-Bāqir played a pivotal role in the intellectual and religious development of early Islamic jurisprudence and theology. His school in Medina became a center for religious learning, attracting students and scholars from various backgrounds. His teachings laid the foundation for the Jafari school of thought - named after his son Imam Ja'far al-Ṣādiq - the jurisprudential school of thought in Shia Islam.

ومَنْ قَرَأَ مِائَةَ آيَةٍ كُتِبَ مِنَ الْقَانِتِينَ،

Whoever recites one hundred verses will be recorded amongst the devout.

ومَنْ قَرَأَ مِائَتَيْ آيَةٍ كُتِبَ مِنَ الْخَاشِعِينَ،

Whoever recites two hundred verses will be recorded amongst the servile.

ومَنْ قَرَأَ ثَلَاثَمِائَةِ آيَةٍ كُتِبَ مِنَ الْفَائِزِينَ،

Whoever recites three hundred verses will be recorded amongst the victors.

ومَنْ قَرَأَ خَمْسَمِائَةِ آيَةٍ كُتِبَ مِنَ الْمُجْتَهِدِينَ،

Whoever recites five hundred verses will be recorded amongst the perseverant.

وَمَنْ قَرَأَ أَلْفَ آيَةٍ كُتِبَ لَهُ قِنْطَارٌ مِن تِبْرٍ.

Whoever recites a thousand verses will be given a qinṭār[22] *of gold.*[23]

These traditions highlight the multifaceted rewards and spiritual benefits of engaging with the Quran regularly. It underscores the transformative potential of Quranic learning, which not only enriches the individual but also benefits the community and contributes to their spiritual elevation.

A steadfast commitment to reading, learning, and engaging with the Quran is not only an act of devotion but also a pathway to spiritual growth, enlightenment, and elevated status in the Hereafter. It is a practice that yields both individual and communal rewards, embodying the profound value of Quranic knowledge in a believer's life.

---

[22] A qinṭār is an ancient unit of measurement. -eds.

[23] Al-ʿĀmilī, *Wasāʾil al-Shīʿah*, 6:202.

Reciting The Noble Quran

How should The Noble Quran be recited?

These noble verses tell us the proper etiquette that a believer should have in reciting the Noble Quran.

Seeking God's Protection

God Almighty says,

فَإِذَا قَرَأْتَ الْقُرْآنَ فَاسْتَعِذْ بِاللَّهِ مِنَ الشَّيْطَانِ الرَّجِيمِ

When you recite the Quran, seek God's protection against the accursed Satan.[24]

The verse instructs us to seek God's protection while reciting the Quran. This can be done by repeating the statement as taught in the verse:

"a 'ūdhu bi'llāh mina al-shayṭāni al-rajīm"

(I seek God's protection against the accursed Satan).

The reason for this is likely to repel Satan from the individual's presence while they are reading the Quran. This allows the reader to better understand the detailed concepts and parables that God teaches through His Holy Book.

Tone of Recitation

God Almighty says,

وَرَتِّلِ الْقُرْآنَ تَرْتِيلًا

and recite the Quran in a measured tone.[25]

The verse instructs us to read the Quran in the style of *tartīl*. This means

---

[24] The Noble Quran, 16:98.

[25] The Noble Quran, 73:4.

that we should enunciate properly and read deliberately and slowly. It is also understood as reading in a measured and soothing tone. In one narration, *tartīl* is described as follows:

[التَرْتيل] أَنْ تَتَمَكَّثَ فِيهِ وتُحَسِّنَ بِهِ صَوْتَكَ.

[*Tartīl* is] to take a slow pace and enhance your voice [in recitation].[26]

The Commander of the Faithful (a) said,

بَيِّنْهُ تِبْيَاناً ولا تَهُذَّهُ هَذَّ الشِّعرِ ولا تَنثُرْهُ نَثرَ الرَّمْلِ، ولكن اقرَعُوا بِهِ قُلُوبَكُمُ القاسِيَةَ ولا يَكُنْ هَمُّ أَحَدِكُمْ آخِرَ السُّورَةِ.

Annunciate it clearly. Do not rush it like poetry or scatter it like sand. Use it to knock on your hardened hearts. Do not let finishing the surah be your concern.[27]

Contemplation

God Almighty says,

أَفَلَا يَتَدَبَّرُونَ الْقُرْآنَ أَمْ عَلَىٰ قُلُوبٍ أَقْفَالُهَا

Do they not contemplate the Quran, or are there locks on the hearts?[28]

Imam Ali (a) said in describing the pious believers,

أَمَّا اللَّيْلَ فَصَافُّونَ أَقْدَامَهُمْ، تَالِينَ لِأَجْزَاءِ الْقُرْآنِ يُرَتِّلُونَهَا تَرْتِيلاً، يُحَزِّنُونَ بِهِ أَنْفُسَهُمْ، وَيَسْتَثِيرُونَ بِهِ دَوَاءَ دَائِهِمْ،

During the night they are standing on their feet reading portions of the Quran and reciting it in a well-measured way, creating through it

---

[26] Al-ʿĀmilī, *Wasāʾil al-Shīʿah*, 4:856.

[27] Ibid.

[28] The Noble Quran, 47:24.

grief for themselves and seeking by it a cure for their ailments.

فَإِذَا مَرُّوا بِآيَةٍ فِيهَا تَشْوِيقٌ رَكَنُوا إِلَيْهَا طَمَعاً، وَتَطَلَّعَتْ نُفُوسُهُمْ إِلَيْهَا شَوْقاً، وَظَنُّوا أَنَّهَا نُصْبَ أَعْيُنِهِمْ

If they come across a verse creating eagerness [for Paradise] they pursue it avidly, their spirits turn towards it eagerly, and they feel as if [Paradise] is in front of them.

وَإِذَا مَرُّوا بِآيَةٍ فِيهَا تَخْوِيفٌ أَصْغَوْا إِلَيْهَا مَسَامِعَ قُلُوبِهِمْ، وَظَنُّوا أَنَّ زَفِيرَ جَهَنَّمَ وَشَهِيقَهَا فِي أُصُولِ آذَانِهِمْ

And when they come across a verse which contains fear [of Hell] they bend the ears of their hearts towards it and feel as though the sound of Hell and its cries are reaching their ears.[29]

It Cannot be Touched by the Impure

God Almighty says,

لَّا يَمَسُّهُ إِلَّا الْمُطَهَّرُونَ

no one touches it except the purified ones.[30]

The verse states that the impure cannot touch the Noble Quran. There are various interpretations for this statement. Nonetheless, there is a clear and undisputed rule that a person cannot touch the words of the Quran without first achieving ritual purity.[31]

---

[29] Al-Raḍī, *Nahj al-Balāghah*, Sermon 193.

[30] The Noble Quran, 56:79.

[31] Ritual purity is attained through performing wuḍū˒ or ghusl, depending on the circumstance. The rulings on this are presented in detail in the fiqh manuals of our scholars. -eds.

Listening Attentively

وَإِذَا قُرِئَ الْقُرْآنُ فَاسْتَمِعُوا لَهُ وَأَنصِتُوا لَعَلَّكُمْ تُرْحَمُونَ

When the Quran is recited, listen to it and be silent, maybe you will receive [God's] mercy.[32]

The verse states that when the Quran is recited, we should listen to it attentively.

Should the verse be understood to say that listening attentively to the Quran is a religious obligation (*wājib*)?

Clearly not. Attentiveness is a difficult thing to control for most people. A person may not be able to stop their mind from dallying or daydreaming. Sleep is also hard to control. What happens if a person falls asleep while the Quran is being recited? Suffice it to say our scholars interpret the verse to mean that listening to the Quran is a religiously recommended (*mustaḥabb*) act.

Interpreting the Quran

There is a view that says interpreting the Quran is something that is beyond our purview. Interpretation is reserved for the Ahl al-Bayt, and we cannot exercise our judgements and opinions when reading the Quran. Is this a valid opinion?

There are numerous traditions that convey a similar understanding. Zayd al-Shaḥḥām narrates that Qutādah ibn Duʿāmah once came to Imam al-Ṣādiq (a). The Imam had heard that Qutādah used to interpret the Quran, so he asked him if this was true. Qutādah told the Imam that he did. To that the Imam said,

---

[32] The Noble Quran, 7:204.

وَيْحَكَ يَا قَتَادَةُ، إِنْ كُنْتَ إِنَّمَا فَسَّرْتَ الْقُرْآنَ مِنْ تِلْقَاءِ نَفْسِكَ، فَقَدْ هَلَكْتَ وأَهْلَكْتَ، وإِنْ كُنْتَ قَدْ فَسَّرْتَهُ مِنَ الرِّجَالِ، فَقَدْ هَلَكْتَ وَأَهْلَكْتَ، وَيْحَكَ يَا قَتَادَةُ إِنَّمَا يَعْرِفُ الْقُرْآنَ مَنْ خُوطِبَ بِهِ.

Woe to you, Qutādah!

If you interpreted the Quran from your [personal opinion], then you have perished and led others to perish.

If you interpreted the Quran from the [opinions] of others, then you have [also] perished and led others to perish.

Woe to you Qutādah!

Surely, [only] those addressed in the Quran know it![33]

In another narration Imam al-Riḍā[34] (a) said,

قَالَ اللهُ جَلَّ جَلَالُهُ مَا آمَنَ بِي مَنْ فَسَّرَ بِرَأْيِهِ كَلَامِي.

God Almighty said, 'One who interprets my words with his opinions has not [truly] believed in me![35]

Let us try to understand these traditions one by one.

The first tradition does not mean that we are incapable of understanding the Quran. The narrations are telling us that the

---

[33] Al-ʿĀmilī, *Wasā'il al-Shī'ah*, 18:136.

[34] Imam Ali al-Riḍā is the eighth Imam in Twelver Shia Islam. He was born in 766 CE in Medina, and he is a direct descendant of the Prophet Muhammad through his father Imam Musa al-Kadhim, the seventh Imam. Imam al-Riḍā's mother Najmah was known as a pious woman and was of non-Arab descent. Imam al-Riḍā lived during the Abbasid Caliphate, specifically during the reigns of several Abbasid caliphs, including Al-Ma'mun. One of the significant events in Imam al-Riḍā's life was his nomination as the heir apparent by Caliph Al-Ma'mun, a move that was politically motivated to legitimize his rule and gain support from the Shia community. This appointment forced Imam al-Riḍā's relocation to Khorasan (in modern-day Iran), where he spent a portion of his life. He was eventually poisoned and killed by the same Abbasids, threatened by his growing popularity with the masses. Imam al-Riḍā is buried in Mashhad, Iran. His shrine is one of the largest in Islam and a destination for pilgrims from all over the world.

[35] Ibid, 18:137.

individuals who know the Quran in all its depth and details – its general and specific, abrogating and abrogated, etc. – are those who are addressed in it. Therefore, only the Prophet (sa) and his household have this deep knowledge of the Quran.

As for the rest of us, we can understand the plain, apparent meanings of the Quran. We go back to the Ahl al-Bayt for a deeper level of understanding. But even without reference to the Ahl al-Bayt, we can read the Quran and understand its apparent meanings. As such, these apparent meanings are a divine proof and part of the divine argument upon us. This assertion is backed by several points:

First, the Quran itself commanded us to ponder on its verses. It states,

أَفَلَا يَتَدَبَّرُونَ الْقُرْآنَ وَلَوْ كَانَ مِنْ عِندِ غَيْرِ اللَّهِ لَوَجَدُوا فِيهِ اخْتِلَافًا كَثِيرًا

Do they not contemplate the Quran? Had it been from [someone] other than God, they would have surely found much discrepancy in it.[36]

If the apparent meaning of the verses could not be properly understood and relied upon, the command to contemplate would be meaningless.

Second, the Quran challenges humankind to come up with a chapter like one of its chapters. If the apparent meaning of the verses could not be properly understood and relied upon, this challenge would also be meaningless.

Third, the Prophet (sa) commanded us in numerous traditions to abide by the teachings of the Quran. For example, in the well-known *ḥadīth al-thaqalayn*[37] he said,

---

[36] The Noble Quran, 4:82.

[37] Hadīth al-Thaqalayn is a well-known saying or tradition of the Prophet Muhammad (sa) in Islam. It revolves around the concept of the "Two Weighty Things" or "Two Precious Trusts" and is considered significant, especially within the Shia Islamic tradition. The hadith is reported in various versions in both Sunni and Shia sources, but its core message remains consistent. It

إنِّي تارِكٌ فيكم الثَّقَلَيْنِ أحَدُهما أكبَرُ مِن الآخَرِ كتابُ اللهِ حبلٌ ممدودٌ مِن السَّماءِ إلى الأرضِ وعِتْرتي أهل بيتي وإنَّهما لن يتفرَّقا حتَّى يرِدَا علَيَّ الحوضَ.

I am leaving among you the Two Weighty Things – one of which is greater than the other – the Book of God, a rope extended from the heavens to the earth, and my kindred (ʿitrah), my household. Indeed, the two will never separate until they come back to me at the Pool [of al-Kawthar on the Day of Judgment].[38]

The Prophet (sa) commands us to hold on to God's book. We cannot hold on to and abide by the Quran if its apparent meanings are not proper and valid.

Moreover, the Ahl al-Bayt would always refer their followers back to the Quran and teach them how to benefit from its verses. For example, in an authenticated tradition, *Zurārah*[39] asked Imam al-Bāqir (a) about the method of *wuḍūʾ* (ablution).[40] The Imam responded,

فَعَرَفْنَا حِينَ قَالَ بِرُءُوسِكُمْ أَنَّ الْمَسْحَ بِبَعْضِ الرَّأْسِ لِمَكَانِ الْبَاءِ.

Thus, we knew when He said 'bi ruʾusikum' that wiping should be

---

emphasizes that the Prophet Muhammad (sa) is leaving behind two precious and weighty things (thaqalayn) among his Ummah (community), and as long as Muslims adhere to both, they will never go astray. The two weighty things are described as the Quran and the Ahl al-Bayt.

[38] Al-Tirmidhī, *Sunan al-Tirmidhī*, 13:200.

[39] Zurārah ibn A'yan was a prominent early Islamic scholar and close companion of Imam al-Bāqir, Imam al-Ṣādiq, and Imam al-Kāẓim, the fifth, sixth and seventh Imams of Twelver Shia Islam, respectively. Zurārah is celebrated for his significant contributions to Hadith and Islamic jurisprudence in the Twelver Shia tradition. He collected and transmitted a vast number of Hadith from Imam al-Ṣādiq, playing a crucial role in the development of Twelver Shia theology and jurisprudence. His recorded Hadith can be found in important Shia collections like "*Wasāʾil al-Shīʿah*" by al-Ḥur Al-ʿĀmilī and "al- Kāfī" by Shaykh al-Kulaynī. Zurārah's dedication to learning and close association with the Imams left a lasting legacy in the history of Islamic scholarship and Twelver Shia thought.

[40] Wuḍūʾ is a ritual ablution or purification process in Islam. It involves the act of washing specific parts of the body before certain acts of worship, such as prayer or touching the Quran, to maintain physical and spiritual purity. The body parts washed during wuḍūʾ are the face, hands and arms, and then ritual wiping on the head and feet.

> *for part of the head because of the letter bāʾ.*[41]

In another tradition, a companion asked Imam al-Ṣādiq (a) how he should perform wuḍūʾ when he had a bandage covering part of his foot. The Imam responded,

يُعْرَفُ هَذَا وأَشْبَاهه، مِنْ كِتَابِ اللهِ عَزَّ وَجَلَّ قَالَ اللهُ تَعَالَى: ما جَعَلَ عَلَيْكُمْ فِي الدِّينِ مِنْ حَرَجٍ، امْسَحْ عَلَيْهِ.

> *[The answer to] that and similar [questions] can be known from the book of God Almighty. God Almighty says, 'He has not placed for you any obstacle in the religion.' Wipe over it.*[42]

If the apparent meanings of the Quran were not proper proof in religious issues, the Imams would not have referred their companions back to it in this way. They would have simply said, 'This is the way it is, and we know because the Quran speaks to us.' Instead, we find the Imams teaching us how to read and understand the Quran. This demonstrates that its meanings, at least at an apparent level, are both attainable and valid.

Fourth, the Prophet (sa) and Imams have instructed us that when there is a conflict amongst their traditions, we should refer to the Noble Quran. We should hold on to what conforms to the Quran and reject what contradicts with it. If the apparent meanings of the Quran were not understandable and proper, then these commands would also be rendered meaningless.

Fifth, it is intuitive that we should read and recite the Quran, and we have been instructed to do so by our religious heritage. This also demonstrates that the Quran is understandable. It is absurd to think that

---

[41] Al-ʿĀmilī, *Wasāʾil al-Shīʿah*, 1:290. In Arabic, the letter *bāʾ* can appear at the beginning of a word and act as a grammatical particle. In this usage, the *bāʾ* can impart numerous meanings depending on the context and intent of the speaker. One of those meanings is referred to as *bāʾ al-tabʿīḍ*, which can be translated as 'part of.' Thus, the phrase *wa amsaḥū bi ruʾusikum* in the Quranic verse can be translated as 'and wipe part of your heads.' -eds.

[42] Al-ʿĀmilī, *Wasāʾil al-Shīʿah*, 1:327.

we were commanded to recite the Quran simply as an incomprehensible movement of the tongue. It is also absurd to think that reading and contemplating on the Quran is not something that God wants. These absurd conclusions would be the natural result of the premise that Muslims cannot understand the Quran. Because this premise leads to such absurd conclusions, we deem it to be false.

The second tradition should be clear in its meaning and intent. To understand a verse according to its plain, apparent meaning is not *tafsīr*[43] (interpretation). Tafsīr is an attempt at bringing out the deep and hidden meanings of a text. The apparent understanding does not need someone to interpret it, as it is plain and clear for everyone.

Moreover, the narrations are not forbidding all interpretation. Rather, they specifically prohibit interpreting the Quran in accordance to personal opinion.[44] Again, the apparent meaning of the verse does not fall into this category, as there is no opinion involved in understanding it.

In summary, it is an error to say that the Quran is meant only for those it spoke of directly. We should not allow this misconception to dissuade us from reading the Quran and contemplating its verses. Neither should we be dissuaded by the prohibition against interpreting the Quran

---

[43] Tafsīr, in the context of Islam, refers to the scholarly interpretation and commentary on the Holy Quran. It involves the detailed explanation, clarification, and commentary on the meanings of Quranic verses, as well as their historical, linguistic, legal, and theological aspects. Tafsīr aims to provide a deeper understanding of the Quranic text, its context, and its application to various aspects of life. Islamic scholars and exegetes (mufassirun) have produced numerous tafsir works throughout Islamic history, each offering their insights and interpretations of the Quran. Tafsīr can vary in style and approach, including linguistic analysis, historical context, jurisprudential rulings (fiqh), and spiritual and moral guidance. These interpretations often draw upon various sources, including Hadith, linguistic analysis of Arabic, and the principles of Islamic jurisprudence.

[44] Interpretation according to opinion occurs when the verse is understood in a way different than its apparent meaning while lacking any objective evidence for such an interpretation. The interpreter is thus providing a subjective interpretation based on personal biases, judgments, and preferences.

according to personal opinions and preferences.

God Almighty

You emphasize the significance of nurturing a connection with God through the Noble Quran. Your words suggest a strong emphasis on remembrance of God Almighty in the journey of self-development. How can individuals take further steps to deepen their connection with God Almighty?

God Almighty emphasizes the concept of remembrance in numerous verses of the Noble Quran. He says,

الَّذِينَ يَذْكُرُونَ اللَّهَ قِيَامًا وَقُعُودًا وَعَلَىٰ جُنُوبِهِمْ

Those who remember God standing, sitting, and lying on their sides.[45]

يَا أَيُّهَا الَّذِينَ آمَنُوا اذْكُرُوا اللَّهَ ذِكْرًا كَثِيرًا

O' you who have faith! Remember God with frequent remembrance.[46]

---

[45] The Noble Quran, 3:191.

[46] The Noble Quran, 33:41.

فَإِذَا أَمِنتُمْ فَاذْكُرُوا اللَّهَ كَمَا عَلَّمَكُم مَّا لَمْ تَكُونُوا تَعْلَمُونَ

When you are safe remember God, as He taught you what you did not know.[47]

فَإِذَا قَضَيْتُمُ الصَّلَاةَ فَاذْكُرُوا اللَّهَ قِيَامًا وَقُعُودًا وَعَلَىٰ جُنُوبِكُمْ

When you have finished the prayers, remember God, standing, sitting, and lying down.[48]

فَإِذَا قُضِيَتِ الصَّلَاةُ فَانتَشِرُوا فِي الْأَرْضِ وَابْتَغُوا مِن فَضْلِ اللَّهِ وَاذْكُرُوا
اللَّهَ كَثِيرًا لَّعَلَّكُمْ تُفْلِحُونَ

And when the prayer is finished, disperse through the land and seek God's grace, and remember God much so that you may be felicitous.[49]

The Importance of Remembering God

The Quran places immense importance on the practice of remembering God, and it extends far beyond mere verbal recitations or supplications. True remembrance of God is a continuous state of mindfulness, a way of life for a believer. It involves being ever aware of His presence and guidance, irrespective of one's activities or surroundings.

In this holistic approach to remembrance, a believer remains constantly attuned to God's presence. This means remembering God whether one is sitting or standing, whether transitioning from one task to another, or even when interacting with friends or bidding them farewell. It is an awareness that encompasses moments of gratitude for His blessings, as well as moments of patience during trials and hardships.

This practice does not require isolation or seclusion from society.

---

[47] The Noble Quran, 2:239.

[48] The Noble Quran, 4:103.

[49] The Noble Quran, 62:10.

Instead, it encourages active participation in the world while maintaining a constant connection with the Divine. It is about finding the balance between one's worldly responsibilities and spiritual mindfulness.

The Quranic verses guide us with the directive to "remember God often," without prescribing specific constraints on when, where, or how to remember Him. This open-ended guidance underscores the universal nature of this practice, urging us to infuse every moment, every place, and every situation with mindfulness of God's presence.

Furthermore, some verses specify that we should "remember God, standing, sitting, and lying down," emphasizing the all-encompassing nature of this practice. It transcends the boundaries of physical posture, demonstrating that remembrance is not limited to a particular setting or circumstance; it is a way of life that permeates every facet of our existence.

Nurturing a connection with God Almighty involves the cultivation of a constant and unwavering remembrance, an awareness that transcends the confines of formal rites and rituals. It is a practice that invites believers to engage with the world actively while remaining anchored in the consciousness of the Divine. By embracing this holistic approach to remembrance, individuals can deepen their connection with God Almighty and infuse their lives with spiritual purpose and mindfulness.

One day, Imam al-Ṣādiq (a) was asked about the verse,

كَانُوا قَلِيلًا مِّنَ اللَّيْلِ مَا يَهْجَعُونَ

They used to sleep a little during the night.[50]

He said,

[50] The Noble Quran, 51:17.

كَانَ الْقَوْمُ يَنَامُونَ، ولَكِنْ كُلَّمَا انْقَلَبَ أَحَدُهُمْ قَالَ، الْحَمْدُ لِلَّهِ وَلَا إِلَهَ إِلَّا اللهُ وَاللهُ أَكْبَرُ.

These were people that would sleep at night. However, whenever they turned [and tossed in bed] they would say, 'Praise be to God. There is no god but God. God is the greatest.'[51]

If constant remembrance is a sign of strong faith, then scant remembrance is a sign of weak faith. Rather, it may even be a sign of hypocrisy. God says,

إِنَّ الْمُنَافِقِينَ يُخَادِعُونَ اللَّهَ وَهُوَ خَادِعُهُمْ وَإِذَا قَامُوا إِلَى الصَّلَاةِ قَامُوا كُسَالَىٰ
يُرَاءُونَ النَّاسَ وَلَا يَذْكُرُونَ اللَّهَ إِلَّا قَلِيلًا

The hypocrites indeed seek to deceive God, but it is He who outwits them. When they stand up for prayer, they stand up lazily, showing off to the people and not remembering God except a little.[52]

When Should You Remember God?

Several Quranic verses provide specific guidance on when and how a person should remember God, emphasizing the importance of this practice throughout various moments in our daily lives. One verse instructs the believers to

وَاذْكُر رَّبَّكَ كَثِيرًا وَسَبِّحْ بِالْعَشِيِّ وَالْإِبْكَارِ

Remember Your Lord much and glorify Him morning and evening.[53]

This directive underscores the significance of remembering God both at the beginning and end of each day, encouraging us to commence and conclude our daily routines with mindfulness of His presence. Another

---

[51] Al-ʿĀmilī, *Wasāʾil al-Shīʿah*, 4:1028.

[52] The Noble Quran, 4:142.

[53] The Noble Quran, 3:41.

verse advises the believers:

وَاذكُر رَّبَّكَ فِي نَفْسِكَ تَضَرُّعًا وَخِيفَةً وَدُونَ الْجَهْرِ مِنَ الْقَوْلِ بِالْغُدُوِّ
وَالْآصَالِ وَلَا تَكُن مِّنَ الْغَافِلِينَ

And remember your Lord within your heart beseechingly and reverentially, without being loud, morning, and evening, and do not be among the heedless.[54]

This verse emphasizes the inner aspect of remembrance, highlighting the need for a heartfelt connection with God, characterized by humility and reverence. It calls for a continuous remembrance that transcends mere verbal recitation, fostering a deeper spiritual connection. God also urges us to be patient. He says,

فَاصْبِرْ عَلَىٰ مَا يَقُولُونَ وَسَبِّحْ بِحَمْدِ رَبِّكَ قَبْلَ طُلُوعِ الشَّمْسِ وَقَبْلَ
الْغُرُوبِ، وَمِنَ اللَّيْلِ فَسَبِّحْهُ وَأَدْبَارَ السُّجُودِ

So be patient at what they say and celebrate the praise of your Lord before the rising of the sun and before the sunset, and glorify Him through part of the night and after the prostrations.[55]

Here, we are reminded to exercise patience in the face of challenges while simultaneously engaging in praise and glorification of God during various phases of the day and night.

By combining these verses, we discern a comprehensive framework for remembrance, encompassing the morning, evening, night, and moments after prayer. These timeframes are deliberately broad, encompassing virtually every minute of our 24-hour day. This expansive

---

[54] The Noble Quran, 7:205.

[55] The Noble Quran, 50:39-40.

approach to remembrance emphasizes that there is no moment too insignificant for remembering God and no aspect of our daily lives that should be devoid of His consciousness.

In essence, these Quranic verses provide a roadmap for infusing our daily routines with mindful remembrance of God, encouraging us to maintain an unbroken connection with Him throughout the day and night. It is a call to weave remembrance into the fabric of our existence, allowing us to lead lives enriched with spiritual purpose and profound consciousness of the Divine.

The same can be understood from the following verse:

فَاصْبِرْ عَلَىٰ مَا يَقُولُونَ وَسَبِّحْ بِحَمْدِ رَبِّكَ قَبْلَ طُلُوعِ الشَّمْسِ وَقَبْلَ غُرُوبِهَا
وَمِنْ آنَاءِ اللَّيْلِ فَسَبِّحْ وَأَطْرَافَ النَّهَارِ

So be patient with what they say and celebrate the praise of your Lord before the rising of the sun and before the sunset and glorify Him in parts of the night and at the day's margins.[56]

There is some dispute over what is meant by "the day's margins." Some say it is another reference to sunrise and sunset, and therefore, an emphasis on the earlier part of the verse. Others say that it is correlated to the phrase directly preceding it; "parts of the night." Thus, the meaning would be that a person should begin their remembrance in the late parts of the night and into dawn.

In another verse God says,

---

[56] The Noble Quran, 20:130.

وَاصْبِرْ لِحُكْمِ رَبِّكَ فَإِنَّكَ بِأَعْيُنِنَا وَسَبِّحْ بِحَمْدِ رَبِّكَ حِينَ تَقُومُ

وَمِنَ اللَّيْلِ فَسَبِّحْهُ وَإِدْبَارَ النُّجُومِ

So, submit patiently to the judgement of your Lord, for indeed you fare before Our eyes. And celebrate the praise of your Lord when you rise and glorify Him during the night and at the receding of the stars.[57]

The verse gives us three times for remembrance: when we "rise," "during the night," and "at the receding of the stars."

There is disagreement over the meaning of the first time, i.e., 'rising.' Some say it is a reference to rising from bed at the beginning of the day. Others say it is a reference to rising after sitting, especially in a gathering. Still, others say it is a reference to rising in prayer.

Perhaps the best understanding is that it is a general reference to rising at all times, whether from bed, from a gathering, or to prayer. Therefore, the verse is general and instructs us to remember God whenever we turn from one state to another.

There are narrations that mention glorification and remembrance specifically when a person rises to leave a gathering. For example, Imam al-Ṣādiq (a) said that when a person is about to leave a gathering, they should recite the following verses:

سُبْحَانَ رَبِّكَ رَبِّ الْعِزَّةِ عَمَّا يَصِفُونَ

Glorified be your Lord, the Lord of Might, above whatever they [falsely] ascribe [to Him].

[57] The Noble Quran, 52:48-49.

وَسَلَامٌ عَلَى الْمُرْسَلِينَ

Peace be to the apostles!

وَالْحَمْدُ لِلَّهِ رَبِّ الْعَالَمِينَ

All praise belongs to God, Lord of all the worlds.[58]

Of course, God should not only be remembered at the end of a gathering but mentioned and remembered throughout it as well.

Imam al-Ṣādiq (a) said,

ما مِنْ مَجْلِسٍ يَجْتَمِعُ فِيهِ أَبْرَارٌ وفُجَّارٌ، فَيَقُومُونَ عَلَى غَيْرِ ذِكْرِ اللهِ عَزَّ وجَلَّ، إِلَّا كَانَ حَسْرَةً عَلَيْهِمْ يَوْمَ الْقِيَامَةِ.

Whenever [both] virtuous and vicious [individuals] hold a gathering for something other than the remembrance of God almighty, they shall regret it on the Day of Resurrection.[59]

This is an issue emphasized in prophetic traditions. In one narration, God Almighty says to Jesus, son of Mary,

يا عِيسَى أَلِنْ لِي قَلْبَكَ، وأَكْثِرْ ذِكْرِي فِي الْخَلَوَاتِ، وَاعْلَمْ أَنَّ سُرُورِي أَنْ تُبَصْبِصَ إِلَيَّ، وَكُنْ فِي ذَلِكَ حَيّاً وَلَا تَكُنْ مَيِّتاً.

O' Jesus! Make your heart soft for Me and remember Me constantly in solitude. Know that My pleasure is in your approach towards Me. Be lively in that, and do not be dead.[60]

Imam al-Ṣādiq (a) also said,

مَا مِنْ شَيْءٍ إِلَّا وَلَهُ حَدٌّ يَنْتَهِي إِلَيْهِ إِلَّا الذِّكْر، فَلَيْسَ لَهُ حَدٌّ يَنْتَهِي إِلَيْهِ، فَرَضَ اللهُ عَزَّ وَجَلَّ الْفَرَائِضَ، فَمَنْ أَدَّاهُنَّ فَهُوَ حَدُّهُنَّ، وَشَهْرَ رَمَضَانَ فَمَنْ صَامَهُ فَهُوَ حَدُّهُ، وَالْحَجَّ فَمَنْ حَجَّ فَهُوَ

[58] The Noble Quran, 37:180-82.

[59] Al-ʿĀmilī, *Wasāʾil al-Shīʿah*, 4:1179.

[60] Ibid, 4:1184.

حَدُّهُ إِلَّا الذِّكْر، فَإِنَّ اللهَ عَزَّ وَجَلَّ لَمْ يَرْضَ مِنْهُ بِالْقَلِيلِ، وَلَمْ يَجْعَلْ لَهُ حَدٌّ يَنْتَهِي إِلَيْهِ.

Everything is subject to a limit, except for remembrance [of God] – it is not subject to a limit. God Almighty made obligatory prayers, such that whomsoever performs them has reached their limit. He made the Month of Ramadan, such that whomsoever fasts it has reached its limit. He made ḥajj, such that whomsoever performs it has reached its limit. However, God Almighty did not accept little remembrance and did not make a limit for it.

The Imam then recited the verse,

يَا أَيُّهَا الَّذِينَ آمَنُوا اذْكُرُوا اللَّهَ ذِكْرًا كَثِيرًا

O' you who have faith! Remember God with frequent remembrance

وَسَبِّحُوهُ بُكْرَةً وَأَصِيلًا

and glorify Him morning and evening.[61]

He continued,

لَمْ يَجْعَلِ اللهُ لَهُ حَدّاً يَنْتَهِي إِلَيْهِ، قَالَ وَكَانَ أَبِي كَثِيرَ الذِّكْرِ، لَقَدْ كُنْتُ أَمْشِي مَعَهُ وَإِنَّهُ لَيَذْكُرُ اللهَ، وَآكُلُ مَعَهُ الطَّعَامَ وَإِنَّهُ لَيَذْكُرُ اللهَ، وَلَقَدْ كَانَ يُحَدِّثُ الْقَوْمَ وَمَا يَشْغَلُهُ ذَلِكَ عَنْ ذِكْرِ اللهِ، وَكُنْتُ أَرَى لِسَانَهُ لَازِقاً بِحَنَكِهِ يَقُولُ لَا إِلَهَ إِلَّا اللهُ، وَكَانَ يَجْمَعُنَا فَيَأْمُرُنَا بِالذِّكْرِ حَتَّى تَطْلُعَ الشَّمْسُ.

God did not set a limit for [remembrance]. My father was a man of constant remembrance. I used to walk with him, and he would be remembering God. I used to eat with him, and he would be remembering God. He used to talk to people, but that would not distract him from remembering God. I saw that his tongue was [constantly moving in remembrance of God], saying, 'There is no god

[61] The Noble Quran, 33:41-42.

but God.' He used to gather us and exhort us to remember God until sunrise...

وَقَالَ رَسُولُ اللهِ(ص) مَنْ أُعْطِيَ لِسَاناً ذَاكِراً، فَقَدْ أُعْطِيَ خَيْرَ الدُّنْيَا وَالْآخِرَةِ.

The Messenger of God (sa) said, 'Whoever is given an oft-remembering tongue has been given the best of this world and the next.'

Remembrance with the tongue is something we should do. However, remembrance within us is also imperative. In fact, it is more potent and important. The authentic narration of *Zurārah* states that Imam al-Bāqir (a) or Imam al-Ṣādiq (a) said,

لَا يَكْتُبُ الْمَلَكُ إِلَّا مَا سَمِعَ وَقَالَ اللهُ عَزَّ وَجَلَّ:

The angel does not write except what it hears. God Almighty says,

وَاذْكُر رَّبَّكَ فِي نَفْسِكَ تَضَرُّعًا وَخِيفَةً

'And remember your Lord within your heart beseechingly and reverentially.'[62]

فَلَا يَعْلَمُ ثَوَابَ ذَلِكَ الذِّكْرِ فِي نَفْسِ الرَّجُلِ، غَيْرُ اللهِ لِعَظَمَتِهِ.

No one knows the reward of that remembrance with a person's self except God due to the greatness [of such remembrance].[63]

Pleading for Forgiveness (*istighfār*)

Are there specific methods of remembrance that we should focus on?

There are several important methods of remembrance, but I will focus on one: pleading for forgiveness (*istighfār*).

[62] The Noble Quran, 7:205.

[63] Al-ʿĀmilī, *Wasāʾil al-Shīʿah*, 4:1188.

Pleading for forgiveness is emphasized in the Noble Quran time and again. All of God's prophets and messengers called their people to plead for forgiveness. Throughout history, God's chosen messengers consistently called upon their people to engage in istighfār as a means of seeking God's forgiveness and mercy. Prophet Nūh[64] called his people, saying,

فَقُلْتُ اسْتَغْفِرُوا رَبَّكُمْ إِنَّهُ كَانَ غَفَّارًا

So, I [Nūḥ] said, 'Plead to your Lord for forgiveness. Indeed, He is all-forgiving.'[65]

The act of seeking forgiveness was associated with God's response in the form of abundant rain, increased wealth, progeny, gardens, and flowing streams—manifestations of His blessings in this world.

Prophet Hūd, Prophet Ṣāliḥ, and Prophet Shuʿayb similarly conveyed the message of istighfār to their communities, emphasizing its transformative power and the accompanying divine rewards. These messages serve as timeless reminders of the efficacy of istighfār as a means of invoking God's benevolence, whether through relief from adversity, material prosperity, or the cultivation of a harmonious and abundant life.

Prophet Hūd[66] said:

---

[64] Prophet Nūh (Noah in English) is regarded as one of the earliest prophets sent to humanity. He played a pivotal role in calling his people to the worship of the One God and to repentance. His mission took place in ancient Mesopotamia, roughly around 2000 BCE. Nūh's people were deeply immersed in idol worship and moral corruption. Despite facing numerous challenges and opposition, Nūh persistently called upon his people to turn away from their sinful ways and seek God's forgiveness through istighfār.

[65] The Noble Quran, 71:10.

[66] Prophet Hud was sent to the people of ʿĀd, who dwelled in the southern Arabian Peninsula around 2000 BCE. The ʿĀd people were known for their arrogance, rejection of God's guidance, and their habit of constructing grand structures. Hud called upon his people to abandon their

وَيَا قَوْمِ اسْتَغْفِرُوا رَبَّكُمْ ثُمَّ تُوبُوا إِلَيْهِ يُرْسِلِ السَّمَاءَ عَلَيْكُم مِّدْرَارًا

O' my people! Plead with your Lord for forgiveness, then turn to Him penitently: He will send copious rains for you from the sky.[67]

Prophet Ṣāliḥ[68] stated:

يَا قَوْمِ اعْبُدُوا اللَّهَ مَا لَكُم مِّنْ إِلَٰهٍ غَيْرُهُ - هُوَ أَنشَأَكُم مِّنَ الْأَرْضِ وَاسْتَعْمَرَكُمْ فِيهَا فَاسْتَغْفِرُوهُ

O' my people! Worship God. You have no other god besides Him. He brought you forth from the earth and made it your habitation. So plead with Him for forgiveness.[69]

Prophet Shuʿayb[70] said to his people:

---

pride and idolatry and to seek God's forgiveness and guidance. He emphasized istighfār as a means to avert God's punishment and receive His blessings. Despite Hud's persistent efforts, most of the ʿĀd people rejected his message, and God's punishment eventually befell them, emphasizing the consequences of ignoring the call to istighfār and repentance.

[67] The Noble Quran, 11:52.

[68] Prophet Ṣāliḥ was sent to the people of Thamud, a civilization that inhabited the Arabian Peninsula in the northwestern region. The Thamud people were known for their arrogance and their remarkable ability to carve homes and structures into the mountains. Ṣāliḥ's mission was to guide the Thamud away from their idolatry and wickedness and toward monotheism and righteousness. He stressed the importance of istighfār as a means to receive God's mercy and blessings. Unfortunately, many among the Thamud people refused to heed Ṣāliḥ's call. They demanded a miraculous sign, and as a result, God provided a miraculous she-camel as a sign of His power. However, the people rejected it and subsequently faced divine punishment.

[69] The Noble Quran, 11:61.

[70] Prophet Shuʿayb, also known as Jethro in the Bible, is a significant prophet in Islamic tradition. He is mentioned in the Quran and is considered one of the prophets sent by God to guide and teach his people. While the Quran provides some information about Prophet Shuʿayb, additional details about his life and mission can be found in Islamic traditions and historical sources.

وَاسْتَغْفِرُوا رَبَّكُمْ ثُمَّ تُوبُوا إِلَيْهِ - إِنَّ رَبِّي رَحِيمٌ وَدُودٌ

Plead with your Lord for forgiveness, then turn to Him penitently. My Lord is indeed all-merciful, all-affectionate.[71]

Our Holy Prophet Muhammad (sa) also received divine guidance regarding istighfār, reinforcing its significance. He was instructed to say,

قُلْ إِنَّمَا أَنَا بَشَرٌ مِّثْلُكُمْ يُوحَىٰ إِلَيَّ أَنَّمَا إِلَٰهُكُمْ إِلَٰهٌ وَاحِدٌ فَاسْتَقِيمُوا إِلَيْهِ وَاسْتَغْفِرُوهُ

Say, 'I am just a human like you. It has been revealed to me that your God is the One God. So, worship Him single-mindedly and plead to Him for forgiveness.'[72]

This command underscores that istighfār is a universal practice that is accessible to all believers.

The benefits of istighfār are multifaceted, beginning with the pardoning and forgiveness of sins. It is a means to seek God's mercy, which is pivotal in the journey towards salvation. Furthermore, it invites divine blessings into our lives, including the bestowal of children and an increase in wealth, as highlighted in the Quranic accounts of Prophet Nūh's mission.

The Noble Quran recounts the following statement from Prophet Nūh,

---

[71] The Noble Quran, 11:90.

[72] The Noble Quran, 41:6.

فَقُلْتُ اسْتَغْفِرُوا رَبَّكُمْ إِنَّهُ كَانَ غَفَّارًا

يُرْسِلِ السَّمَاءَ عَلَيْكُم مِّدْرَارًا

وَيُمْدِدْكُم بِأَمْوَالٍ وَبَنِينَ وَيَجْعَل لَّكُمْ جَنَّاتٍ وَيَجْعَل لَّكُمْ أَنْهَارًا

I told [them], 'Plead to your Lord for forgiveness. Indeed, He is all-forgiving.

He will send for you abundant rains from the sky,

and aid you with wealth and sons, and provide you with gardens and provide you with streams.'[73]

The verse clearly states that a believer should plead with God for forgiveness, and there are great rewards for a person who does so. Most importantly, pleading for forgiveness is a reason for God Almighty to forgive us and grant us a home in His paradise in the hereafter. But the benefits of pleading for forgiveness start in this world. It allows us to receive more and more of God's blessings, including children and wealth.

The Quranic emphasis on istighfār also provides guidance for individuals seeking specific blessings. When one desires offspring or improved financial circumstances, scholars often recommend engaging in istighfār as a means to invoke God's favor. Imam al-Bāqir's counsel to plead for forgiveness for a year during the final hours of each night, as well as the hadiths attributed to Imam al-Ḥasan, align with this practice. These traditions underscore the comprehensive nature of istighfār and its universal applicability.

In one tradition, a man said to Imam al-Bāqir (a), "I am a wealthy man, but I am not blessed with offspring. What can I do?" The Imam (a) responded,

---

[73] The Noble Quran, 71:10.

اسْتَغْفِرْ رَبَّكَ سَنَةً فِي آخِرِ اللَّيْلِ مِائَةَ مَرَّةٍ، فَإِنْ ضَيَّعْتَ ذَلِكَ بِاللَّيْلَةِ فَاقْضِهِ بِالنَّهَارِ، فَإِنَّ اللهَ يَقُولُ "اسْتَغْفِرُوا رَبَّكُمْ".

Plead with your Lord for forgiveness for a year in the final hours of every night. If you miss a night, make up in the day. God says, 'Plead to your Lord for forgiveness....'[74]

A man approached Imam al-Ḥasan[75] (a) and complained of an illness. The Imam (a) said,

اسْتَغْفِرِ اللهَ.

Plead with God for forgiveness.

Another man came to him and complained of poverty. The Imam (a) responded,

اسْتَغْفِرِ اللهَ.

Plead with God for forgiveness.

A third man came and asked the Imam (a) to pray for him because he was not able to have any children. The Imam (a) told him,

اسْتَغْفِرِ اللهَ.

Plead with God for forgiveness.

The people around Imam al-Ḥasan (a) were astonished. Different people

---

[74] Al-ʿĀmilī, *Wasāʾil al-Shīʿah*, 4:1199.

[75] Imam Ḥasan ibn Ali (a) belonged to the Ahl al-Bayt, the family of the Prophet Muhammad, as he was the grandson of the Prophet (sa) through his daughter Lady Fatimah (a) and son-in-law Imam Ali (a). He was born in the year 625 CE in Medina, a few years after the migration of the Prophet to the city. He grew up in the household of his parents, Imam Ali and Fatimah, and was known for his piety, kindness, and close relationship with his grandfather, the Prophet Muhammad. Imam Ḥasan is revered by Muslims for his commitment to justice, his sacrifices for the unity of the Muslim community, and his unwavering adherence to the principles of Islam. His legacy continues to inspire Muslims worldwide. His life serves as an example of patience, wisdom, and peaceful resolution in the face of challenging circumstances.

came asking for different things, but the response was always the same. When they asked the Imam (a) about this he said,

مَا قُلْتُ ذَلِكَ مِنْ ذَاتِ نَفْسِي، إِنَّمَا اعْتَبَرْتُ فِيهِ قَوْلَ اللهِ "اسْتَغْفِرُوا رَبَّكُمْ إِنَّهُ كَانَ غَفّاراً".

I did not say that from my [personal opinion]. Rather, I relied on the word of God, 'Plead to your Lord for forgiveness. Indeed, He is all-forgiving...'[76]

The same meaning can be found in a few Quranic verses. For example, the Quran states that Prophet Hūd said to his people,

وَيَا قَوْمِ اسْتَغْفِرُوا رَبَّكُمْ ثُمَّ تُوبُوا إِلَيْهِ يُرْسِلِ السَّمَاءَ عَلَيْكُم مِّدْرَارًا وَيَزِدْكُمْ قُوَّةً إِلَىٰ قُوَّتِكُمْ وَلَا تَتَوَلَّوْا مُجْرِمِينَ

O' my people! Plead with your Lord for forgiveness, then turn to Him penitently: He will send copious rains for you from the sky and add power to your [present] power. So do not turn your backs [on Him] as guilty ones.[77]

Similarly, God says,

وَأَنِ اسْتَغْفِرُوا رَبَّكُمْ ثُمَّ تُوبُوا إِلَيْهِ يُمَتِّعْكُم مَّتَاعًا حَسَنًا إِلَىٰ أَجَلٍ مُّسَمًّى

Plead with your Lord for forgiveness, then turn to Him penitently. He will provide you with a good provision for a specified term.[78]

Istighfār is an act of devotion that carries immense spiritual and practical significance. It serves as a means of seeking God's forgiveness, inviting His blessings, and ensuring a harmonious and abundant life. It is a practice accessible to all believers, embodying the concept of seeking

---

[76] Al-ʿĀmilī, *Wasāʾil al-Shīʿah*, 4:1199.

[77] The Noble Quran, 11:52.

[78] The Noble Quran, 11:3.

God's mercy and grace in every aspect of our existence. As the Quranic verses and prophetic traditions demonstrate, istighfār is a fundamental aspect of a believer's relationship with God, one that can profoundly influence their life's course and spiritual journey.

We see that some people, despite their continuous remembrance of God pleading for forgiveness, are still living with poverty and lack of offspring.

How can we reconcile between what you are saying, and this observed reality?

Certainly, let's delve further into the concept of causal relationships and how they apply to the act of pleading for forgiveness (istighfār) as prescribed in the Quran.

The Quranic prescription of 'pleading for forgiveness' can be likened to a medical prescription in its causal relationships. Just as a doctor might recommend a patient to eat more fruits and vegetables or prescribe a specific medication to prevent or alleviate certain ailments, the act of istighfār is a component in a broader equation that generates spiritual and worldly benefits.

To understand this concept more deeply, we can explore two key notions in causality: sufficient causality and component causality.

A sufficient cause is one whose effect follows necessarily. It is an indispensable factor, and the presence of this cause guarantees the occurrence of the effect. For example, the presence of fire is a sufficient cause for burning. Fire and the chemical reaction of burning are inherently linked, and you cannot have fire without the burning effect.

In the context of istighfār, it serves as a component cause rather than a sufficient cause. While it is a crucial element, it may not, on its own, guarantee a specific outcome. Istighfār is essential for seeking God's forgiveness, but other factors, both internal and external, come into play to determine the final result.

A component cause is a part of a larger equation that generates an effect.

It contributes to the overall process but is not the sole determinant of the outcome. For instance, if a doctor advises a patient to avoid coming into contact with someone who has an infectious disease, it is a component cause in preventing illness. However, other factors like the patient's immune system, prior vaccinations, hygiene practices, or environmental factors may also play a role.

Similarly, istighfār is a component cause in the broader equation of seeking God's mercy and blessings. While it is an integral part of the process, other factors, both observable and unobservable, may influence the final result. These factors could include one's sincerity in seeking forgiveness, the state of their heart, the acceptance of their supplication by God, and the divine wisdom behind the response.

Thus, the act of istighfār prescribed in the Quran is indeed a significant component cause in a causal relationship that can lead to numerous benefits and rewards, both in the spiritual and worldly domains. However, it is essential to acknowledge that istighfār is not a standalone sufficient cause, but part of a larger equation influenced by various internal and external factors.

Just as medical prescriptions may not prevent or cure illnesses in every individual due to diverse circumstances and health conditions, istighfār's impact can also be influenced by a range of factors. Nevertheless, practicing istighfār remains a powerful and spiritually enriching act, aligning believers with God's guidance and mercy while acknowledging the complexity of causal relationships in human experiences.

Now, consider the following verse:

وَإِذْ قَالُوا اللَّهُمَّ إِن كَانَ هَـٰذَا هُوَ الْحَقَّ مِنْ عِندِكَ فَأَمْطِرْ عَلَيْنَا حِجَارَةً مِّنَ السَّمَاءِ أَوِ ائْتِنَا بِعَذَابٍ أَلِيمٍ

وَمَا كَانَ اللَّهُ لِيُعَذِّبَهُمْ وَأَنتَ فِيهِمْ - وَمَا كَانَ اللَّهُ مُعَذِّبَهُمْ وَهُمْ يَسْتَغْفِرُونَ

And when they said, 'O' God, if this be the truth from

You, rain down upon us stones from the sky, or bring us a painful punishment.'

But God will not punish them while you are in their midst, nor will God punish them while they plead for forgiveness.[79]

The verses of The Noble Quran highlight yet another important benefit of pleading of forgiveness; namely, that God Almighty will not send his worldly punishment on a people who plead for forgiveness. Believers should not be heedless of the importance of pleading with God, as it could be their salvation if worldly punishment was ever decreed for them.

Incorporating istighfār into one's life, as highlighted in the Quran, is a comprehensive approach that addresses both the avoidance of divine punishment and the attraction of divine blessings. It is a constant reminder for believers to maintain humility, self-awareness, and a close connection with God.

Moreover, istighfār is not limited to a specific ritual or moment but can be practiced throughout one's daily life. This continuous act of seeking forgiveness fosters a deep and enduring relationship with the Divine, enhancing one's spirituality and moral character.

The Quranic verses emphasize that pleading for forgiveness is not only a means to seek God's pardon but also a powerful tool to avert divine punishment and attract His abundant blessings. It underscores the dynamic and multifaceted nature of istighfār in shaping a believer's spiritual journey and relationship with the Divine.

---

[79] The Noble Quran, 8:32-33.

The Hidden Imam (a) and Being Spared Punishment

This raises an important question regarding our Twelfth Imam (a). We believe that he lives in a state of occultation (ghaybah), making it impossible for us to have direct visual or auditory contact with him.

In what ways can we derive spiritual and practical benefits from the presence of Imam Mahdi (a) during his occultation when he is not accessible to us through conventional means?

This question slightly deviates from our current focus, but let's briefly address it. Some of our traditions use metaphors to describe the hidden presence of Imam Mahdi (a), referring to it as 'a safety for the people of the earth' or 'like the sun behind the clouds.' These descriptions may appear enigmatic at first glance, but when we consider the verses we've discussed, a clearer understanding begins to take shape.

In the verse mentioned earlier, it is stated that people were spared from worldly punishment as long as the Holy Prophet (sa) was present among them.[80] This implies that they were not subjected to catastrophic disasters like sinkholes, storms, or other calamities that could potentially annihilate them.

Such divine punishments were inflicted upon nations that rejected their prophets. Similarly, the hidden presence of our Twelfth Imam (a) serves as a safeguard, much like the presence of the Holy Prophet (sa). Even though he remains in occultation, his existence acts as a deterrent against catastrophic disasters where entire nations were annihilated from earth, reminiscent of those experienced by the people of Nūh, Hūd, Ṣāliḥ, and Lūṭ.[81]

---

[80] The Noble Quran, 8:33.

[81] Prophet Lūṭ (Lot in English) is a significant figure in Abrahamic religions, including Islam, Christianity, and Judaism. He is a prophet and a relative of Prophet Abraham (Ibrahim in Islam).

When to Plead for Forgiveness

Back to the focus of this topic, what are some specific times or situations where pleading for forgiveness is recommended?

God Almighty says in The Noble Quran,

ثُمَّ أَفِيضُوا مِنْ حَيْثُ أَفَاضَ النَّاسُ وَاسْتَغْفِرُوا اللَّهَ، إِنَّ اللَّهَ غَفُورٌ رَّحِيمٌ

Then stream out [of 'Arafāt] from where the people stream out, and plead to God for forgiveness; indeed, God is all-forgiving, all-merciful.[82]

There are various specific times and situations in which pleading for forgiveness is highly recommended in Islamic tradition. One such instance is during the annual pilgrimage (ḥajj), particularly when pilgrims are leaving the sacred site of Mount 'Arafāt.[83]

In the verse above, God Almighty emphasizes the significance of seeking His forgiveness during the ḥajj pilgrimage. Here, the reference to "streaming out of 'Arafāt" pertains to an essential ritual of ḥajj, where pilgrims gather at Mount 'Arafāt to stand in prayer, repentance, and supplication. Afterward, as they depart from this sacred location, they are encouraged to engage in fervent pleading for forgiveness from God.

The act of seeking forgiveness during the ḥajj pilgrimage holds

---

His story is primarily associated with his mission to the people of Sodom and Gomorrah. In the Islamic tradition, Prophet Lut is highly regarded as a righteous and pious servant of God. He is mentioned in the Quran in several chapters, including Surah Al-Ankabut (Chapter 29) and Surah Hud (Chapter 11), where his story is recounted in detail.

[82] The Noble Quran, 2:199.

[83] Mount 'Arafāt is located in the plain of Arafat, which is situated about 20 kilometers (12.5 miles) east of the holy city of Mecca in present-day Saudi Arabia. The plain itself covers an area of approximately 20 square kilometers. Mount 'Arafāt is one of the most sacred sites in Islam and holds immense religious significance. It is the place where the pinnacle of the Ḥajj pilgrimage occurs, known as the "Stay at Arafat" (Wuqūf al-'Arafāt). This ritual takes place on the 9th day of Dhul-Ḥijjah, the twelfth month of the Islamic lunar calendar.

profound spiritual significance. It is a time when millions of pilgrims from around the world come together to fulfill one of the ritual tenants of Islam, and their collective prayers and repentance symbolize unity and humility before God. By sincerely pleading for forgiveness, pilgrims express their acknowledgment of their own shortcomings and sins while seeking God's pardon and mercy.

This practice during the ḥajj pilgrimage serves as a reminder of the broader concept of seeking forgiveness in Islam. It underscores the idea that seeking God's forgiveness is not limited to one's personal prayers but can also be a communal and deeply spiritual experience.

In addition to the ḥajj, there are many other occasions and situations in daily life where believers are encouraged to engage in pleading for forgiveness. These moments can include daily prayers, before and after acts of worship, when seeking God's help and guidance, and during moments of reflection and repentance. Seeking forgiveness is seen as a means of purifying one's soul, strengthening one's connection with God, and striving for spiritual growth.

Are Believers Free of Sin?

Some individuals may assume that a devout believer lives a life completely free from sin and in unwavering obedience to God. While it is true that striving for such a state is an ideal, the Noble Quran acknowledges that believers may occasionally falter and commit sins. However, this does not contradict their status as believers.

When a believer does stray from the path of righteousness, it is imperative that they promptly acknowledge their errors, feel genuine remorse, and turn to God in humble supplication, seeking His forgiveness. This act of seeking forgiveness from God is highly emphasized in Islam, and the Quran provides guidance on this matter. God Almighty states:

إِنَّ الَّذِينَ اتَّقَوْا إِذَا مَسَّهُمْ طَائِفٌ مِّنَ الشَّيْطَانِ تَذَكَّرُوا فَإِذَا هُم مُّبْصِرُونَ

When those who are Godwary are touched by a visitation of Satan, they remember [God] and, behold, they perceive.[84]

This verse underscores that even the most pious individuals, the "Godwary," may occasionally face moments of spiritual weakness due to the influence of Satan. However, their strength lies in their ability to remember God and regain their spiritual clarity and consciousness.

Moreover, believers are encouraged to express their remorse and seek forgiveness from God. The Quran states:

الَّذِينَ يُنفِقُونَ فِي السَّرَّاءِ وَالضَّرَّاءِ وَالْكَاظِمِينَ الْغَيْظَ وَالْعَافِينَ عَنِ النَّاسِ -
وَاللَّهُ يُحِبُّ الْمُحْسِنِينَ

وَالَّذِينَ إِذَا فَعَلُوا فَاحِشَةً أَوْ ظَلَمُوا أَنفُسَهُمْ ذَكَرُوا اللَّهَ فَاسْتَغْفَرُوا لِذُنُوبِهِمْ

[The Godwary are] those who spend in ease and adversity, and suppress their anger, and excuse [the faults of] the people, and God loves the virtuous;

and those who, when they commit an indecent act or wrong themselves, remember God, and plead [to God seeking His] forgiveness for their sins.[85]

This passage highlights that true believers demonstrate several key attributes:

1. They are charitable, giving to those in need, regardless of their own circumstances.
2. They control their anger, demonstrating patience and

[84] The Noble Quran, 7:201.

[85] The Noble Quran, 3:134-135.

forgiveness.

3. They excuse the faults of others.

Crucially, when they commit sins or engage in indecent acts, they promptly remember God and earnestly plead for His forgiveness.

These verses illustrate the essential quality of seeking forgiveness as a means of rectifying one's relationship with God after wrongdoing. Seeking God's forgiveness is an integral part of a believer's journey towards spiritual growth and moral development.

Furthermore, the Quran emphasizes God's readiness to forgive those who are God-fearing and sincere in their repentance:

يَا أَيُّهَا الَّذِينَ آمَنُوا إِن تَتَّقُوا اللَّهَ يَجْعَل لَّكُمْ فُرْقَانًا وَيُكَفِّرْ عَنكُمْ سَيِّئَاتِكُمْ وَيَغْفِرْ لَكُمْ - وَاللَّهُ ذُو الْفَضْلِ الْعَظِيمِ

O' you who have faith! If you are wary of God, He shall appoint a criterion for you, and absolve you of your misdeeds, and forgive you, for God is dispenser of a great grace.[86]

وَمَن يَتَّقِ اللَّهَ يُكَفِّرْ عَنْهُ سَيِّئَاتِهِ وَيُعْظِمْ لَهُ أَجْرًا

And whoever is wary of God, He shall absolve him of his misdeeds and give him a great reward.[87]

In addition, a believer should ask God to forgive others, especially their parents. God says,

---

[86] The Noble Quran, 8:29.

[87] The Noble Quran, 65:5.

رَبِّ اجْعَلْنِي مُقِيمَ الصَّلَاةِ وَمِن ذُرِّيَّتِي - رَبَّنَا وَتَقَبَّلْ دُعَاءِ

رَبَّنَا اغْفِرْ لِي وَلِوَالِدَيَّ وَلِلْمُؤْمِنِينَ يَوْمَ يَقُومُ الْحِسَابُ

My Lord! Make me a maintainer of prayer, and my descendants [as well]. Our Lord, accept my supplication.

Our Lord! Forgive me and my parents, and all the faithful, on the day when the reckoning is held.[88]

These verses emphasize the importance of caring for fellow believers and extending one's supplications for their well-being. It reflects the noble moral character of Islam, fostering mutual affection, and selflessness among believers.

While it is ideal for believers to avoid sin and remain steadfast in their faith, the Quran acknowledges the human propensity for error. It encourages believers to seek God's forgiveness sincerely and humbly, both for themselves and for others, fostering a sense of unity and shared responsibility among the faithful.

Did you suppose that We created you aimlessly?

We should remember that God Almighty gave us life and a chance to strive towards excellence. We must therefore build our lives on a solid foundation. Let us remember God's words,

أَفَحَسِبْتُمْ أَنَّمَا خَلَقْنَاكُمْ عَبَثًا وَأَنَّكُمْ إِلَيْنَا لَا تُرْجَعُونَ

Did you suppose that We created you aimlessly, and that you will not be brought back to Us?[89]

---

[88] The Noble Quran, 14:40-41.

[89] The Noble Quran, 23:115.

We must realize the purpose of our existence. Otherwise, our entire life may be a waste of time. Let us turn again to the Quran. God says,

وَمَا خَلَقْتُ الْجِنَّ وَالْإِنسَ إِلَّا لِيَعْبُدُونِ

I did not create the jinn and the humans except that they may worship Me.[90]

Our purpose is stated explicitly.

We were created to worship!

But what is true worship?

That is the real question that needs to be addressed.

A true worshipper and servant must connect with their Lord. A servant must align his wants and desires to the wishes of God. A servant must show the utmost manifestations of servitude and submission to God Almighty.

Servitude is a concept that, if it takes hold of our minds, will dictate how we seek the truth.

True Servitude

When you understand servitude, you find that it obliges you to thank your Lord. This will lead you on a search within yourself.

- Who is your Lord and Creator?
- Who must you worship?
- What are His attributes?
- What does He want of us?

Each one of us needs to search for answers to these questions. We must all ponder on these questions to know what we are doing in our lives and where we are headed.

---

[90] The Noble Quran, 51:56.

Servitude allows humankind to reach towards excellence and inch closer in proximity to God Almighty. True servitude is unconditional obedience. God says,

يَا أَيُّهَا الَّذِينَ آمَنُوا أَطِيعُوا اللَّهَ وَأَطِيعُوا الرَّسُولَ وَلَا تُبْطِلُوا أَعْمَالَكُمْ

O' you who have faith! Obey God and obey the Apostle, and do not render your works void.[91]

That raises another question. How should we exemplify servitude and worship our Lord?

A person must base their actions on a deep understanding of their beliefs and ensure that their actions mirror those beliefs and concepts. If they do so, their actions will have a deeper and more complete meaning. Their actions will have a greater influence on their souls.

If a person lives their life without understanding their purpose, they would surely be wasting their time. This is why we should give understanding our purpose the highest importance. This will allow us to reach the true goal of our creation.

Note that God Almighty described our purpose as "worship." Of course, we are His servants by creation. However, we worship Him when we exercise our free will and follow His commands.

Everything in the universe was created by God and is sustained by Him. God says,

وَتَرَى الْجِبَالَ تَحْسَبُهَا جَامِدَةً وَهِيَ تَمُرُّ مَرَّ السَّحَابِ - صُنْعَ اللَّهِ الَّذِي أَتْقَنَ
كُلَّ شَيْءٍ - إِنَّهُ خَبِيرٌ بِمَا تَفْعَلُونَ

You see the mountains, which you supposed to be stationary, while they drift like passing clouds—the handiwork of God who has made everything faultless.

---

[91] The Noble Quran, 47:33.

He is indeed well aware of what you do.[92]

God created everything perfectly and without fault. Every single being is perfect, faultless, and consistent in its creation.

Everything in the universe needs Him and is dependent on Him – not only in creation, but in continued existence and being.

Servitude and worship are a crown given to humankind to wear as a manifestation of our highest excellence. God says,

يَا أَيُّهَا الَّذِينَ آمَنُوا كُلُوا مِن طَيِّبَاتِ مَا رَزَقْنَاكُمْ وَاشْكُرُوا لِلَّهِ إِن كُنتُمْ إِيَّاهُ تَعْبُدُونَ

O' you who have faith! Eat of the good things We have provided you, and thank God, if it is Him that you worship.[93]

Servitude is manifested in a human being through actions undertaken by free will.

Signs of Servitude

The verse that we just mentioned lists some of the signs of servitude that a believer needs to exemplify. One of these signs is that a believer should consume the good things that God provides, and stay away from everything forbidden, evil, and vile. To do so, the believer needs to be able to distinguish between the good and bad – between what is permissible and what is forbidden. Another sign is that a believer is thankful and grateful towards the One who gave us countless blessings.

The need to distinguish and make the right choice is a result of humankind having freewill in the first place. Of course, freewill itself is

---

[92] The Noble Quran, 27:88.

[93] The Noble Quran, 2:172.

one of the greatest blessings that God Almighty gave us and distinguished us with. It is because of our freewill that we become deserving of rewards or punishment.

To make the right decisions and choices, a believer needs to have the proper tools.

Making the Right Choices

How can we make the right choices? Is it up to us to exercise judgement on what the best choice is, or is there something beyond that?

In order to make informed choices and decisions in life, it is essential for us to understand and align ourselves with God's divine guidance. Knowing what God expects of us is the first step towards leading an ideal and purposeful life.

Consider these questions:

- Should we consume whatever we desire without restraint?
- Should we interact with others solely based on our own preferences?
- Should we treat our families as we see fit, or is there a set of moral and ethical principles that we should follow?
- Does God provide us with clear instructions and a roadmap to excel spiritually and intellectually, enabling us to fulfill the purpose of our existence?

God Almighty did not create us aimlessly; He did not abandon us without direction. In the Noble Quran, we find that God called upon the Holy Prophet (sa) with a profound mission:

لَقَدْ مَنَّ اللَّهُ عَلَى الْمُؤْمِنِينَ إِذْ بَعَثَ فِيهِمْ رَسُولًا مِّنْ أَنفُسِهِمْ يَتْلُو عَلَيْهِمْ آيَاتِهِ
وَيُزَكِّيهِمْ وَيُعَلِّمُهُمُ الْكِتَابَ وَالْحِكْمَةَ وَإِن كَانُوا مِن قَبْلُ لَفِي ضَلَالٍ مُّبِينٍ

God certainly favored the faithful when He raised up

among them an apostle from among themselves to recite to them His signs and to purify them and teach them the Book and wisdom, and earlier they had indeed been in manifest error.[94]

This verse highlights that God, in His infinite mercy, bestowed His favor upon the believers by appointing a Prophet from among them. This chosen Prophet, Muhammad (sa), was entrusted with the divine responsibility of conveying God's messages, reciting His signs, purifying the souls of the believers, and imparting the knowledge and wisdom of the Book. Before receiving this guidance, humanity had wandered in clear error.

The Holy Prophet (sa) was granted the Noble Quran, a sacred scripture filled with verses that serve as a source of divine guidance and a pathway to self-purification. Achieving self-purification involves making righteous decisions and resisting the temptations of Satan—a vital pursuit that leads to success in both this world and the Hereafter. This process of purification is captured succinctly in God's words:

قَدْ أَفْلَحَ مَن زَكَّاهَا

One who purifies it is felicitous.[95]

True happiness and eternal felicity are attained through self-purification, which, in turn, hinges upon understanding and adhering to God's teachings. God emphasizes this connection when He says:

وَمَا آتَاكُمُ الرَّسُولُ فَخُذُوهُ وَمَا نَهَاكُمْ عَنْهُ فَانتَهُوا - وَاتَّقُوا اللَّهَ - إِنَّ اللَّهَ شَدِيدُ الْعِقَابِ

Take whatever the Apostle gives you, and refrain from whatever he forbids you, and be wary of God. Indeed,

---

[94] The Noble Quran, 3:164.

[95] The Noble Quran, 91:9.

God is severe in retribution.[96]

God has entrusted us with commandments and prohibitions conveyed through the Holy Prophet (sa). To attain the promised eternal happiness, we must diligently purify ourselves by adhering to these divine directives. Our self-purification journey is inextricably linked to the teachings of the Holy Prophet (sa) and the guidance contained within the Noble Quran.

Knowing God's commands and following His guidance is the compass that steers us towards a purposeful and righteous life. Through sincere adherence to God's teachings and self-purification, we strive for success in this world and the Hereafter, aligning our choices and actions with His divine will.

Ḥalāl and Ḥarām?

Building on above, is this a reference to the matters of ḥalāl and ḥarām, as discussed in our scholars' books of fiqh[97]?

Expanding upon the previous discussion, we delve into the significance of adhering to the teachings of Islam, which encompass matters beyond the realm of ḥalāl (permissible) and ḥarām (forbidden) as expounded in the books of fiqh (Islamic jurisprudence). While the ḥalāl and ḥarām aspects are indeed integral to Islamic guidance, the teachings of our Holy Prophet (sa) extend far beyond these boundaries, encompassing a broader spectrum of theological, ethical, and moral principles.

---

[96] The Noble Quran, 59:7.

[97] *Fiqh* is an Arabic term that translates to "Islamic jurisprudence" or "Islamic law." It refers to the interpretation of Islamic legal principles and rules derived from The Noble Quran and Hadith (sayings and actions of the Prophet Muhammad). Fiqh encompasses a wide range of legal, ethical, and moral issues, addressing matters such as religious rituals, family law, contracts, commerce, and criminal law within the framework of Islamic teachings.

It is crucial for us, as believers, to recognize that the guidance provided by the Holy Prophet (sa) transcends mere dietary restrictions or legalistic rules. Islam offers a comprehensive framework that guides every aspect of our lives, addressing theological beliefs, ethical conduct, interpersonal relationships, and more. This guidance serves as a roadmap for believers to navigate the complexities of the human experience while remaining steadfast in their faith.

The central tenet lies in returning to God Almighty by delving into the Quranic verses revealed to His messenger, the Holy Prophet (sa). Within these verses, God has enjoined upon us the imperative to follow "those who are vested with authority" among us. This divine directive underscores the importance of recognizing and obeying the appointed leaders whom God has chosen to guide and govern the affairs of the Muslim community.

The Quranic verse unequivocally states:

يَا أَيُّهَا الَّذِينَ آمَنُوا أَطِيعُوا اللَّهَ وَأَطِيعُوا الرَّسُولَ وَأُولِي الْأَمْرِ مِنكُمْ

O' you who have faith! Obey God and obey the Apostle and those vested with authority among you.[98]

By emphasizing obedience to "those vested with authority," God highlights the significance of recognizing legitimate leadership within the Islamic community. These leaders, divinely appointed and guided by the teachings of the Holy Prophet (sa), play a pivotal role in interpreting and applying Islamic principles in various contexts.

Hence, while ḥalāl and ḥarām form a fundamental component of the practice of our faith, they are intricately interwoven with a broader tapestry of teachings. These encompass the entirety of our spiritual journey, molding our beliefs, shaping our ethics, and influencing our behavior. Through a comprehensive understanding of the Quranic

---

[98] The Noble Quran, 4:59.

verses and the guidance of the Holy Prophet (sa) and Ahl al-Bayt, we strive to lead lives that are not only compliant with legal and dietary regulations but are also characterized by moral excellence, ethical conduct, and the pursuit of spiritual enlightenment.

Therefore, adhering to the teachings of Islam involves a holistic commitment to God's guidance as conveyed through His messenger and those vested with authority. It is a journey that encompasses all facets of life, both individual and communal, ensuring that our actions, beliefs, and choices align with the divine will. In this way, we seek not only to fulfill our religious obligations but also to lead lives of virtue, compassion, and righteousness.

Divine Leadership

God says,

يَا أَيُّهَا الَّذِينَ آمَنُوا أَطِيعُوا اللَّهَ وَأَطِيعُوا الرَّسُولَ وَأُولِي الْأَمْرِ مِنكُمْ

"O' you who have faith! Obey God and obey the Apostle and those vested with authority among you."[1]

Who are these individuals that God 'vested with authority' and commanded us to obey?

The concept of obeying those "vested with authority" is deeply rooted in Islamic teachings and holds paramount significance in the lives of Muslims. It is crucial to understand who these individuals are, as they play a central role in guiding the Muslim community.

In the Quranic verse, "O' you who have faith! Obey God and obey the Apostle and those vested with authority among you," the individuals referred to as "those vested with authority" are none other than the Imams (a) from the family of Prophet Muhammad (sa). This understanding is based on the unconditional nature of the obedience commanded in the verse. Unconditional obedience implies that these individuals must be entirely in alignment with God's will and free from

---

[1] The Noble Quran, 4:59.

any sin or error. This exalted status of immaculateness, or ʿiṣmah, is exclusively attributed to the Imams (a) of the Ahl al-Bayt.

The Quran also provides further evidence of the Imams' (a) elevated status in the verse of purification (*ayat al-taṭhīr*), where God explicitly designates them as purified and free from impurities. This divine purification underscores their exceptional character and unwavering adherence to God's commands.

These Imams (a) are not just historical or political figures; they are the divinely appointed leaders chosen by God to guide humanity after the Prophet Muhammad (sa). Their authority transcends mere leadership; it encompasses spiritual guidance, moral exemplification, and preservation of the authentic teachings of Islam. Their lives serve as a model for Muslims to emulate, as they provide profound insights into the interpretation of the Quran and the implementation of Islamic principles.

By obeying and following these Imams (a), Muslims are not only safeguarding their faith but also ensuring that they remain on the true path of Islam. Through their wisdom, knowledge, and piety, the Imams (a) provide guidance on issues ranging from theology and jurisprudence to ethics and spirituality. Their teachings continue to serve as a beacon of light, helping Muslims navigate the complexities of life while upholding the principles of faith and righteousness.

The Imams (a) of the Ahl al-Bayt are the divinely appointed authorities whom God has commanded Muslims to obey and follow unconditionally. Their immaculate character, as indicated in the Quran, sets them apart as exemplars of Islamic values and principles. Embracing their guidance is not just an act of religious devotion; it is a means to attain spiritual elevation and draw closer to God in the pursuit of a righteous and fulfilling life.

Obedience

The rest of the verse states,

فَإِنْ تَنَازَعْتُمْ فِي شَيْءٍ فَرُدُّوهُ إِلَى اللَّهِ وَالرَّسُولِ

"If you dispute concerning anything, refer it to God and the Apostle." [2]

The reference to 'those vested with authority' is plainly missing from the second part which commands us to refer to God and the Prophet (sa) in issues of dispute. Why is this the case?

The verse, which commands believers to obey God, the Prophet (sa), and "those vested with authority," also includes guidance on dispute resolution. It states, "If you dispute concerning anything, refer it to God and the Apostle." However, the reference to 'those vested with authority' is notably absent in this context. To comprehend this omission, we must first consider the nature of the disputes that may arise within the Muslim community.

One possible interpretation is rooted in the understanding of the nature of the dispute in question. If the dispute pertains to matters concerning the Imams or their teachings and directives, then it becomes imperative to refer to them. This aligns with the commandment to obey them unconditionally. Referring to the Imams in such disputes is a fundamental aspect of obedience to God's divine order.

Conversely, when disputes concern legislative matters, it is prescribed to refer to God and the Prophet (sa). The authority to legislate, particularly with regard to what is ḥalāl (permissible) and ḥarām (forbidden), is a prerogative exclusively held by God and the Prophet (sa). Under normal circumstances, the Imams do not possess the

---

[2] The Noble Quran, 4:59.

authority to legislate in this domain.

Nonetheless, it is crucial to recognize that the Imams serve as a conduit to access divine and prophetic teachings. This role does not contradict the command to refer to God and the Prophet (sa) in matters of ḥalāl and ḥarām; rather, it complements it. In situations where direct access to God and the Prophet (sa) is not feasible, the Imams (a) act as representatives who provide guidance.

When seeking answers or clarification on matters, believers turn to the Imams (a), who serve as the embodiments of divine knowledge and wisdom. The Imams, in their responses, consistently upheld the importance of grounding their teachings in the Quran. As exemplified by Imam al-Bāqir (a), who encouraged his followers to inquire about any matter and seek support for their questions from the Book of God, the Quran remains the ultimate source of guidance. He told his followers:

إذَا حَدَّثْتُكُم بِشَيءٍ فاسْأَلُونِي مِنْ كِتَابِ اللهِ.

If I speak to you about any matter, ask me [for its support] from the Book of God.[3]

Thus, through the guidance of the Imams, believers effectively return to God and the Prophet (sa), as their teachings are firmly rooted in divine revelation.

Perhaps the most crucial disagreement amongst Muslims is concerning who 'those vested with authority' are. Knowing this, we cannot turn to 'those vested with authority' to tell us who is vested with authority. Instead, we need to turn to the Quran and the Prophet (sa) to tell us who they are. This is what we see when we turn to Prophetic traditions and find countless examples of him naming Imam Ali (a) as his deputy, vicegerent, and Imam after him.

---

[3] Al-Kulaynī, *al-Kāfī*, 1:60.

Moreover, all Muslims agree that the Quran and the Sunnah are the primary sources of guidance. This is the essence of Islam. The role of the Imam is to preserve this guidance, and to guide people to it.

In essence, the absence of the phrase 'those vested with authority' in the context of dispute resolution signifies the role of the Imams (a) in elucidating divine teachings and the ultimate authority of God and the Prophet (sa) in matters of legislation. Believers are encouraged to seek knowledge and understanding by referring to the Imams and grounding their inquiries in the Quran, thus maintaining a harmonious relationship between divine guidance and human understanding.

Why Twice?

The Quranic verse states, "Obey God and obey the Apostle and those vested with authority among you." Why is the word "obey" mentioned twice? Why not just once at the beginning of the sentence? Why not three times, once before every subject?

The Quranic verse, which instructs believers to "Obey God and obey the Apostle and those vested with authority among you," may initially raise the question of why the word "obey" is repeated and why it is not placed before each subject individually. However, a deeper understanding reveals the wisdom behind this phrasing.

The repetition of the word "obey" serves to emphasize the distinct nature of obedience in each case. Obedience to God stands independently as the highest and ultimate form of obedience. It is absolute and intrinsic, requiring no external decree or authority. Believers are inherently bound to obey God's commands, reflecting their devotion and submission to the Divine Will.

In contrast, obedience to the Prophet (sa) and the Imams (a) is contingent upon God's divine decree and appointment. It is a derived form of obedience, emanating from God's designation of the Prophet (sa) and the Imams (a) as guides and leaders of the community. Therefore, the repetition of the word "obey" serves to underline that while obedience to God is inherent and self-evident, obedience to the Prophet (sa) and the Imams (a) is established through God's divine authority and decree.

At its core, this repetition underscores the fundamental concept of worship and servitude to God. It reminds believers that adherence to God's commands, as well as those of His chosen messengers and divinely appointed leaders, is an essential aspect of their worship. Through obedience, believers express their devotion, submission, and acknowledgment of God's authority in both its direct and delegated forms.

Essentially, the dual mention of "obey" in the verse serves as a reminder of the hierarchy of obedience, with God at its pinnacle and the Prophet (sa) and the Imams (a) occupying roles of authority and guidance by God's divine design. It reinforces the profound concept that obedience to God is the foundation of faith and that obedience to His chosen representatives is an integral part of the believers' devotion and service to Him.

Referring to the Prophet (sa)

Is obedience the main reason for us to refer to the Holy Prophet Muhammad (sa)?

The obedience to and emulation of the Holy Prophet Muhammad (sa) hold profound significance in the lives of believers, as emphasized by many Quranic verses and prophetic traditions. God says in the Holy Quran:

لَقَدْ كَانَ لَكُمْ فِي رَسُولِ اللَّهِ أُسْوَةٌ حَسَنَةٌ لِمَنْ كَانَ يَرْجُو اللَّهَ وَالْيَوْمَ الْآخِرَ

There is certainly a good exemplar for you in the Apostle of God—for those who look forward to God

***and the Last Day.*[4]**

The Quran directs us to consider the Prophet (sa) as a role model, setting an excellent example for those who look forward to God and the Last Day. This guidance implies that the actions and conduct of the Prophet (sa) should serve as a model for believers unless there is evidence to the contrary.

One illustrative example from the Prophet's (sa) life is his practice of preparing his siwāk (toothbrush) and water for wuḍū' (ritual ablution) after his evening prayer before retiring for the night. Upon awakening, he would use the siwāk, perform wuḍū', and offer a four-unit prayer, then return to sleep. Upon awakening again, he would repeat the same routine.[5]

While this specific practice pertained to the Prophet (sa) himself, the Quranic directive to take him as a role model implies that believers may generalize from his actions in contexts that do not contradict established teachings. In other words, emulating the Prophet's (sa) practices, when applicable, can be seen as a means of seeking God's pleasure and following the guidance of the Quran.

This principle extends beyond the Prophet (sa) to the Imams from the Ahl al-Bayt, as affirmed by Twelver Shia Muslims. Just as the Quran presents the Prophet (sa) as an exemplar due to his immaculacy, the same rationale applies to the Imams, who are also regarded as immaculate figures within Shia Islam. Thus, the Quranic command to follow the Prophet (sa) as a role model naturally extends to the Imams, making them exemplary guides for the faithful.

Moreover, prophetic traditions, such as the Hadith Al-Thaqalayn, reinforce this principle by emphasizing the inseparable connection between the Quran and the Prophet's (sa) progeny.

---

[4] The Noble Quran, 33:21.

[5] Al-ʿĀmilī, *Wasāʾil al-Shīʿah*, 1:356.

إنّي قَدْ تَرَكْتُ فِيكُم الثَّقلَيْنِ أَحَدُهُمَا أَكْبَرُ مِنَ الآخَرِ، كِتَابُ اللهِ تعالى وَعِتْرَتِي، فَانْظُرُوا كَيفَ تَخْلفونِي فِيهِمَا فإنَّهُمَا لَن يَفْتَرِقَا حَتّى يَرِدَا عَلَيَّ الحَوْض.

Verily, I am leaving among you the Two Weighty Things – one of which is greater than the other – the Book of God and my kindred ('itrah), my household. Take care of how you treat them after me. Indeed, the two will never separate until they come back to me at the Pool [of al-Kawthar on the Day of Judgment].[6]

In this well-known tradition, the Prophet (sa) highlights the significance of upholding both the Quran and his kindred ('itrah), referring to his household and the Imams. This affirmation underscores the enduring unity of these two sources of guidance until the Day of Judgment.

Obedience to and emulation of the Holy Prophet Muhammad (sa) is a fundamental aspect of the faith, and this principle extends to the Imams from the Ahl al-Bayt as well. Believers are encouraged to take the actions and teachings of both the Prophet (sa) and the Imams as exemplars for their lives, in accordance with the guidance of the Quran and prophetic traditions. This practice reflects a commitment to seeking God's pleasure and following the path of righteousness.

Our Role Models

Does this principle – that we must take the Immaculates as role models – apply in every aspect of our lives? Does it extend to even everyday actions, like when to eat and when to sleep?

The principle of taking the Immaculates as role models, as directed by the Quran, raises an important question: does this principle extend to every aspect of our lives, including mundane actions like our daily

[6] Ibn Ḥanbal, *Musnad Aḥmad*, 3:18. See also: al-Tirmidhī, *Sunan al-Tirmidhī*, 13:200. For a list of many other references, see: al-Fayrūzābādī, *Faḍā'il al-Khamsah*, 2:43.

routines, eating habits, and sleep patterns? While the answer is not a simple 'yes' or 'no,' it is crucial to clarify the scope and implications of this principle.

When we speak of the Immaculates as our role models, it does not imply that every action they performed becomes an obligation for us or elevates routine activities to the level of religious duty. Instead, there is a nuanced understanding of how this principle applies. Some scholars suggest an exception to the role model principle, stating that it does not encompass general permissible actions, such as eating and sleeping, which are dictated by human nature.

The core focus of following the Immaculates as role models pertains to devotional matters and religious practices. In these areas, their actions serve as a source of guidance for believers. To understand the application of this principle, it is essential to consider the context and intent behind the Immaculates' actions.

If the Immaculates performed an action, we would thus learn of its permissibility and that would dismiss any idea that it may be prohibited. If they performed an action considering it to be recommended (mustaḥabb), the believers would follow suit and deem it to be recommended. This principle allows for a practical application of their guidance in areas of religious significance.

For instance, if an Imam observed a recommended fast on a specific day, it indicates that fasting on that day is also recommended for the believers. In this way, the actions of the Immaculates provide a model for believers to align their religious practices with the teachings and traditions of the Prophet (sa) and the Imams.

In summary, the principle of taking the Immaculates as role models primarily applies to religious and devotional matters. While it does not impose a strict obligation to replicate every aspect of their lives, it serves as a valuable guide for believers in aligning their religious practices and actions with the teachings and traditions of these revered figures. This nuanced approach ensures that the principle is understood and applied in a balanced and contextually appropriate manner.

If the Imam engages in an action that is confirmed as recommended, permissible, or obligatory, we can infer that it holds the same status for us as believers. The principle of following their example extends to actions that are categorically defined in the same way for both the Immaculates and the believers.

However, uncertainty arises when we are unsure about the motivation behind an Immaculate's actions. For instance, if we cannot determine whether an action was performed out of religious obligation or as a recommended act, or if we are aware that the Imam refrained from a particular action but are uncertain about whether it was due to its prohibition or for another reason.

The principle of permissibility, obligation, and recommendation in relation to the actions of the Immaculates carries profound implications for understanding and practicing our faith. When an action is observed to be performed by an Immaculate, it signifies that within the scope of human behavior, that action is considered permissible. This means that it doesn't contravene any religious laws or moral boundaries and can be undertaken without reservation.

However, when it comes to acts of worship and devotion, the classification becomes more nuanced. Acts of worship, such as prayers, fasting, and supplication, are not merely permissible but are further categorized into two distinct types: obligatory (wājib) and recommended (mustaḥabb). The determination of whether a specific act of worship is obligatory or recommended depends on the specific circumstances and context surrounding that act.

When historical accounts or traditions indicate that an Immaculate did not undertake a particular act, it implies that this action is not considered obligatory in the realm of religious practice. In other words, the absence of their engagement in that specific action suggests that it does not carry the same level of religious duty as obligatory acts of worship.

This intricate framework guides believers in their religious practices, offering insights into which actions are required, recommended, or simply permissible. It underscores the importance of discerning the specific context and circumstances surrounding the actions of the Immaculates to properly categorize them within the framework of Islamic jurisprudence and ethics.

Commands and Prohibitions

We have been bestowed with the divine command to obey God, the Prophet (sa), and the Imams, which encompasses a comprehensive code of conduct that guides every facet of our lives. However, the question arises: how do we discern and comprehend these commands, knowing what we are obligated to do and what we are forbidden from doing?

The foundational reservoir of these divine commands lies within the primary sources of Islamic teachings. These sources were meticulously compiled, explained, and elucidated by the Prophet Muhammad (sa) and subsequently by the Imams from the Ahl al-Bayt. It is through this rich corpus of ḥadīth, the recorded sayings, actions, and approvals of these revered figures, that we receive the profound wisdom and guidance that illuminate our spiritual journey.

To extract the authentic and authoritative commands from these sources, we turn to the invaluable work of our scholarly tradition. The vast body of Islamic disciplines was established by early Shia scholars and has evolved over the centuries under the diligent efforts of successive generations of specialists. These disciplines serve as the methodical tools that enable us to distinguish between what is trustworthy and what is unreliable within the vast sea of narrations.

Among these disciplines, some are dedicated to the critical evaluation of narrators' integrity, reliability, and precision, aiding the scholar in the classification of the narration, and evaluating the strength of its reliability and authority. Others focus on the contextual and linguistic analysis of the primary sources, shedding light on the subtle nuances and deeper meanings encapsulated within them.

A scholar of Islamic jurisprudence, theology, and ethics must be well-versed in these disciplines, as they embark on the noble journey of deciphering and interpreting the divine commands. It is through this rigorous and critical scholarly endeavor that we inch closer to a profound understanding of our faith and a more faithful adherence to the commands of God, the Prophet (sa), and the Imams, nurturing our spiritual growth and connection to the divine. This ongoing intellectual and spiritual pursuit continues to thrive within the hallowed halls of Islamic seminaries, ensuring that the light of knowledge and guidance continues to shine brilliantly for all those who seek it.

The Scholars

There are many questions about the seminaries, scholars, and seeking knowledge.

Is it obligatory on the believers to study the Islamic disciplines to become specialists who others can refer to in religious issues? If there is such an obligation, is it incumbent on every believer or only some?

Is the matter of taqlid – referring to a scholar and following their edicts – obligatory? Is a jurist's verdict binding on the believer? If a jurist is asked about an issue, is it obligatory on them to respond? Or can they choose to remain silent on the issue? Is there an obligation to educate the people about jurists' edicts?

Certainly, these are significant questions surrounding the roles of seminaries, scholars, and the pursuit of knowledge within the context of Islamic practice. These inquiries delve into the obligations and responsibilities of believers, specialists, and jurists in the realm of religious education and guidance.

First and foremost, it is essential to address the question of whether it is obligatory for believers to study the Islamic disciplines with the aim of becoming specialists who can guide others in religious matters. In this regard, we turn to a Quranic verse that states,

وَمَا كَانَ الْمُؤْمِنُونَ لِيَنفِرُوا كَافَّةً ۚ فَلَوْلَا نَفَرَ مِن كُلِّ فِرْقَةٍ مِّنْهُمْ طَائِفَةٌ لِّيَتَفَقَّهُوا فِي الدِّينِ وَلِيُنذِرُوا قَوْمَهُمْ إِذَا رَجَعُوا إِلَيْهِمْ لَعَلَّهُمْ يَحْذَرُونَ

Yet it is not for the faithful to go forth en masse. But why should there not be a group from each of their sections to go forth and become learned in religion, and to warn their people when they return to them, so that they may beware?[105]

This verse carries several implications.

Firstly, it underscores the obligation of seeking an understanding of religion, as evident in the phrase "but why should there not be." This phrase serves as a clear and compelling rallying call to action for believers. Secondly, it emphasizes that this obligation persists even when individuals must undertake extensive journeys to acquire knowledge.

Lastly, it signifies that this obligation is of the nature of wujūb kifā'ī, meaning that it is a general obligation on all believers, and it is fulfilled when a sufficient number of them step forward to undertake it. The verse does not demand the participation of 'all believers' but rather encourages 'a group' to emerge and delve into a comprehensive understanding of the religion. Consequently, it becomes an obligation for certain believers to specialize in the Islamic disciplines, with the number of such specialists being sufficient to meet the educational needs of society.

Turning to the second question concerning taqlid, the act of referring to a scholar and following their religious edicts, we must assess whether taqlid is obligatory and whether a jurist's verdict holds binding authority over the believer. The Quran instructs believers to

---

[105] The Noble Quran, 9:122.

فَاسْأَلُوا أَهْلَ الذِّكْرِ إِن كُنتُمْ لَا تَعْلَمُونَ

"Ask the People of the Reminder if you do not know."[106]

While this verse emphasizes seeking knowledge when you do not know, it is the preceding verse that adds depth to the discussion. Consequently, it is not solely about asking questions but also about adhering to the guidance provided by jurists out of devotion and obedience to God. This implies that the words of a jurist possess a binding authority for non-specialist believers. In essence, the command to "beware" of religious guidance and rulings cannot be effectively fulfilled without following the verdicts and counsel of jurists.

These Quranic verses offer valuable insights into the obligations and responsibilities of believers, scholars, and jurists concerning the acquisition and dissemination of religious knowledge. These obligations extend to various facets of life and are grounded in the pursuit of a comprehensive understanding of Islamic disciplines.

If You Do Not Know!

As you mentioned, God says,

فَاسْأَلُوا أَهْلَ الذِّكْرِ إِن كُنتُمْ لَا تَعْلَمُونَ

Ask the People of the Reminder if you do not know.[107]

---

[106] The Noble Quran, 21:7.

[107] The Noble Quran, 21:7.

Can we use this verse to prove the necessity of taqlid and the binding nature of a mujtahid's[108] edicts?

The apparent meaning of this Quranic verse encourages seeking guidance. It does not provide a conclusive proof for the necessity of taqlid or the binding nature of a mujtahid's edicts.

However, this verse has a deeper meaning that is explained to us by the narrations of Ahl al-Bayt. It calls upon believers to follow the Imams, the People of the Reminder, not merely for the sake of inquiry but out of devotion and obedience to God.

The previous verse - the one which commands a group of believers to become learned in religion[109] - is more relevant to this question. It implies that the words and rulings of qualified jurists carry a binding authority for non-specialist believers. While a detailed discussion of the indications of these verses exists, a comprehensive exploration would lead us into a separate conversation.

Moving on to your third question, the Quranic verse you mentioned indicates that issuing religious edicts is indeed an obligation. It explicitly commands the subjects of this verse to "warn their people," emphasizing the responsibility of knowledgeable individuals to clarify and convey religious guidance to the community.

The same can be understood from the following verse,

إِنَّ الَّذِينَ يَكْتُمُونَ مَا أَنزَلْنَا مِنَ الْبَيِّنَاتِ وَالْهُدَىٰ مِن بَعْدِ مَا بَيَّنَّاهُ لِلنَّاسِ فِي الْكِتَابِ أُولَٰئِكَ يَلْعَنُهُمُ اللَّهُ وَيَلْعَنُهُمُ اللَّاعِنُونَ

Indeed, those who conceal what We have sent down of

---

[108] A mujtahid is a qualified Islamic jurist who possesses the expertise to independently derive legal rulings (fatwas) from Islamic sources. They undergo rigorous training in Islamic law, theology, and jurisprudence. Mujtahids are of varying levels, with the highest-ranking mujtahids referred to as Maraje' or sources of emulation, in Twelver Shia Islam. Following a mujtahid's guidance - emulation - is typically referred to as taqlid.

[109] The Noble Quran, 9:122.

> ***manifest proofs and guidance, after We have clarified it in the Book for mankind, they shall be cursed by God and cursed by the cursers.***[110]

This verse serves as a stark reminder of the obligation to convey and clarify the detailed commandments of our religion.

While these Quranic verses may not provide an exhaustive proof of taqlid or the binding nature of a mujtahid's edicts on their own, they collectively contribute to a holistic understanding of these concepts within the broader framework of Islamic teachings. They highlight the importance of seeking knowledge, following qualified jurists, issuing religious edicts, and conveying religious guidance to the community as essential components of religious duty and obedience to God's commandments.

The answer to your fourth question should be clear now. The verses make it an obligation to "warn" and clarify the detailed commandments of our religion.

Perhaps failing to deliver these edicts could be understood as a form of "concealing" of truth and guidance. If so, the obligation to convey this guidance can be understood from this verse as well:

وَلَا تَلْبِسُوا الْحَقَّ بِالْبَاطِلِ وَتَكْتُمُوا الْحَقَّ وَأَنْتُمْ تَعْلَمُونَ

> ***Do not mix the truth with falsehood, nor conceal the truth while you know.***[111]

The verse clarifies the following issues: One, it is prohibited to conceal the truth. Two, it is also prohibited to mix truth with falsehood, thus creating confusion. Three, whoever conceals the truth or intentionally creates confusion is cursed by God.

---

[110] The Noble Quran, 2:159.

[111] The Noble Quran, 2:42.

Concealing the Truth

What is the meaning of "concealing the truth"? Is it simply not to speak it out loud? Or is it intentionally hiding and suppressing it?

When we examine the verses of the Holy Quran, they seem to convey the second meaning. God says,

وَلَا تَكْتُمُوا الشَّهَادَةَ - وَمَن يَكْتُمْهَا فَإِنَّهُ آثِمٌ قَلْبُهُ

And do not conceal your testimony; anyone who conceals it, his heart will indeed be sinful.[112]

إِنِّي أَعْلَمُ غَيْبَ السَّمَاوَاتِ وَالْأَرْضِ وَأَعْلَمُ مَا تُبْدُونَ وَمَا كُنتُمْ تَكْتُمُونَ

I know the Unseen of the heavens and the earth, and that I know whatever you disclose and whatever you conceal.[113]

لَتُبَيِّنُنَّهُ لِلنَّاسِ وَلَا تَكْتُمُونَهُ

You shall explain it for the people, and you shall not conceal it.[114]

The Quran advises against concealing one's testimony, emphasizing that those who do so commit a sin of the heart. This implies that concealing essential information, especially in legal matters, is morally and spiritually wrong.

God's omniscience is highlighted in the Quranic verse, indicating that He knows both what is disclosed and what is concealed. This underscores the futility of attempting to hide the truth from God, as

---

[112] The Noble Quran, 2:283.

[113] The Noble Quran, 2:33.

[114] The Noble Quran, 3:187.

nothing escapes His knowledge.

The Quran also instructs believers to explain the truth to others and not to conceal it. This reinforces the idea that sharing knowledge and guidance with fellow human beings is an essential aspect of conveying the truth.

Delivering the 'Warning'

There are two distinct approaches to fulfilling the duty of warning people through educating them about religious edicts:

First, a jurist can make themselves available within the community and take measures to ensure that their edicts are well-understood. For instance, they may choose to be present in the mosque, readily answering any questions posed to them. Additionally, they could open their doors to the community, making themselves accessible for individuals seeking guidance.

Second, a jurist may opt for a more proactive approach by actively engaging with the community to impart knowledge. For instance, if they come across someone who is unfamiliar with how to perform prayers, they would take the initiative to personally teach them. In this approach, the jurist doesn't simply wait for individuals to seek them out but actively goes out to disseminate edicts to the people.

The first method of delivering these rulings is undeniably a part of the process of "warning" the people about religious obligations.

However, the second approach raises an important question: Is it obligatory for a jurist to venture into the community and ensure that people are well-informed about the rules of Islamic practices?

The verse from the Quran indeed commands believers to "warn" their people without specifying the mode of warning. Consequently, the act of warning is not limited to the first approach, where a jurist makes themselves available for inquiries within the community.

However, it's important to note that the obligation does not extend to the second mode – that is, requiring jurists to actively go door-to-door to ensure that individuals are well-versed in the religious rulings of their faith. This approach of proactive proselytizing, involving visiting people's homes to disseminate religious knowledge, was not practiced by the Immaculate Imams, nor was it a historical norm among scholars.

Hence, there is no binding obligation for jurists to engage in such extensive proselytization efforts. While the duty to "warn" remains, it can be fulfilled through various means, including responding to inquiries, offering guidance when sought, and educating the community, but it does not necessitate the rigorous, proactive outreach akin to door-to-door evangelism.

Referring to the Jurists

There are people who say that we do not need to refer to the jurists and marājiʿ. They even claim there is no proof that the concepts of ijtihād (the process of extrapolating rulings from the sources of legislation) and taqlīd (emulation) are valid.

What is the response to such claims?

What we have said so far should be enough to answer this question.

But to clarify the issue further, let us start by asking the following question:

- What is the evidence that a sick person should see a doctor?
- If your car breaks down, why should you go to a mechanic?
- If you want to build a house, why hire an architect?
- If you have a legal question, why would you consult a lawyer?

You can ask the same question about every profession. To put it more generally, why do we refer to experts in their fields of specialization?

My question applies to every aspect of human life.

- So why do we rely on doctors, engineers, lawyers, and other professionals?

- What is the evidence there?

The answer is simple: This does not need evidence.

If you are ill, you refer to a person with the knowledge and skill to treat your illness – a physician. In the field of engineering, you must refer to the engineer who has the knowledge and skill to address your problem. Thus, in every field, the ignorant person refers to the specialists in the field.

This is a rational case that does not need evidence.

The same logic applies when we say that individuals without specialized knowledge in religious disciplines – laypeople[115] – must refer to jurists in understanding their faith.

Who should a layperson – who is unaware of the legal ruling – refer to? They must refer to the expert who knows the details of the ruling. This expert is the mujtahid, a person whose expertise derives rulings from the primary sources of the religion. Also, if the layperson returns to a mujtahid, then he becomes his reference, or the reference that he imitates – his *marji'*.

To those who claim that there is no need to refer to experts in religious disciplines, let me ask the following question:

- What should a layperson do if they wish to perform ḥajj?
- Would you come up with your own rules?
- Would you refer to other laypeople?
- Would you give up on knowing the rules and decide not to perform ḥajj altogether?

The answer to all these questions is clearly "no." Your only viable option is to refer to an expert on these issues or put the time and effort into

[115] In this text, we will use layperson is as a translation for the Arabic "mukallaf" – i.e., a person who is responsible and will be held accountable for their actions. This refers to every individual who is of sound mind and has reached the age of majority. The detailed definitions and rulings regarding this concept can be found in the books of fiqh.

becoming an expert yourself.

The case is clear and logical. No further evidence is necessary.

The same goes for the rulings on prayers, fasting, and other acts of worships. Where do people who are ignorant of the rules of the *sharīʿah*, or Islamic law, get acquainted with it? They must refer to the specialists and experts in the discipline. In other words, a layperson must follow the jurist (*faqīh*).

This is a clear rational issue.

In addition, in the Islamic seminary, we say this issue is supported by "*sīrat al-ʿuqalāʾ*" – i.e., it is the practice of rational people throughout history.

By that, we mean rational people refer to individuals of expertise when they themselves do not have the knowhow to address an issue they face. Rational people have done so throughout history. Thus, a rational historical precedence has been set on the issue.

We can also assume that God Almighty does not disapprove of this precedence. Why?

Because if God Almighty did disapprove, He would have communicated that disapproval through prohibition and deterrence. There is no evidence of that in the Noble Quran or the corpus of ḥadīth. To the contrary, we find sources that encourage reference back to experts when it comes to religious knowledge. Of course, every area of expertise, including religious knowledge, requires a dedicated course of study.

What would happen if you or I, for example, object to a surgeon who is exercising his medical judgement when operating on a patient?

We would be told: You are not qualified in this specialty!

The surgeon has dedicated years to the study and practice of medicine, and therefore has the necessary qualifications to exercise professional judgement.

Religious knowledge needs a dedicated course of study as well. A person who has no knowledge of religious rulings should refer to the specialized mujtahid.

So, we do not need to refer to the corpus of ḥadīth to come to a conclusion about this issue. Still, let us take one example of a narration that supports this conclusion.

In one narration, Imam al-Riḍā (a) was asked, "Sometimes I am unable to reach you and ask you about what I need [to know] from the teachings of my religion. Is Yūnus ibn ʿAbdu'l-raḥmān trustworthy so I might ask him about what I need [to know] from the tenets of my religion?"

The Imam (a) responded,

نَعَم.

Yes.[116]

In summary, the layperson – the *mukallaf* – must learn the detailed rulings on issues affecting his life. In this case, they must refer to a jurist who has met the necessary preconditions. This is because reason dictates that a person who does not have specialized knowledge in any area should refer to the expert in the field. Since there is no religious deterrent against this conclusion, this indicates divine approval and acceptance. Of course, this answer is a short, generalized, and simplified answer. Otherwise, the issue deserves a broader and more detailed study.

What if someone does not believe that ijtihād and taqlīd have a role in our understanding of the religion?

Those who hold such skepticism are entitled to their opinions, but they should also consider the implications of their stance. It's analogous to someone asserting that they do not believe in the legitimacy and value of consulting a physician when they are ill.

---

[116] Al-ʿĀmilī, *Wasāʾil al-Shīʿah*, 27:147.

Imagine if a person falls ill – would they freely take any medication without a prescription? Would they attempt to perform surgery on themselves? The answer is unequivocally no. Such actions would not be considered rational or safe.

Likewise, in the realm of legal disputes, if someone found themselves embroiled in a critical legal matter, they would likely seek the services of a qualified attorney rather than representing themselves.

This principle extends across various professions and fields of expertise, including religion. As previously discussed, the same logic applies to those seeking religious guidance. Every layperson is encouraged to refer to a qualified mujtahid to gain insight into the religious rulings that shape their faith.

In essence, ijtihād and taqlīd play vital roles in ensuring that individuals receive accurate and well-informed guidance on religious matters, just as consulting a physician or hiring an attorney is essential in their respective domains of expertise.

Meeting the Preconditions

You mentioned that a jurist should meet the necessary preconditions. Can you explain what this phrase means? What are some of the preconditions that must be met?

Let me elaborate on what some of these preconditions entail and why they are significant.

First and foremost, a jurist must possess the essential qualifications. These qualifications primarily encompass two key aspects: ijtihād and ʿadālah.

Ijtihād refers to the jurist's ability to derive religious rulings from the primary sources of Islamic jurisprudence. This capacity is not inherent but is developed through rigorous study, training, and practice in the

Islamic disciplines. It entails an in-depth understanding of Islamic jurisprudence, theology, and other relevant fields.

The second precondition, ʿadālah, revolves around the concept of righteousness. A jurist must lead a life characterized by piety and adherence to the sharīʿah in all aspects. This includes performing acts of worship, such as prayer and fasting, with sincerity and devotion. It also extends to their moral conduct, necessitating that they do not engage in dishonesty, deceit, or any transgressions against others. In essence, ʿadālah signifies a jurist's commitment to upholding Islamic ethical and moral values.

These are some of the preconditions, which are essential because they ensure that the jurist possesses the necessary knowledge and moral integrity to interpret and guide others on matters of Islamic jurisprudence. With that, a jurist can provide reliable and trustworthy religious guidance to the community, thus upholding the integrity and authenticity of the Islamic legal tradition.

The Most Knowledgeable

It is indeed a crucial point that when choosing a jurist to follow in matters of religious guidance, one should prioritize the selection of the most knowledgeable and competent individual. In Shia Islam, this principle of choosing the most knowledgeable jurist, also known as the "most learned" or "*al-Aʿlam*," is considered paramount.

The concept of "most knowledgeable" is rooted in the rationality of the decision-making process. When faced with complex religious or legal questions, it is logical to seek guidance from the most competent expert available. While the religious texts may not explicitly state the necessity of following the most knowledgeable jurist, the rational basis for this practice is evident.

Reason dictates that if a more knowledgeable and competent expert is accessible, it is one's duty to refer to them for guidance. There is no religious evidence to suggest otherwise, so adhering to the rule of reason is both a practical and rational approach.

Historically, the precedence of seeking guidance from the most knowledgeable scholars and jurists has been a common practice in Shia communities. This practice has not been prohibited by religious texts, reinforcing the notion that it aligns with the divine approval. Therefore, it is not only a rational choice but also a well-established tradition within Shia Islamic jurisprudence to prioritize the most knowledgeable jurist for religious guidance.

Theology or Fiqh?

When deciding whom to follow, should one prioritize a person with more expertise in theological matters or someone with a deeper understanding of fiqh and uṣūl al-fiqh?

The crucial factor in determining whom to follow lies in understanding the needs of a layperson. Laypeople do not necessarily require an in-depth comprehension of the intricate theological intricacies regarding the Immaculate Imams' (a) exalted status in the eyes of God Almighty. Instead, knowing that there are Immaculate Imams (a) divinely appointed to guide humanity suffices. Delving into the finer points of Imamate is not obligatory, as these details will not be a subject of scrutiny in the hereafter.

What will be questioned, however, are matters related to worship, such as prayers, fasting, and ḥajj, as well as one's interactions and transactions with others. The questions posed will revolve around why an individual did not pray or why they performed prayers incorrectly. Inquiries will also touch on issues like dishonesty and injustice in one's actions.

When it comes to theological matters, a fundamental understanding of the general concept is sufficient. Laypeople should be aware that there is always a living Immaculate Imam safeguarding the purity of God's religion. For matters related to the rules of worship and transactions, it is essential to follow a marjiʿ who is an expert in the disciplines of fiqh and uṣūl al-fiqh.

This response offers a simplified perspective on the question, as it can be explored in much greater detail if desired.

Is the issue of following the most knowledgeable a matter of conviction? Or is it a rule that must be followed? Must a layperson be convinced of it before they begin looking for the most knowledgeable and following him?

In essence, this matter can be likened to the process of referring a patient to a doctor. It is fundamentally rational and governed by intellect. When a patient is advised to consult a doctor, or even a specific specialist, they typically accept and comply without hesitation. However, it appears that a distinction is made when it comes to religious rulings concerning acts such as prayer, fasting, and pilgrimage. Why is it not equally evident that these religious obligations demand a level of expertise that only specialized jurists can provide?

If seeking expert medical advice is deemed necessary for a patient's well-being, then it follows that a layperson seeking to understand and fulfill the religious obligations of prayer, fasting, and pilgrimage should equally turn to knowledgeable jurists for guidance. After all, these religious duties are required of individuals, and it becomes impossible to fulfill them correctly without a clear understanding of their rules and procedures.

The clarity of this principle is often corresponding to the seriousness of the issue in question. Rational people may not have an issue with someone self-medicating a common cold. But what about a respiratory virus? What about a possible cancerous tumor?

The more there is at stake, the more evident and pressing the need to refer to an expert becomes. The question we need to ask ourselves is this: How much is at stake when it comes to our religion? How much importance do we give to our prayers and fasting?

If we understand that our eternal life hangs in the balance - that whether we spend it in everlasting happiness or eternal regret depends on our understanding and application of God's laws - then we will make our best attempt to get the answer to these questions right. This requires us either to refer to the experts, or to become experts ourselves.

When Experts Disagree

Now what do we do when the experts disagree? Which expert do we follow? Knowing what is at stake, we need to put our best effort into ensuring that whoever we follow will get us the closest to the correct understanding of God's teachings. We need a way to find the most qualified, competent, and proficient expert. We do this by referring to the peer community of experts, because they are the ones capable of identifying the most proficient amongst them.

Thus, we say that a person should follow the 'most knowledgeable' jurist.

Again, this is in line with the conduct of rational people in any other aspect of life. If - God forbid - your child needs a complicated open-heart surgery, would you trust any cardiologist to perform the procedure? Would you not try to find the most competent surgeon? Clearly, something this important deserves putting in the effort to improve the chances of a positive outcome.

Therefore, it is imperative to rely on the expertise of jurists in matters of jurisprudence. The question of personal conviction should not be a factor in this equation, as it pertains to a practical necessity rather than a matter of personal preference.

What makes an individual jurist more knowledgeable than others?

When it comes to determining the knowledge and competence of a jurist, experience plays a vital role in assessing a jurist's knowledge and competence. A jurist who has spent decades studying and practicing Islamic jurisprudence is likely to have encountered a wide range of legal and ethical dilemmas, thereby gaining a deeper understanding of the complexities of human life and being able to provide a more nuanced guidance.

Thus, the choice of a jurist to follow should be made with careful consideration of their knowledge, qualifications, and experience. This rational approach ensures that individuals receive accurate and reliable guidance in accordance with the teachings of Shia Islam.

How Do We Know the Most Knowledgeable?

What are the elements of knowledge? How do we recognize the most knowledgeable? What are the criteria for the experts to identify ijtihad and scholarly merit?

Before we answer the question, we must first agree on the need to refer to the jurist in the rulings of *Sharī'ah*. It is an obvious matter, such as one plus one equals two. No one can disagree with that.

If we agree that it is necessary to refer to the most knowledgeable jurist, then the criterion for identifying the most knowledgeable and diligent is the same method in identifying the most knowledgeable and most skilled physicist. We must refer to other experts in the field.

Take this example. If we were to ask, Name one of the most brilliant physicists of the twentieth century? Most people would name Albert Einstein. Why? Was it the world's blue-collar workers who decided that Einstein was an ingenious physicist? Was it lawyers? Physicians? Of course not. It was other physicists who assessed and tested his theories, then gave him the recognition that he deserved.

If physicists testify that there is a skillful and brilliant physicist among them, their testimony is credible because they are the ones with experience. We do not refer to a person outside the field of physics and take their word, as this has no meaning. We refer to the experts within the field.

Yes, people of a specialization may have differing opinions. For example, if you ask some physicists about who is more skilled, you may get different answers. This is only natural.

The same process and principles apply when trying to identify the most knowledgeable jurist. If the testimonies regarding one person are more and are all trustworthy, while in another person the testimonies are few and weak, then there is a preponderance of evidence in favor of the former.

Identifying the Most Knowledgeable

Is it possible for a non-expert in the religious disciplines to identify a mujtahid or the most knowledgeable marjaʿ?

Let's explore this question from a different perspective.

Consider this: Can someone without any medical background, such as the average person – you or I, for example – identify the doctor who possesses the highest level of skill and knowledge in their medical specialty?

If one were to concede that this is an unrealistic expectation, then the same principle applies to the realm of jurisprudence and the identification of the most knowledgeable among jurists. Just as non-medical individuals are ill-equipped to determine the most competent physician, those without expertise in jurisprudence are similarly unequipped to make informed judgments regarding jurists' levels of knowledge and expertise.

It becomes evident that only experts within a specific field are capable of recognizing and distinguishing the most skilled and knowledgeable individuals in that field. In the context of religious jurisprudence, only qualified scholars and jurists possess the requisite knowledge and discernment to identify their peers' expertise and competence.

Conflicting Testimony

If experts give conflicting testimony on who the most knowledgeable mujtahid is, can the layperson follow any of the possible candidates?

This question becomes clearer when we draw parallels with other areas of expertise. For instance, when medical experts disagree on how to treat a particular disease, what steps should a patient take?

In such situations, the logical course of action is to revisit and assess the testimonies and opinions presented by these experts. Similarly, when it comes to identifying the most knowledgeable jurist, a layperson should examine the various testimonies and opinions put forth by experts in the field of religious jurisprudence. This process allows for a more informed and conscientious decision in selecting a mujtahid to follow.

In essence, the principle remains the same: when experts within a specialized field disagree, seeking further clarification and informed guidance from these experts is the rational and prudent approach.

Who is the Judge?

Sometimes it is difficult for the experts to decide who is more knowledgeable. Naturally, people outside of scholarly circles will have an even tougher time with the issue. What are people to do?

Navigating the question of who is the most knowledgeable jurist can indeed be challenging, even for experts, let alone individuals outside of scholarly circles. In such cases, it's essential to adopt a rational approach to address this issue effectively.

Imagine you are inquiring about the most knowledgeable jurist, and two jurists are being considered—one known by a specific group of experts and the other known by a different group of experts. Here lies a critical consideration: do the experts you consult have knowledge of both jurists in question? Were they asked to make a direct comparison between the two, or were they simply providing opinions based on their own knowledge and expertise?

If the experts were not acquainted with one of the jurists, it means that particular jurist was not part of their comparative analysis. The crucial point here is that when faced with conflicting testimonies, we must explore ways to weigh these testimonies against each other, just as we would approach any significant matter in our lives. This process requires a rational and measured approach, free from emotional bias.

If, despite these efforts, one is unable to conclusively identify the most knowledgeable jurist due to conflicting expert opinions, the best course of action is to practice precaution in matters where the candidates for the most knowledgeable differ. This cautious approach ensures that one adheres to the most reliable and stringent opinions available within the religious framework. However, if no clear resolution is reached, the individual retains the freedom to choose from among the candidates based on their judgment and conscience.

Knowledgeability

What is the meaning of being "the most knowledgeable"? Is there a precise definition?

The concept of being "the most knowledgeable" in the context of Islamic jurisprudence does not have a rigid or precisely defined definition. It hinges on the ability to scrutinize intricate arguments and extract nuanced interpretations from religious texts.

When two individuals read the same religious text, one may uncover more detailed and subtle insights than the other. This variation arises from differences in their knowledge, experience, and expertise in various Islamic disciplines. It's important to note that knowledgeability, in this sense, is not about proximity to absolute truth, which only God Almighty has.

The process of deduction within Islamic jurisprudence relies on a broad spectrum of tools and resources. A competent jurist draws from the knowledge of the Arabic language and the Quran, the principles of juristic reasoning (uṣūl), the biographies of narrators, the science of hadith, and various other disciplines that aid in understanding religious texts.

A highly knowledgeable jurist possesses a deep understanding of these disciplines and can deduce what appears to be the most appropriate ruling based on their educated approximation of God's will. The depth of their knowledge is a result of their continuous study, experience, and commitment to sorting out nuanced arguments.

For instance, consider two jurists examining the reports[117] of esteemed scholars like Sayyid al-Khoei and Sayyid Muḥsin al-Hakim. Each jurist might derive different conclusions from the same reports, highlighting the diverse interpretations possible within Islamic jurisprudence. Thus, a jurist who can delve into the text with greater nuance and depth, offering more profound and well-supported arguments, is generally regarded as more knowledgeable in this complex field.

---

[117] Reports (*taqrīrāt*, singular *taqrīr*) are a distinctive and important part of studying in the Islamic seminary at all levels of study. Students are encouraged – and sometimes required – to make a 'report' for each of their courses, where they compile and annotate their pre-lesson preparation, lesson notes, questions, and relevant discussions. A teacher may review a student's report to gauge their understanding of the subject matter. These reports are especially important when they are compiled by a jurist's brightest students during *al-baḥth al-khārij*.

Following a Deceased Scholar

There are some questions about the validity of following a deceased scholar. If experts say that the deceased scholar is more knowledgeable then the currently living ones, should he be followed?

The question of whether it is valid to follow a deceased scholar in Islamic jurisprudence has sparked some debate. Generally, there is a consensus among scholars that following a deceased jurist is not permissible. However, scholars have outlined an exception to this rule.

According to this exception, if a layperson was previously following a jurist and that jurist passes away, they are allowed to continue following the deceased jurist, even after their demise, under specific circumstances. The crucial condition for this exception is that the deceased jurist must be more knowledgeable in Islamic jurisprudence than the currently living ones.

In essence, if the deceased jurist is recognized as more knowledgeable than any living jurist, a layperson may continue to follow the teachings and rulings of the deceased scholar, even after their passing. This exception is widely accepted among scholars and might even be considered a point of consensus within the Islamic jurisprudential tradition. It reflects the importance placed on knowledge and expertise in determining who should be followed in matters of religious guidance.

The Juristic Process

How does a jurist deduce a ruling on any issue? Can you shed some light, even briefly, on juristic methodology?

To comprehend how a jurist deduces rulings on various issues, it is essential to explore the methodology they employ. Jurists follow a structured approach that is deeply rooted in specific sources and principles. This process is neither arbitrary nor isolated; rather, it is grounded in a rich tradition and guided by certain principles.

Jurists do not operate in isolation; they are part of a broader institution and school of thought. They draw upon a vast array of resources in their deductive process, which can be considered a sacred and continuous chain of knowledge transmission. This chain links them to the Twelfth Imam (a), who is believed to be the divinely appointed leader and guide for Muslims.

Several critical disciplines come into play as jurists engage in this process. Firstly, they must have a comprehensive understanding of the Arabic language, encompassing all its intricate details, since primary sources are in Arabic. Moreover, they need to critically assess the authenticity of these sources before relying on them for deductions.

In essence, a jurist's methodology involves a thorough examination of various sources, including the Quran, hadith (sayings and actions of the

Prophet Muhammad and Ahl ul-Bayt), and the writings of previous scholars. They apply their linguistic expertise and scrutinize the authenticity of these sources to derive comprehensive and well-founded rulings.

This methodology represents a profound and systematic approach to understanding Islamic jurisprudence and serves as a means to ensure that the rulings they deduce are rooted in the teachings of Islam and the guidance of their religious authorities.

These are specialized discussions in the discipline of uṣūl al-fiqh, correct?

Indeed, these discussions delve into the intricate realm of uṣūl al-fiqh, the principles of juristic reasoning. They constitute the bedrock upon which the entire edifice of Islamic jurisprudence stands. These principles guide jurists in navigating the complex web of sources and traditions, ensuring that their deductions are firmly grounded in the tenets of the faith.

These discussions encompass a wide array of topics, each bearing significant weight in the realm of jurisprudence. Initially, they grapple with the question of the authoritative status of the apparent meanings of the Noble Quran, the traditions of the Prophet Muhammad and the Ahl al-Bayt (a).

Furthermore, these deliberations extend to the realm of scholarly consensus, a crucial aspect of jurisprudential determination. The consensus of scholars holds a profound role in validating legal rulings, as it represents a collective agreement within the scholarly community.

Additionally, this discipline explores the role of reason in the process of juristic deduction, a topic of paramount importance for jurists. There are many other wide-ranging discussions in uṣūl al-fiqh.

Authoritativeness of Ḥadīth

Can you give us an example of the authoritativeness of prophetic ḥadīth?

The discussion on the authoritativeness of ḥadīth, or prophetic tradition, falls into two stages:

In the first stage, how do we prove the authenticity of a particular prophetic tradition or practice? How do we prove who said this or did that?

This is where the jurist studies the authoritativeness of traditions. If authoritativeness is proven, then we must follow those traditions out of devotion to God and His selected Messenger (sa).

If authoritativeness is established, then we move on to the second stage; how do we prove that the Prophet's (sa) words, actions, and omittances are binding on us Muslims?

There are many verses in The Noble Quran that we can turn to at this stage. God Almighty says,

يَا أَيُّهَا الَّذِينَ آمَنُوا أَطِيعُوا اللَّهَ وَأَطِيعُوا الرَّسُولَ وَأُولِي الأَمْرِ مِنكُمْ

O you who have faith! Obey God and obey the Apostle and those vested with authority among you.[118]

وَمَا يَنطِقُ عَنِ الْهَوَىٰ

Nor does he speak out of [his own] desire:

إِنْ هُوَ إِلَّا وَحْيٌ يُوحَىٰ

it is just a revelation that is revealed [to him],[119]

---

[118] The Noble Quran, 4:59.

[119] The Noble Quran, 53:3-4.

لَّقَدْ كَانَ لَكُمْ فِي رَسُولِ اللَّهِ أُسْوَةٌ حَسَنَةٌ

There is certainly a good exemplar for you in the Apostle of God[120]

وَمَا كَانَ لِمُؤْمِنٍ وَلَا مُؤْمِنَةٍ إِذَا قَضَى اللَّهُ وَرَسُولُهُ أَمْرًا أَن يَكُونَ لَهُمُ الْخِيَرَةُ
مِنْ أَمْرِهِمْ - وَمَن يَعْصِ اللَّهَ وَرَسُولَهُ فَقَدْ ضَلَّ ضَلَالًا مُّبِينًا

A faithful man or woman may not have any option in their matter, when God and His Apostle have decided on a matter, and whoever disobeys God and His Apostle has certainly strayed into manifest error.[121]

قُلْ إِن كُنتُمْ تُحِبُّونَ اللَّهَ فَاتَّبِعُونِي يُحْبِبْكُمُ اللَّهُ وَيَغْفِرْ لَكُمْ ذُنُوبَكُمْ - وَاللَّهُ غَفُورٌ
رَّحِيمٌ

Say, 'If you love God, then follow me; God will love you and forgive you your sins, and God is all-forgiving, all-merciful.'[122]

فَآمِنُوا بِاللَّهِ وَرَسُولِهِ النَّبِيِّ الْأُمِّيِّ الَّذِي يُؤْمِنُ بِاللَّهِ وَكَلِمَاتِهِ وَاتَّبِعُوهُ لَعَلَّكُمْ
تَهْتَدُونَ

So have faith in God and His Apostle, the untaught prophet, who has faith in God and His words, and follow him so that you may be guided.[123]

---

[120] The Noble Quran, 33:21.

[121] The Noble Quran, 33:36.

[122] The Noble Quran, 3:31.

[123] The Noble Quran, 7:158.

وَمَا آتَاكُمُ الرَّسُولُ فَخُذُوهُ وَمَا نَهَاكُمْ عَنْهُ فَانتَهُوا

Take whatever the Apostle gives you, and refrain from whatever he forbids you.[124]

These verses clearly prove the obligation to follow the Messenger (sa). Some of the verses command us to listen to the Prophet's (sa) words. Moreover, the explicit meaning of some verses, and the implicit meaning of others, clearly proves the obligation to follow him in the broadest sense.

Moreover, the authoritativeness of the Prophet's (sa) words and actions should be evident to every Muslim. If that was not the case, a Muslim would not be able to practice the rituals of the religion and would not be guided to its most basic tenets. There should be no need to deduce it by listing the above verses, but we do so to lift even the slightest doubt or misconception.

Essentially, if we do not accept the authoritativeness of prophetic traditions, then we have stripped Islam of all its teachings and practices.

Some people claim that the Book of God is sufficient and there is no need for prophetic traditions. What would we say to that?

After the foregoing discussion, it should be obvious how mistaken that opinion is. Clearly, we cannot abandon prophetic traditions on the claim that the Noble Quran contains everything we need.

It is true that the Noble Quran was revealed as a clarification of everything. However, it does not exist in a vacuum. It clearly instructs us to follow the Prophet (sa). That is part of its comprehensive nature.

God says,

---

[124] The Noble Quran, 59:7.

وَأَنزَلْنَا إِلَيْكَ الذِّكْرَ لِتُبَيِّنَ لِلنَّاسِ مَا نُزِّلَ إِلَيْهِمْ وَلَعَلَّهُمْ يَتَفَكَّرُونَ

We have sent down the reminder to you [Prophet Muhammad (sa)] so that you may clarify for the people that which has been sent down to them, so that they may reflect.[125]

It is strange that, after all this, there are some who doubted the authoritativeness of the Prophet's (sa) sunnah.

For example, ʿAbdu'lāh ibn ʿAmr[126] ibn al-ʿĀṣ[127] said,

> *I used to write everything I heard from the Messenger of God (sa). Quraysh forbade me to do so and said, 'You write everything you hear from the Messenger of God (sa) while he is a man who speaks out of anger or contentment?' I stopped writing and mentioned this to the Messenger of God (sa).*

Upon hearing this, the Prophet (sa) pointed to his mouth and said,

اكتُب فَوالَّذي، نَفسي بِيَدِهِ مَا خَرَجَ مِنْهُ إِلَّا حقٌّ.

Write! By the One in who holds my soul in His hands, nothing but truth comes out of [this mouth].[128]

---

[125] The Noble Quran, 16:44.

[126] ʿAbdu'lāh ibn ʿAmr ibn al-ʿĀṣ was a companion of the Holy Prophet Muhammad, having accepted Islam at a young age. He was known to be one of the first companions to record the sayings and actions of the Prophet, making him one of the early narrators of Hadith.

[127] ʿAmr ibn al-ʿĀṣ (573 – 664 CE) was a wealthy member of the Banū Sahm clan of the tribe of Quraysh and an early opponent of Islam in Mecca. He eventually accepted Islam in 630 CE with the dwindling power of the Meccans and the rise of the Muslims. He would become a close ally of the Umayyads and a staunch opponent of Imam Ali (a) and his caliphate, under the banner of Muʿāwiyah bin Abi Sufyan in the Battle of Siffin (657 CE).

[128] Sunan al-Dārimī, 1:125.

The Messenger's (sa) Words

Another example comes from the final days of the Prophet (sa). When he was on his deathbed, he said,

آتوني أَكْتُبْ لَكُمْ كِتَابًا لَنْ تَضِلُّوا بَعْدَهُ أبداً.

Bring me [a pen and paper] and I will write for you a letter after which you will never be misguided.

They said, "The Messenger of God (sa) is delusional!"[129]

Al-Bukhārī[130] also recounted the following account on the authority of Ibn ʿAbbās:[131] As the Prophet (sa) was in his home during the last days of his life, his companions gathered around him. The Prophet (sa) said,

هَلُمَّ أَكْتُبْ لَكُمْ كِتَابًا لَنْ تَضِلُّوا بَعْدَهُ.

Let me write for you a letter after which you will never be misguided.

Some said, "The Prophet (sa) has been overtaken by pain. You have the Book of God, and it will suffice us."

The guests began to dispute amongst themselves on whether they should give the Prophet (sa) a pen or not. The Prophet (sa) was angered by their disrespect and said,

قُومُوا عَنِّي، ولَا يَنْبَغِي عِندِي التَّنَازُعُ.

---

[129] Ṣaḥīḥ al-Bukhārī, 3:358.

[130] Shaykh Muhammad ibn Ismail al-Bukhārī, born in 810 CE in Bukhara (modern-day Uzbekistan), was a 9th century Sunni Muslim muhaddith, or hadith compiler. He is best known for his collection of hadith called "Sahih al-Bukhārī," considered one of the most authentic and comprehensive compilations of hadith in Sunni Islam. In Sunni Muslim scholarship, he is one of the most highly regarded compilers of hadith in Islamic history.

[131] Abdullah Ibn ʿAbbās (619 – 687 CE) was a prominent Islamic scholar and cousin of the Holy Prophet (sa). He was born just a few years before the *hijra* (migration of the Prophet from Mecca to Medina) and thirteen years old at the death of the Holy Prophet (sa) in 632 CE. Ibn ʿAbbās is highly regarded in Islamic scholarship, for his deep knowledge of the Quran and as a direct narrator of the Prophet's tradition.

Get up and leave me! It is inappropriate to argue in my presence.[132]

The same doubts that emerged during the life of the Prophet (sa) were reiterated after his passing as well. *Al-Dhahabī*[133] recounts that *Abū Bakr* gathered the Muslims after the death of the Holy Prophet (sa) and gave a speech. In his sermon he said,

> *You narrate from the Messenger of God (sa) traditions which you dispute about. People after you will be in even greater dispute about them.*
>
> *Thus, do not narrate anything from the Messenger of God (sa). If anyone asks you, say, 'This is the Book of God between us and you. Take what is permissible in it to be permissible and take what is forbidden in it to be forbidden.'*[134]

Ibn Sa'd[135] also wrote the following in his notable work, Kitab Ṭabaqāt al-Kubra (Book of the Major Classes):

> *Narrations had spread during the caliphate of 'Umar ibn al-Khaṭṭāb. He commanded the people to bring their written narrations down. He burned what he could gather.*[136]

---

[132] Ṣaḥīḥ al-Bukhārī, 8:515.

[133] Al-Dhahabī was a Sunni Muslim scholar and historian born in Damascus, Syria, in 1274 CE, and he passed away in 1348 CE. He was known for various Islamic disciplines, including hadith, biography, theology, and jurisprudence. His most notable work, "Siyar A'lam al-Nubala," is a comprehensive biographical dictionary of important figures in Islamic history, particularly scholars, jurists, and hadith narrators in Sunni Islam. Al-Dhahabī was influenced by the likes of Ibn Taymiyya, Ibn Asakir and al-Khaṭīb al-Baghdādī.

[134] Tadhkirat al-Ḥuffāẓ, 1:2-3.

[135] Abū 'Abd Allāh Muḥammad ibn Sa'd ibn Manī' al-Baṣrī al-Hāshimī or simply Ibn Sa'd and nicknamed Scribe of Waqidi, was a scholar and Arabian biographer. Ibn Sa'd was born in 784/785 CE and died in 845 CE. One of his most notable works was Kitab Ṭabaqāt al-Kubra (Book of the Major Classes).

[136] Ibn Sa'd, *al-Ṭabaqāt*, 5:140.

And the ban continued until the reign of *'Umar ibn 'Abdu'l-'Azīz*[137], who lifted it and wrote to the people of Medina, "Find the ḥadīth of the Messenger of God (sa) and write it down. I fear the demise of knowledge and the passing of its people."

Ibn Shihāb al-Zuharī[138] was the first to write down ḥadīth by order of 'Umar ibn 'Abdu'l-'Azīz. Writing of ḥadīth and authorship of compendiums became widespread after that.[139]

But this was not enough. There were efforts to distort the intentions of the Prophet (sa) by saying that he was not interested in his words, actions and traditions being written down. Some even invented fabrications, claiming that he forbade his companions from recording his words. They claim that he said,

لَا تَكْتُبُوا عَنِّي وَمَنْ كَتَبَ عَنِّي غَيْرَ الْقُرْآنِ فَلْيَمْحُهُ.

Do not write what I say. Anyone who writes what I say other than the Quran should erase it.[140]

Al-Dārami[141] also recounts, "The companions asked the Prophet (sa)

---

[137] 'Umar ibn 'Abd al-'Azīz (682 – 720 CE) was an Umayyad caliph known for his brief (2.5 years) but impactful reign. Beyond political and economic reforms that he instituted during his rule, he is credited by historians as having ordered the first official collection of hadith sanctioned by the state. He is sometimes referred to as Umar II distinguishing him from the more well-known Umar ibn al-Khattab (d. 644 CE).

[138] Ibn Shihāb al-Zuharī, full name 'Abdullah ibn Shihāb al-Zuharī (c. 672 – 741 CE), was an early Islamic scholar and historian. Ibn Shihāb al-Zuharī played a crucial role in preserving and transmitting hadith traditions, commissioned by the Umar II (d. 720 CE) to create a record and compile hadith.

[139] Fatḥ al-Bārī, 281, #113.

[140] Ṣaḥīḥ Muslim, 4:2298.

Ṣaḥīḥ Muslim is widely regarded in Sunni Islam to be one of the most authoritative books of hadith. The term "Ṣaḥīḥ" in Islamic context means "authentic," "genuine," or "reliable." It is used to describe hadith collections or individual hadiths that are considered to be authentic and trustworthy in terms of their chain of narration and content.

[141] Al-Dāramī, also known as Abū Muḥammad 'Abd Allāh ibn 'Abd al-Raḥmān al-Dāramī, was

permission to write down what he said, but he denied them permission."[142]

Abū Hurayrah[143] narrates that the Prophet (sa) saw some of his companions writing some things down. He asked them what it was. They replied that they had been writing down what he said. He exclaimed,

اكْتُبُوا كِتَابَ اللَّهِ أَمْحِضُوا كِتَابَ اللَّهِ، أَكِتَابٌ غَيْرُ كِتَابِ اللَّهِ ؟ أَمْحِضُوا كِتَابَ اللَّهِ.

> *Write down the Book of God. Favor the Book of God. Will there be a book aside from the Book of God? Favor the Book of God.*

The companions collected what they wrote and burned it.[144]

But this completely contradicts what was reported from the Holy Prophet (sa) in other sources…

Yes. Although all these traditions were attributed to the Prophet (sa), they contradict many other clear and agreed upon traditions. For example, both sects narrate that the Prophet (sa) said during his Farewell Pilgrimage,

نَضَّرَ اللَّهُ عَبْداً سَمِعَ مَقَالَتِي فَوَعَاهَا وبَلَّغَهَا مَنْ لَمْ يَسْمَعْهَا- فَرُبَّ حَامِلِ فِقْهٍ إِلَى مَنْ هُوَ أَفْقَهُ مِنه.

> *God bless a servant who hears my words and understands them, then delivers them to whoever did not hear them. How many a carrier of*

---

an early Islamic scholar and hadith compiler who lived around the late 8th century to the mid-9th century CE. He was born in Rayy, present-day Iran, and is known for his contributions to the field of hadith literature in Sunni Islam. Al-Dāramī is best known for his work "Sunan al-Dāramī," a collection of hadiths that covers various aspects of Sunni jurisprudence, ethics, and theology.

[142] Sunan al-Dārimī, 1:119.

[143] Abu Hurayrah, whose full name was Abu Hurayrah Abdur-Rahman ibn Sakhr ad-Dawsi al-Yamani (c. 603-681 CE), is considered to be a prolific narrator of hadith in Sunni Islam. His narrations are found in most notable Sunni works such as Ṣaḥīḥ Muslim, Ṣaḥīḥ al-Bukhārī, and Musnad Ahmad. His nickname "Abu Hurayrah" came from his love for cats.

[144] Musnad Aḥmad, 3:16.

knowledge delivers it to someone who is more knowledgeable![145]

In another tradition, the Holy Prophet (sa) said,

اللَّهُمَّ ارْحَمْ خُلَفَائِي، اللَّهُمَّ ارْحَمْ خُلَفَائِي، اللَّهُمَّ ارْحَمْ خُلَفَائِي.

O' God, have mercy on my successors! O' God, have mercy on my successors! O' God, have mercy on my successors!

He was asked, "Who are your successors, O' Messenger of God (sa)?"

He replied,

الَّذِينَ يَأْتُونَ مِنْ بَعْدِي ويَرْوُونَ أَحَادِيثِي وَسُنَّتِي.

They are those who come after me and narrate my ḥadīth and my sunnah.[146]

Authoritativeness of the Ahl al-Bayt (a)

We spoke about the authoritativeness of prophetic traditions. What about the sayings and actions of the Ahl al-Bayt (a)?

Let us turn to a noble verse which allows us to prove the authoritativeness of the Ahl al-Bayt's (a) words and actions. God says,

إِنَّمَا يُرِيدُ اللَّهُ لِيُذْهِبَ عَنكُمُ الرِّجْسَ أَهْلَ الْبَيْتِ وَيُطَهِّرَكُمْ تَطْهِيرًا

Indeed, God desires to repel all impurity from you, O People of the Household, and purify you with a thorough purification.[147]

Impurity here refers to every deviation and error. Thus, according to the

---

[145] Sunan Abī Dawūd, 563.

[146] Abū Na'īm, Akhbār Aṣbahān, 1:81.

[147] The Noble Quran, 33:33.

verse, the Ahl al-Bayt (a) are free from any deviation or error. In other words, they are *ma ʿṣūm* (immaculate). That proves the authoritativeness of their sunnah, as the words and actions of an immaculate individual are surely a binding authority.

There is no dispute about this. The only dispute regarding this verse concerns the identity of the 'Ahl al-Bayt' who are mentioned in it.

Who are the Ahl al-Bayt (a)?

Who are the Ahl al-Bayt (a), the People of the Household, referred to in this verse? Are they the wives of the Prophet (sa), his relatives in general, or his direct family members and progeny?

This question has elicited various opinions, but explicit traditions have clarified the intended recipients of this divine designation.

One well-documented tradition is found in Ṣaḥīḥ Muslim. It narrates an incident when the Prophet (sa) wore a black fur cloak with embossing. His beloved grandsons, al-Ḥasan and al-Ḥusayn [148], approached him, and he enveloped them within the cloak. Subsequently, Lady Fāṭimah[149] (a), his cherished daughter, joined them,

---

[148] Imam Ḥusayn ibn ʿAlī, also known as Imam Ḥusayn or simply Ḥusayn (626-680 CE), was the grandson of the Prophet Muhammad (sa) and the son of Imam ʿAlī ibn Abī Ṭālib and Lady Fāṭimah, the daughter of the Prophet Muhammad. Imam Ḥusayn is celebrated within the Shia tradition for his pivotal role in safeguarding and revitalizing the essence of Islam. His life and death (massacre at Karbala in 680 CE) are a profound testament to his dedication to preserving the sanctity of life and rescuing the religion from deviations. This renaissance and revival of Islamic principles, which Imam Ḥusayn championed, serve as a timeless source of inspiration for individuals worldwide, transcending religious boundaries.

[149] Lady Fāṭimah al-Zahrā, was born between 605 CE and 615 CE (scholars differ on this) and martyred in 632 CE months after the death of her father Prophet Muhammad (sa). She is highly esteemed among all Muslims. She is the daughter of Prophet Muhammad and Khadījah, known as "the Radiant" or "the Pure" due to her exceptional character. Her life exemplifies devotion, piety, and selflessness. Lady Fāṭimah's unwavering support for her father and husband, Imam ʿAlī, played a crucial role in early Islam. She holds titles like "Sayyidatu Nisāʾ al-Janna" (Leader of

and he included her under the cloak as well. Finally, Imam Ali (a), his trusted cousin and son-in-law, came to him, and he enveloped him within the same cloak. It was at this moment that the Prophet (sa) proclaimed:

إِنَّمَا يُرِيدُ اللَّهُ لِيُذْهِبَ عَنكُمُ الرِّجْسَ أَهْلَ الْبَيْتِ وَيُطَهِّرَكُمْ تَطْهِيرًا

Indeed, God desires to repel all impurity from you, O People of the Household, and purify you with a thorough purification.[150]

This tradition illustrates the specific individuals whom God designates as the Ahl al-Bayt (a). Moreover, the famous Ḥadīth al-Kisā'[151], recorded in Musnad Aḥmad[152] and narrated by Umm Salamah[153], further emphasizes the divine purifying grace bestowed upon this noble household.

In this tradition, Lady Fāṭimah (a) brought a meal to the Prophet (sa) while he was at Umm Salamah's house. The Prophet (sa) requested that Imam Ali (a), their sons, and Lady Fāṭimah (a) join him for the meal.

---

the Women of Paradise) and "Sayyidatu Nisā' al-'Ālamīn" (Leader of the Women of the World). She was the mother of Imam Ḥasan, Imam Ḥusayn, Lady Zaynab and Um Kulthum – the grandchildren of the Prophet Muhammad and his surviving lineage.

[150] Ṣaḥīḥ Muslim, 4:1883.

[151] Ḥadīth al-Kisā' is included in both Shia and Sunni sources. It is pointed to and emphasized within Shia culture more profoundly though. Shia Muslims hold this hadith dear as further evidence of the significance and distinction of the Ahl al-Bayt. It emphasizes the doctrine of Imamate, where Imams are divinely chosen and immaculate leaders of humanity. The hadith is frequently recited and commemorated in Shia religious and cultural events, underscoring the importance of the Ahl al-Bayt in Shia Islam.

[152] Musnad Ahmad is a widely regarded compendium of hadith in Sunni Islam, compiled by the Sunni jurist Ahmad ibn Hanbal (780-855 CE). A prominent Sunni jurist, he was the founder of the Hanbali school of thought, one of the four Sunni jurisprudential schools (the other three are the Hanafi, Shafi'i and Maliki).

[153] Umm Salamah, full name Hind bint Abi Umayya (580/596 – 680/682 CE), was one of the most regarded wives of the Prophet Muhammad (sa). She is known for her piety and commitment to the Prophet and his family, as well as being a narrator of his hadith.

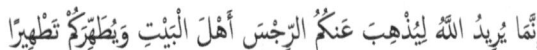

As they gathered together, the Prophet (sa) covered them all with a cloak from Khaybar[154]. While Umm Salamah was engaged in prayer, God revealed the verse of purification. With its revelation, the Prophet (sa) invoked a special supplication, indicating the exceptional status of this select group:

اللهم إن هؤلاء أهلُ بيتي وخاصتي فأذهِب عنهم الرجسَ وطَهِّرهم تطهيراً.

> *O' God, these are my Ahl al-Bayt (a) and nearest kinfolk. [Please] remove from them all impurity and purify them a thorough purification.*

When Umm Salamah inquired about her own status, the Prophet (sa) kindly reassured her that she was well but not counted among this particular group.[155]

That was not the only time that the Prophet (sa) made this clear indication regarding this verse. *Al-Ṣuyūṭī*[156] recounts that *Abū al-Ḥamrā'*, a companion of the Prophet (sa), had accompanied him for eight months in Medina. Every day, the Prophet (sa) would set out for the noon prayer and pass by the door of Imam Ali's (a) home. He would put his hand on the door and say,

---

[154] Khaybar was an oasis with Jewish settlements in the northwestern Arabian Peninsula during the time of the Prophet Muhammad (sa). Tensions arose due to breaches of treaties from some Jewish tribes in the region. In 628 CE, the Holy Prophet (sa) led a campaign to conquer Khaybar, resulting in Muslim control. The conquest was facilitated by the heroic acts of Imam Ali (a), who famously lifted the gate of Khaybar singlehandedly, demonstrating immense strength and determination in the way of God. Jewish inhabitants were allowed to stay but had to pay a portion of their produce as a tax. The conquest of Khaybar marked a significant event in early Islamic history, showcasing justice, power and equity in the Prophet's leadership and growing community.

[155] Musnad Aḥmad, 6:325.

[156] Jalal al-Din Abd al-Rahman Al-Ṣuyūṭī, commonly known as Al-Ṣuyūṭī (1445–1505 CE), was a prominent Sunni scholar and polymath who lived in the 15th century in Cairo, Egypt. Regarding in various fields of Islamic studies, including hadith, tafsir, fiqh, theology, and Arabic literature, he was applauded within Sunni scholarship as the Mujtahid and Mujaddid of his era.

الصَّلَاةَ الصَّلَاةَ، إِنَّمَا يُرِيدُ اللَّهُ لِيُذْهِبَ عَنكُمُ الرِّجْسَ وَيُطَهِّرَكُمْ تَطْهِيرًا

Prayer! Prayer!

Indeed, God desires to repel all impurity from you, O People of the Household, and purify you with a thorough purification.[157]

These traditions unequivocally identify the Ahl al-Bayt (a) as those individuals chosen by God to be the recipients of His divine purification, highlighting their exalted status in Islam.

What about the claim that the context of the verse proves that the intention is the wives of the Prophet (sa)?

God says,

يَا أَيُّهَا النَّبِيُّ قُل لِّأَزْوَاجِكَ إِن كُنتُنَّ تُرِدْنَ الْحَيَاةَ الدُّنْيَا وَزِينَتَهَا فَتَعَالَيْنَ أُمَتِّعْكُنَّ وَأُسَرِّحْكُنَّ سَرَاحًا جَمِيلًا

O Prophet! Say to your wives, 'If you desire the life of the world and its glitter, come, I will provide for you and release you in a graceful manner.

وَإِن كُنتُنَّ تُرِدْنَ اللَّهَ وَرَسُولَهُ وَالدَّارَ الْآخِرَةَ فَإِنَّ اللَّهَ أَعَدَّ لِلْمُحْسِنَاتِ مِنكُنَّ أَجْرًا عَظِيمًا

But if you desire God and His Apostle and the abode of the Hereafter, then God has indeed prepared a great reward for the virtuous among you.'

يَا نِسَاءَ النَّبِيِّ مَن يَأْتِ مِنكُنَّ بِفَاحِشَةٍ مُّبَيِّنَةٍ يُضَاعَفْ لَهَا الْعَذَابُ ضِعْفَيْنِ وَكَانَ ذَٰلِكَ عَلَى اللَّهِ يَسِيرًا [...]

O wives of the Prophet! Whoever of you commits a

---

[157] Al-Dur al-Manthūr, 5:378.

> *gross indecency, her punishment shall be doubled, and that is easy for God. [...]*

وَقَرْنَ فِي بُيُوتِكُنَّ وَلَا تَبَرَّجْنَ تَبَرُّجَ الْجَاهِلِيَّةِ الْأُولَى وَأَقِمْنَ الصَّلَاةَ وَآتِينَ الزَّكَاةَ وَأَطِعْنَ اللَّهَ وَرَسُولَهُ إِنَّمَا يُرِيدُ اللَّهُ لِيُذْهِبَ عَنكُمُ الرِّجْسَ أَهْلَ الْبَيْتِ وَيُطَهِّرَكُمْ تَطْهِيراً

> *Stay in your houses and do not flaunt your finery like the former [days of pagan] ignorance. Maintain the prayer and pay the zakat and obey God and His Apostle. Indeed, God desires to repel all impurity from you, O People of the Household, and purify you with a thorough purification.*

وَاذْكُرْنَ مَا يُتْلَى فِي بُيُوتِكُنَّ مِنْ آيَاتِ اللَّهِ وَالْحِكْمَةِ إِنَّ اللَّهَ كَانَ لَطِيفاً خَبِيراً

> *And remember what is recited in your homes of the signs of God and wisdom. Indeed, God is all-attentive, all-aware.*[158]

Some have claimed that the context of the Quranic verse in question (Surah Al-Ahzab, 33:33) suggests that the intended recipients are the wives of the Prophet (sa). The verse mentions two distinct groups: those who desire the worldly life and its adornments and those who desire God, His Messenger, and the Hereafter. Each group is promised a corresponding reward.

However, it is crucial to examine the presence of clear and definitive evidence that transcends the perceived context. One significant factor to consider is the shift in pronouns within the verse itself. The verses preceding and following the verse of purification utilize feminine pronouns, while the verse of purification uses masculine pronouns. This abrupt change in pronouns holds intentional significance.

---

[158] The Noble Quran, 33:28-34.

The change in pronouns suggests that the subject of the verse of purification is not feminine, i.e., it is not referring to the wives of the Prophet (sa). This indication is compelling and cannot be overlooked.

Ibn Hajar[159], a renowned Sunni scholar, affirmed this interpretation in his work *al-Sawā ʿiq*. He wrote that most commentators concur that this verse was revealed concerning Ali, Fatimah, Hasan, and Husayn, primarily due to the use of masculine pronouns in the phrase "from you" and what follows it. [160]

In essence, while some may argue for a contextual interpretation, the change in pronouns within the verse itself strongly supports the belief that the verse of purification is not exclusively addressing the wives of the Prophet (sa).

Ḥadīth al-Thaqalayn

There is also the ḥadīth of the Two Weighty Things *(ḥadīth al-thaqalayn)*, which was mentioned by the Prophet (sa) on multiple occasions and passed down through numerous chains of narrators.

One of the most prominent examples of this is included by *al-Ḥākim al-Nīsābūrī*[161] who recounts the narration of *Zayd ibn Arqam*[162] on the

---

[159] Ibn Ḥajar al-Haytamī was a renowned Egyptian Sunni scholar from the Shāfiʿī tradition. He was expert in Hadith, Islamic history, and theology. One of his famous works, *al-Ṣawāʿiq al-Muḥriqah,* was authored specifically as a refutation of the beliefs of Shia Muslims. He died in 974 AH.

[160] Al-Ṣawāʿiq al-Muḥriqah, 143.

[161] Al-Ḥākim al-Nīsābūrī was a prominent Sunni scholar and hadith compiler born in 933 CE in Nishapur, Iran. He is known for his work titled "Al-Mustadrak ʿAla al-Ṣaḥīḥayn," (trans. Supplement for What is Missing From al-Bukhârî and Muslim) in which he aimed to identify hadiths meeting the standards of authenticity set by Bukhari and Muslim but that were not included in their works.

[162] Zayd ibn Arqam al-Ansari al-Khazraji was a notable companion of the Prophet Muhammad (sa) and a close associate of Imam Ali (a). He played a significant role in transmitting the Hadith of al-Ghadir. Zayd participated in 19 battles, primarily alongside the Prophet Muhammad (sa),

event of *Ghadīr Khumm*[163]. As the Holy Prophet Muhammad (sa) was returning to Medina after the culmination of his Farewell Pilgrimage, an event of immense significance took place at a location known as Ghadir Khumm. Recognizing the gravity of this moment, the Prophet paused the Muslim caravan, calling for a makeshift pulpit to be constructed from saddles and rocks. Climbing atop this humble platform, he ensured that all those present could hear his words. With a sense of solemnity, the Prophet told his people,

كَأَنِّي قَدْ دُعِيتُ فَأَجَبْتُ.

It seems that I have been called [by God to His side] and I [will soon] answer.

The atmosphere was charged with anticipation as the Prophet continued,

إنِّي قد تَرَكتُ فيكم الثَّقَلَيْنِ أحَدُهما أكبَرُ مِن الآخَرِ كتابُ اللهِ تعالى وعِتْرَتي

I am leaving for you two weighty things, one of which is greater than the other. They are the Book of God and my progeny, my Ahl al-Bayt (a).

فانظُروا كيفَ تخلُفوني فيهِما.

Take heed how you succeed me in regard to them.

In these profound words, the Prophet emphasized the vital role of the Quran and his family in guiding the Muslim community. He urged those gathered to pay careful attention to how they would succeed him

---

starting with the Battle of Muraysi'. Due to his young age, he did not join the battles of Uhud and Badr. Following the Battle of Karbala, he strongly objected to the mistreatment of Imam Husayn's (a) head by Ibn Ziyad, the Umayyad governor of Kufa.

163 The event of Ghadir Khumm is a consequential incident in Islamic history that took place in the final year of the Prophet's (sa) life (632 CE) shortly after his Farewell Pilgrimage to Mecca. Ghadir Khumm was a pond (ghadir) fed by a nearby spring in a *wadi*, or valley, known as Khumm, situated between the cities of Mecca and Medina, in the Arabian Peninsula.

in upholding these two weighty trusts. Importantly, the Prophet declared,

فإنَّهما لن يتفرَّقا حتَّى يرِدَا عليَّ الحوضَ.

Surely, the two shall never separate until they reach me at the Pool [of Paradise].

This statement underscored the inseparable connection between the Quran and his family, implying that they would always be intertwined in guiding the believers. The Holy Prophet (sa) then made a profound declaration, affirming,

إن الله عز وجلَ مولاي وأنا وَلِيُّ كل مؤمنٍ.

Surely, God Almighty is my master, and that I am the master of every believing man and woman.

With these words, he emphasized the divine appointment of his leadership and that of his family, particularly Imam Ali (a), whom he designated as the guardian and leader of the believers. In a powerful gesture, the Prophet raised the hand of Imam Ali (a) and proclaimed,

من كنتُ وليَّهُ فهذا وليَّه اللهمّ والِ من والاهُ وعادِ من عاداهُ.

Whomever I am his master, this [Ali (a)] is also his master. O' God, befriend whoever befriends him and take as an enemy whoever takes him as an enemy.[164]

This declaration of Imam Ali's (a) authority and guardianship was a clear indication of his pivotal role in guiding the Muslim community after the Prophet's departure.

From this momentous event, several essential conclusions can be drawn:

---

[164] Al-Nīsābūrī, *al-Mustadrak*, 3:109.

The Ahl al-Bayt (a) hold a unique and profound knowledge of the Holy Quran due to their close association with it.

Adhering to both the Quran and the Progeny of the Prophet (sa) is the safeguard against falling into misguidance.

Neglecting or abandoning the guidance of the Ahl al-Bayt is strictly forbidden, as it would inevitably lead to failure. This reinforces the concept of Imamate being exclusive to them.

The Ahl al-Bayt have maintained an unwavering adherence to the Quran, ensuring that they remain true to its teachings until the Day of Resurrection.

The evidence establishing the authoritativeness of the words and actions of the Ahl al-Bayt extends beyond the verse of purification and the hadith of the Two Weighty Things (ḥadīth al-thaqalayn). Numerous other verses and traditions corroborate this fundamental point.

The event at Ghadir Khumm serves as a pivotal moment in Islamic history, highlighting the vital role of the Ahl al-Bayt in guiding the Muslim community and underscoring their unwavering connection to the Holy Quran. This event remains a source of reflection, inspiration and guidance for Muslims worldwide, emphasizing the importance of upholding both the Quran and the teachings of the Prophet's family.

Text and Opinion

Let us delve further into the discussion regarding the interpretation of the verse of purification. Some argue that the term "household of the Prophet" (sa) refers specifically to his wives rather than his progeny. Are these the two main schools of thought on this matter?

The Prophet (sa) only passed away after he delivered his message completely and perfectly. As the Noble Quran says,

الْيَوْمَ أَكْمَلْتُ لَكُمْ دِينَكُمْ وَأَتْمَمْتُ عَلَيْكُمْ نِعْمَتِي وَرَضِيتُ لَكُمُ الْإِسْلَامَ دِينًا

Today I have perfected your religion for you, and I have completed My blessing upon you, and I have approved Islam as your religion.[165]

Two schools emerged: *madrasat al-naṣṣ* (the school of text) and *madrasat al-ra'y* (the school of opinion).

The school of text is the school of Ahl al-Bayt (a), represented in the person of Imam Ali (a) at its helm. The distinctive trait of this school of thought is its reliance on the primary sources – the Noble Quran and the Sunnah. Any juristic reasoning (*ijtihād*) must be confined within the scope of these sources.

This is based on the idea that the Quran and the hadith contain everything that the Muslims need in terms of deriving the religious rulings. The Prophet (sa) entrusted his knowledge to Imam Ali (a), who then passed it on to the Imams (a) after him. Every rule that Muslims need can be derived from these sources.

The second school, the school of opinion, is the school of the caliphs. This school was initially launched and led by the second caliph. It expanded after him and reached new heights at the hands of *Abū Ḥanīfah*[166]. In fact, this school developed so much so that Abū Ḥanīfah would intentionally rule in opposition to the primary sources in favor of his own opinion and personal judgement. *Al-Khaṭīb al-Baghdādī*[167]

---

[165] The Noble Quran, 5:3.

[166] Abū Ḥanīfah, full name Nu'mān ibn Thābit ibn Zūṭā ibn Marzubān was born in Kufa in 689/699 CE (historians differ on the exact year of his birth) and died in 767 CE. He was a Sunni theologian and jurist who became the eponymous founder the Hanafi school of Sunni jurisprudence. He emphasized the use of al-ra'y (juristic opinion) in deriving legal rulings and essentially became the leader of that school of thought. His jurisprudential school, Hanafi, became one of the four major Sunni schools of jurisprudence which are still followed today. Abū Ḥanīfah's most notable works include *al-Fiqh al-Akbar*, *Musnad Abu Hanifa*, and *Kitab al-Athar*.

[167] Al-Khaṭīb al-Baghdādī (1002 – 1071 CE), full name Abū Bakr Aḥmad ibn 'Alī ibn Thābit ibn

recounted in one of his seminal works that Abū Ḥanīfah used to say, "If the Messenger of God (sa) were to live in my time or I were to live in his time, he would take many of my sayings. Is religion anything but sound opinion?!"[168]

You will find that this school relies on *al-ra'y* (juristic opinion) in addition to the Quran and noble traditions. *Ijtihad* in this school is not confined to the parameters of the primary sources. Rather, it goes beyond and deduces rulings based on opinions and preferences as well.

This school bases these ideas on their beliefs surrounding the Quran and the noble traditions, and they are not adequate to fulfill the jurisprudential needs of the Muslims.

The origins of *madraset al-ra'y* can be traced back to the time of the Prophet (sa) and the early years of the Islamic message. Instances were recorded in which companions made judgments based on their personal opinions, sometimes conflicting with the Prophet's statements. While nothing but revelation came from the Holy Prophet,[169] the heralds of this school of thought would outwardly contradict him with their own personal opinions.

Notable examples include the actions of Abū Bakr, 'Umar, and Zayd ibn Thābit. Some scholars identify 'Umar ibn al-Khaṭṭāb as a prominent figure associated with this school or doctrine, known for his reliance on personal reasoning in religious matters.

Aḥmad Amīn[170] writes,

Aḥmad ibn Mahdī al-Shāfi'ī, was a leading Sunni scholar of his time, known for hadith, history, and jurisprudence. His title, Al-Khaṭīb al-Baghdādī, means "the lecturer from Baghdad."

[168] Tārīkh Baghdād, 13:390.

[169] Shia Muslims believe that the Holy Prophet (sa) was immaculate and guided by the Divine. Thus, what Prophet Muhammad (sa) said and did was from God, not of his own opinion or preference to be negated or contradicted by others. God says, "He does not speak of his own desire; It is not but a revelation that is revealed." (Quran 53:3-4)

[170] Ahmad Amīn (1886–1954) was a prominent Egyptian intellectual and historian known for his

> *There are many accounts of the companions making judgements by their own opinion. Such was the case with Abū Bakr, 'Umar, and Zayd ibn Thābit. We believe that the standard-bearer of this school or doctrine was 'Umar ibn al-Khaṭṭāb.*[171]

During the time of the Prophet Muhammad (sa) and in the years following his passing, a new dimension of Islamic jurisprudence emerged - the reliance on juristic opinion as a third source of legislation. This development had political motivations behind it and was shaped by specific historical circumstances.

A Third Source

Why did this idea of relying on opinion as a third source develop in this way?

One of the key factors that contributed to the development of this idea was the prohibition of recording the prophetic sunnah (traditions and practices of the Prophet). This prohibition, instated by the early caliphs, was in place until the caliphate of 'Umar ibn 'Abdu'l-'Azīz. As discussed previously, this posed challenges to the authoritativeness of the prophetic sunnah.

A Dangerous Slope

During the reign of *Mu'āwiyah ibn Abi Sufyan*[172], a concerning trend

---

contributions to literature and historical scholarship. Amīn's most notable work, "Fajr al-Islam" (The Dawn of Islam), explored the history and development of Islamic civilization, highlighting the contributions of Muslim scholars and thinkers throughout history.

[171] Fajr al-Islām, 240.

[172] Mu'āwiyah ibn Abi Sufyan (602 – 680 CE) began the Umayyad dynasty with his rule as caliph in 661 CE after the Peace Accord of Imam al-Hassan (a). His father, Abu Sufyan, was a prominent

emerged – the fabrication of hadiths (narrations) that extolled the virtues of the caliphs. This phenomenon aimed to vilify Imam Ali (a) while glorifying the previous caliphs. Mu'āwiyah appointed individuals like *al-Mughīrah ibn Shu'bah*[173], instructing them to promote this narrative. Such actions further fueled the divergence between the two schools of thought.

Al-Ṭabarī[174] reported the following in one of his seminal works:

> *Mu'āwiyah appointed al-Mughīrah ibn Shu'bah as governor of Kufa in 41 AH. He summoned him and said, 'There were many things that I wished to instruct you with,*

---

leader in Mecca and an adversary of the Prophet Muhammad (sa). His mother, Hind bint 'Utba, is infamously known for her role in the killing of Hamza ibn Abdulmuttalib, the Prophet's uncle, during the Battle of Uhud. Mu'āwīya converted to Islam, along with this father Abu Sufyan and the defeated Meccans, during the bloodless conquest of Mecca. Mu'āwiyah played a role in the conquest of the Levant during the time of Abu Bakr. Later, during the caliphate of 'Umar, Mu'āwiyah served as the governor of Jordan and eventually became the governor of all of the Levant. During the rebellion against 'Uthman ibn 'Affan, Mu'āwiyah did not respond to 'Uthman's request for assistance. However, when Imam Ali (a), was elected by the people as the new caliph, Mu'āwiyah refused to pay allegiance to him and initiated the Battle of Siffin under the pretext of seeking revenge for 'Uthman's death. After the martyrdom of Imam 'Ali (a) in 661 CE, at the hands of Mu'āwiyah's agents, and the Peace Accords with Imam al-Hassan, Mu'āwiyah assumed the caliphate and established Damascus as his capital.

[173] Al-Mughīrah ibn Shu'bah (612 – 671 CE) was a young companion of the Holy Prophet Muhammad (sa), having been born a couple years after the beginning of the Prophet's mission in 610 CE. Al-Mughīrah becomes a contentious figure in Islamic history given his early involvement in attacks on the Prophet's family. According to the great theologian and scholar of the 10th and 11th centuries, *Shaykh al-Mufid* (948 – 1022 CE), Al-Mughīrah participated in the attack on Lady Fatima's (a) home after the Prophet's death. This was during the caliphate's attempt to compel Imam Ali's (a) allegiance to the new caliphate. Al-Mughīrah would later be rewarded for his loyalty to the caliphate through political appointments as governor of Bahrain, Basra and Kufa during the reign of the second caliph, 'Umar ibn al-Khattab (582 – 644 CE), who ruled from 634 to 644 CE. Al-Mughīrah would later be appointed as the governor of Kufa, under the reign of Mu'awiya who ruled from 661 to 680 CE.

[174] Shaykh al-Ṭabarī (839 – 923 CE), full name Abū Ja'far Muḥammad ibn Jarīr ibn Yazīd al-Ṭabarī, was a Muslim historian and scholar of the 9th and 10th centuries from Amol, Tabaristan. He eventually settled in Baghdad, Iraq which was an intellectual center of the Muslim world during the Abbasid empire. Al-Ṭabarī is most known for his comprehensive historical work, "*Tarikh al-Tabari*" (The History of al-Tabari), which is considered one of the earliest and most significant works of Islamic historiography.

> *but I am leaving them up to your judgement. However, I will not neglect to instruct you with a single command: Do not stop cursing and slandering Ali, remember 'Uthmān and seek forgiveness for him, harass Ali's companions and exile them, and flatter 'Uthmāns followers and bring them close to you.'* [175]

This trend aligned with the school of opinion, a school of thought that expanded in scope, particularly under the influence of scholars like Abū Ḥanīfah. This school allowed for juristic opinion (al-ra'y) in addition to the Quran and noble traditions, which infused the effects of individual preferences and personal judgments into the law. The school of Ahl al-Bayt was on the other side of the spectrum, emphasizing the Quran and Hadith and not allowing for such personal opinions to take hold. Imam al-Ṣādiq (a) said,

اعْرِفُوا مَنَازِلَ النَّاسِ عَلَى قَدْرِ رِوَايَاتِهِمْ عَنَّا.

Know the status of people by how much they narrate from us.[176]

In addition to all of this, the Imams (a) stressed the importance of writing down their traditions and documenting the knowledge and guidance they are passing down to the Muslims. The process of documenting and collecting the hadith was both significant and controversial in the history of Islam, as we discussed earlier. The Imams (a) always emphasized the need to preserve knowledge through writing. Imam al-Ṣādiq (a) said,

اكْتُبُوا فَإِنَّكُمْ لَا تَحْفَظُونَ حَتَّى تَكْتُبُوا.

Write! Surely, you will not remember unless you write.[177]

---

[175] Al-Ṭabarī, Tārīkh al-Ṭabarī, 2:112.

[176] Al-'Āmilī, Wasā'il al-Shī'ah, chapter 8 on the traits of a judge, tr. #7.

[177] Al-'Āmilī, Wasā'il al-Shī'ah, chapter 8 on the traits of a judge, tr. #16.

احْتَفِظُوا بِكُتُبِكُمْ فَإِنَّكُمْ سَوْفَ تَحْتَاجُونَ إِلَيْهَا.

Safeguard your books, for you will need them.[178]

Ahl al-Bayt (a) and the School of Opinion

Imam al-Ṣādiq (a) guided his companions and followers to true value and knowledge in faith. As shown above, he emphasized the importance of documenting knowledge, advised the safeguarding of books, and highlighted the significance of understanding people's positions based on their narrations from the Ahl al-Bayt.

Imam al-Ṣādiq (a) engaged in numerous discussions with scholars from the school of opinion. One day, the Imam (a) asked *Abū Ḥanīfah*,

أَيُّمَا أَعْظَمُ قَتْلُ النَّفْسِ أَوِ الزِّنَا ؟

Which is greater in the sight of God, murder, or adultery?

Abū Ḥanīfah said, "Murder."

The Imam (a) responded,

فَكَيْفَ رَضِيَ فِي الْقَتْلِ بِشَاهِدَيْنِ، وَلَمْ يَرْضَ فِي الزِّنَا إِلَّا بِأَرْبَعَةٍ؟

Then why did He accept two witnesses in cases of murder, but in cases of adultery did not accept less than four?

الصَّلَاةُ أَفْضَلُ أَمِ الصِّيَامُ؟

Is prayer better or fasting?

Abū Ḥanīfah said, "Prayer is better."

The Imam (a) said,

فَيَجِبُ عَلَى قِيَاسِ قَوْلِكَ عَلَى الْحَائِضِ، قَضَاءُ مَا فَاتَهَا مِنَ الصَّلَاةِ فِي حَالِ حَيْضِهَا دُونَ

---

[178] Al-ʿĀmilī, Wasāʾil al-Shīʿah, chapter 8 on the traits of a judge, tr. #17.

الصِّيَامِ، وقَدْ أَوْجَبَ اللهُ عَلَيْهَا قَضَاءَ الصَّوْمِ دُونَ الصَّلَاةِ.

Based on your qiyās [analogical reasoning], a menstruating woman should make up for the prayers she missed during her cycle rather than the fasting [which she missed]. However, God has made it obligatory for her to make up her fasting but not her prayers.

The Imam (a) continued to pose similar questions until he said,

تَزْعُمُ أَنَّكَ تُفْتِي بِكِتَابِ الله، ولَسْتَ مِمَّنْ وَرِثَهُ، وَتَزْعُمُ أَنَّكَ صَاحِبُ قِيَاسٍ، وَأَوَّلُ مَنْ قَاسَ إِبْلِيسُ، وَلَمْ يُبْنَ دِينُ الله عَلَى الْقِيَاسِ.

Do you claim that you rule according to the Book of God, while you are not one of its inheritors?

Do you claim that you are a man of qiyās when the first to perform qiyās was Satan?

God's religion was not built on qiyās![179]

This is the knowledge and wisdom of the Imams. Is it not appropriate for him to say regarding *al-Ḥakam ibn ʿUtaybah*[180],

فَلْيُشَرِّقِ الْحَكَمُ ولْيُغَرِّبْ، أَمَا وَالله لَا يُصِيبُ الْعِلْمَ إِلَّا مِنْ أَهْلِ بَيْتٍ نَزَلَ عَلَيْهِمْ جَبْرَئِيلُ.

Let al-Ḥakam look to the east and west. By God, knowledge is not reached except by the people of a household where Gabriel descended.[181]

The Imam's wisdom and knowledge challenged the scholars of opinion and questioned the validity of their *qiyās* (analogical reasoning). He emphasized that God's religion was not built on qiyās, highlighting the

---

[179] Al-ʿĀmilī, Wasāʾil al-Shīʿah, chapter 6 on the traits of a judge, tr. #28.

[180] Al-Ḥakam ibn ʿUtaybah (668 – 733 CE) was a contemporary of Imam al-Baqir and Imam al-Sadiq during the 8th century. He died in Kufa, Iraq, during the era of the Umayyad caliph Hisham ibn Abd al-Malik (691 – 743 CE). Al-Hakam ibn ʿUtaybah is regarded amongst the early Muslim jurists.

[181] Al-ʿĀmilī, Wasāʾil al-Shīʿah, chapter 7 on the traits of a judge, tr. #23.

distinctive wisdom and knowledge of the Ahl al-Bayt.

Imam al-Ṣādiq's assertion that true knowledge is inherited by those upon whom Gabriel descended underscores the unique position of the Ahl al-Bayt in preserving and conveying the authentic teachings of Islam.

The Book of Ali (a)

How did the school of Ahl al-Bayt (a) use and have enough prophetic traditions when most of the Imams (a) did not live during his time?

Some might wonder how the school of Ahl al-Bayt (a) managed to preserve and transmit prophetic traditions when most of the Imams (a) did not live during the time of the Prophet Muhammad (sa). The answer lies in the meticulous preservation and transmission of knowledge within the family of the Prophet (sa).

The Ahl al-Bayt (a) inherited their knowledge directly from their grandfather, the Prophet Muhammad (sa). This knowledge was passed down from father to son through a carefully maintained tradition. This tradition included the preservation of various books and scrolls that contained valuable teachings and narrations.

One such significant book is known as *Kitab Ali*, or the "Book of Ali", which plays a central role in the intellectual and spiritual heritage of the Ahl al-Bayt (a). According to narrations, this book was dictated by the Messenger of God (sa) and transcribed by the hand of the Commander of the Faithful, Imam Ali (a).

Imam al-Baqir (a) engaged in a discussion with Al-Ḥakam ibn ʿUtaybah, and a disagreement arose between them. In response, Imam al-Baqir (a) instructed one of his sons to bring out *Kitab Ali*. This book contained a wealth of knowledge, including the specific issue they were debating.

Imam al-Baqir (a) examined the contents of the book and confirmed its authenticity, stating that it was in the handwriting of Imam Ali (a) and had been dictated by the Prophet Muhammad (sa). He then emphasized the unparalleled authority of the knowledge contained within the book. He said,

هذا خطّ عليّ وَإمْلاء رَسُولِ اللّه صلّى الله عَلَيْه وَآلِه وَسَلَّم.

يا أبامُحَمَّد، اذْهَب أَنت وسلمة وأَبُو المقدام حَيْثُ شِئْتُم يميناً وَشمالاً، فوالله لاتَجِدُون العلمَ أوثَق مِنْهُ عنْدَ قَوْمٍ كانَ ينْزِلُ عَلَيهِم جَبْرَئِيل.

> *This is the handwriting of Ali (a) as dictated by the Messenger of God (sa). O' Abū Muhammad, go – you, Salamah, and Abū al-Miqdām – wherever you like, right or left. By God, you will not find knowledge to be well established in a people more than the people of a household upon whom Gabriel used to descend.*[182]

The preservation of such books and scrolls, along with the continuous transmission of knowledge from one generation of the Ahl al-Bayt to the next, ensured that the prophetic traditions and teachings remained intact within the family of the Prophet (sa). This knowledge was regarded as highly reliable and authoritative, providing a solid foundation for jurisprudence, theology, and spirituality within the school of Ahl al-Bayt (a).

Al-Jāmiʿah

The Ahl al-Bayt (a) also possess a book called *al-Jāmiʿah*. It is described in an authentic tradition relayed by *Abū Baṣīr*[183]. He asked Imam al-

---

[182] Rijāl al-Najāshī, Biography of Muhammad ibn ʿUdhāf.

[183] Abū Baṣīr (d. 767 CE) was a significant figure in early Islamic history, known for his close companionship with the fifth and sixth Imams, Imam al-Baqir and Imam al-Sadiq, respectively. He played a crucial role in transmitting Hadith and teachings from the Imams, contributing to the development of Shia jurisprudence and theology. Abū Baṣīr's enduring legacy lies in his dedication to preserving and passing on the traditions of the Imams, despite facing persecution and challenges during his lifetime under the Umayyads and Abbasids.

Ṣādiq (a) about a tradition stating that the Prophet (sa) had taught Imam Ali (a) a gate of knowledge from which a thousand gates open. The Imam (a) responded,

علّمَ رسولُ الله صَلّى اللّهُ عليه وآلِه وَسَلَّمَ عَليّاً عليه السلام ألفَ بابٍ يفتح مِنْ كُلِّ بابٍ ألف بابٍ [...] وإنّ عندَنا الجامِعَة وَما يُدْرِيهم مَا الجَامِعَة ؟

The Messenger of God (sa) taught Ali (a) a thousand gates [of knowledge], each gate opens to a thousand more. [...] We have al-Jāmiʿah! And how would they know what al-Jāmiʿah is?

Abū Baṣīr asked, "What is al-Jāmiʿah?" The Imam (a) replied,

صحيفةٌ طُولُها سَبْعُونَ ذِرَاعاً بذراعِ رسولِ الله صلى الله عليه وآله وسَلم وَإمْلَائِه من فَلْقِ فيه وخَطِّ عَليّ بيمينه، فيها كلّ حَلالٍ وحَرامٍ وكُلّ شيءٍ يَحتَاجُ الناسُ اليْه حَتى الأرشَ في الخدْش.

It is a scroll seventy arm spans long, measured by the arms of the Messenger of God (sa). It was dictated by him directly and written by ʿAlī's (a) right hand. It contains every matter of ḥalāl and ḥarām and everything that people will need, even the penalty of a scratch.[184]

Al-Jafr

It is also narrated that Imam al-Ṣādiq (a) said,

وإنّ عندَنا الجفر وَمَا يُدْرِيهم مَا الجَفْر ؟ [...] وعَاءٌ مِنْ أَدَمٍ فيه عِلْمُ النبيّين والوصيّين وعِلْمُ العلماءِ الّذين مَضُوا مِنْ بَنِي إسْرَائِيل.

We have al-Jafr! And how would they know what al-Jafr is? [...] [It is] a leather vessel which contains the knowledge of the prophets and their vicegerents, and the knowledge of the scholars who passed from the Children of Israel.[185]

---

[184] Al-Kulaynī, *al-Kāfī*, 1:239.

[185] Ibid.

The Imam's Knowledge

The Imams of Ahl al-Bayt (a) possessed a unique source of knowledge that extended beyond conventional means. Their knowledge was not solely acquired through ordinary channels but was enriched by unseen divine sources. Numerous traditions attest to this extraordinary aspect of their knowledge.

One tradition highlights this divine connection, stating that when an Imam sought knowledge, God Almighty would facilitate its acquisition.

إذَا أَرادَ الإمامُ أنْ يعلمَ شيئاً أعْلَمَهُ اللهُ ذلكَ.

If the Imam wants to know something, God will let him know it.[186]

This indicates that their knowledge was not limited to what they learned through conventional education but extended to insights and wisdom granted directly by God.

How does knowledge get to the Imams (a)? How do they inherit it?

While divine means played a significant role, there were also tangible methods through which knowledge was transferred within the family of the Prophet (sa).

One essential means of knowledge transmission was through the circulation of specific books and written materials. The Book of Ali (a), al-Jāmiʿah, and al-Jafr, which we mentioned briefly, are examples of this material transmission. These books contained a wealth of wisdom, traditions, and teachings, and they were carefully preserved within the family of Ahl al-Bayt (a). *Sulaym ibn Qays*[187], a witness to Imam Ali's (a)

---

[186] Al-Kulaynī, *al-Kāfi*, 1:258.

[187] Sulaym ibn Qays (d. 713 CE) was considered a companion of Imam Ali towards the end of the latter's life. He also transmitted Hadith, becoming a link in the chain of narrators in some of the narrations in the corpus of hadith. Sulaym lived to be a loyal companion of Imam Ali's sons Imam Hasan and Imam Husayn, the latter's son Imam Ali Zayn al-'Abidin, and Imam Muhammad al-Baqir.

will to his sons, recounted an important moment. In his will, Imam Ali (a) turned to his son, Imam al-Hasan (a), and emphasized the significance of this knowledge transfer.

يا بُنيّ، أَمَرني رسولُ الله صلى الله عليه وآله وسَلم، أنْ أُوصيَ إليكَ وأنْ ادفعَ اليك كُتُبِي وسِلاحِي كَما أوصى إلي رسولُ الله صلى الله عليه وآله وسلم وَدَفَعَ إليّ كتبَه وسِلاحَه، وأمرني أن آمرَك إذا حَضَرَكَ الموتُ أن تَدْفعَهَا إلى أخيك الحسين عليه السلام.

O' my son, the Messenger of God (sa) instructed me to bequeath to you and to give you my books and my weapon, just as the Messenger of God (sa) had bequeathed to me and given me his books and weapon. He instructed me to instruct you that when death approaches you, to give them to your brother al-Ḥusayn (a).[188]

This tradition highlights the meticulous preservation and circulation of essential written materials among the Imams of Ahl al-Bayt (a). These books served as a crucial repository of knowledge, ensuring the continuity and accessibility of divine teachings and traditions within their noble lineage.

Consensus and Reason

We spoke about various matters regarding the sources of legislation in the jurisprudence of Ahl al-Bayt (a). Why did you not mention consensus and reason?

It is clear from the foregoing that there are two sources that can be relied upon in the jurisprudential process of Ahl al-Bayt (a): the Quran and the Sunnah.

As for consensus, considering it an independent source would be inaccurate. Consensus has no value in the jurisprudential process if it does not reveal the approval of the Imam (a). We do not believe in the

---

[188] Al-Kulaynī, *al-Kāfī*, 1:297.

saying that 'this nation will not agree on misguidance.'

Thus, authoritativeness here stems from the sunnah. Consensus has no value other than the revelatory value in indicating the position of the Prophet or Imam on an issue.

As for reason, it does not have the right to legislate. Nor is it possible to obtain definitive conclusions about divine commandments and forbiddances through reason alone. Reason can only give us definitive conclusions in two cases.

Reason can define correlations, such as defining the correlation between the obligation of a thing and the obligation of its prerequisites. Reason makes a definitive judgement in such a situation. However, the judgement here is not about the ruling, but about the correlation. If this rational judgement is combined with God's command that a certain thing is obligatory, reason allows us to deduce that its prerequisite is obligatory as well. For example, reason tells us that because prayer is an obligation, a person is also obliged to perform its prerequisites, such as wuḍū' (ablution).

Reason also allows us to identify clear and self-evident rulings, which are universally agreed upon by rational human beings across all societies and throughout time. For example, reason allows us to identify the obligation of justice and the prohibition of injustice. However, such rulings are also supported by evidence from the Quran and noble traditions. Considering reason as a source of legislation in such matters becomes a superfluous claim.

We must stress that the role of reason in these matters – correlation and axiomatic rulings – is one of identification and discovery, not legislation. The Quran and the Sunnah are the sources of legislation. Reason is a tool that allows us to discover the corollaries and premises of laws legislated in these sources.

Let us go back to the example of prayer. There are countless instances that the Quran and Sunnah commanded us to pray. We also know that prayer requires ritual purity through wuḍūʾ. If a person does not have the purity of wuḍūʾ, should they simply ignore the command to pray? Should they pray without wuḍūʾ? Or do we understand that the Quran and Sunnah want us to perform wuḍūʾ then pray? Clearly, the latter is the correct understanding, even though there may not be an explicit command to perform wuḍūʾ. In this instance, reason did not legislate the need to perform wuḍūʾ. However, it did allow us to discover that performing wuḍūʾ is an obligation because it is a prerequisite of prayer.

The Practices of People of Sound Mind

What about sīrat al-ʿuqalāʾ (i.e., the practices of the people of sound mind)? What about sīrat al-mutasharriʿah (i.e., the practices of people who mindfully abide by the sharīʿah)? Are these appropriate to count as sources of legislation?

As you suggested in the question, there is a distinction between *sīrat al-ʿuqalāʾ* (i.e. the practices of the people of sound mind) and *sīrat al-mutasharriʿah* (i.e. the practices of people who mindfully abide by the *sharīʿah*).

The practices of the sound-minded are authoritative regardless of their faith. Rather, it is guided by human reason and nature. The practices of the sound-minded are a common matter among all people, so we look at the entirety of humanity to judge whether a consistent practice emerges. The reasoning is that if all of humanity agree on a certain thing, then it must be rooted in humankind's innate nature which God Almighty gave to us all.

As for the practices of the '*sharīʿah*-abiding', they are the practices of Muslims and stem from their faith. It may also apply to the practices of members of a certain sect, so long as it stems from the tenets of their school of thought. The common denominator between those who share a practice is their shared belief, and it is assumed to be the reason behind their shared practice. As such, scholars say that the practices of the *sharīʿah*-abiding are only binding when it is a common practice amongst those who adhere to the rules of their religion. There is no consideration to the practices of people who proclaim a faith and act contrary to its teachings.

However, the requirement of being *sharīʿah*-abiding does not equate the requirement of 'justice' in its jurisprudential sense. Rather, its extent is to give confidence that the particular practice has its roots in the beliefs of the faith-group.

There are two reasons for this categorization.

When it comes to the practices of the *sharīʿah*-abiding, there is no possibility for a religious prohibition against the practice. If there was a prohibition, the *sharīʿah*-abiding would have abided by that prohibition. On the other hand, the practices of the sound-minded can potentially be prohibited by the divine legislator. There is nothing to preclude this possibility.

In addition, the practices of the sound-minded can be proven without a requirement for us to look at and assess people's actions. So long as we can show that rational people would behave in a particular way, that is enough to prove the practices of the sound minded. On the other hand, the practices of the *sharīʿah*-abiding cannot be proven without proof of a course of action taken by a group of people. We must investigate history and ensure that the companions of the Imams (a) and early generations abided by the same practice.

To answer the question: both the practices of the sound-minded and the *sharīʿah*-abiding cannot be considered an independent source of legislation. They both have value in their indicatory power, allowing us to discover the position of the Imam (a) on an issue, but this is in fact a reference to the sunnah and a way of understanding it.

How do these practices reveal the approval of the Immaculate Imam?

If a practice was rational and widely practiced at the time of the

Immaculate Imam, then the lack of a prohibition against it indicates approval.

If it was a practice of the *sharīʿah*-abiding which was present during the time of the Immaculate Imam, then it directly reveals his approval. Otherwise, it cannot be considered a practice of the *sharīʿah*-abiding.

The Sunnah of the Companions

Other schools believe in the authority of the companions and what they practiced. They quote the following verses as evidence:

كُنْتُمْ خَيْرَ أُمَّةٍ أُخْرِجَتْ لِلنَّاسِ تَأْمُرُونَ بِالْمَعْرُوفِ وتَنْهَوْنَ عَنِ الْمُنْكَرِ

You are the best nation [ever] brought forth for mankind: you bid what is right and forbid what is wrong.[189]

وَكَذٰلِكَ جَعَلْنَاكُمْ أُمَّةً وَسَطاً لِتَكُونُوا شُهَداءَ عَلَى النَّاسِ وَيَكُونَ الرَّسُولُ عَلَيْكُمْ شَهِيداً

Thus We have made you a middle nation that you may be witnesses to the people, and that the Apostle may be a witness to you.[190]

---

[189] The Noble Quran, 3:110.

[190] The Noble Quran, 2:143.

Some have inferred the authoritativeness of the sunnah of the companions in several ways, among which were the two noble verses above. They say that the first verse proves the superiority of Muslims over all other nations, and this requires the companion's integrity in every case. The second verse proves their righteousness generally.[191] **How do we respond to these statements?**

This line of reasoning is clearly debatable. The verses indicate that the Muslim ummah has superiority over other nations, but this does not prove the authoritativeness of the companions' words or actions.

In fact, this line of reasoning would lead us to believe that every member of the Muslim ummah is superior and their words and actions are authoritative. Nothing in the verses limit their applicability to the companions. Such a conclusion is absurd, so the line of reasoning is clearly flawed.

To say that the sunnah of the companions is authoritative would require us to believe that all companions are immaculate. However, this cannot be the case. God Almighty says,

وَما مُحَمَّدٌ إِلَّا رَسُولٌ قَدْ خَلَتْ مِنْ قَبْلِهِ الرُّسُلُ أَفَإِنْ ماتَ أَوْ قُتِلَ انْقَلَبْتُمْ عَلى أَعْقابِكُمْ وَمَنْ يَنْقَلِبْ عَلى عَقِبَيْهِ فَلَنْ يَضُرَّ اللَّهَ شَيْئاً وَسَيَجْزِي اللَّهُ الشَّاكِرِينَ

Muhammad is but an apostle; [other] apostles have passed before him. If he dies or is slain, will you turn back on your heels? Anyone who turns back on his heels, will not harm God in the least, and soon God will reward the grateful.[192]

Is this verse just making a hypothetical statement? Or were there

[191] See: al-Shāṭibī, *al-Muwāfaqāt*, 4:74.

[192] The Noble Quran, 3:144.

companions that did turn back on their heels? God Almighty says,

يا أَيُّهَا الَّذِينَ آمَنُوا مَا لَكُمْ إِذَا قِيلَ لَكُمُ انْفِرُوا فِي سَبِيلِ اللَّهِ اثَّاقَلْتُمْ إِلَى الْأَرْضِ أَرَضِيتُمْ بِالْحَيَاةِ الدُّنْيَا مِنَ الْآخِرَةِ فَمَا مَتَاعُ الْحَيَاةِ الدُّنْيَا فِي الْآخِرَةِ إِلَّا قَلِيلٌ

> *O you who have faith! What is the matter with you that when you are told: 'Go forth in the way of God,' you sink heavily to the ground? Are you pleased with the life of this world instead of the Hereafter? But the wares of the life of this world compared with the Hereafter are but insignificant.*

إِلَّا تَنْفِرُوا يُعَذِّبْكُمْ عَذَابًا أَلِيمًا وَيَسْتَبْدِلْ قَوْمًا غَيْرَكُمْ وَلَا تَضُرُّوهُ شَيْئًا وَاللَّهُ عَلَى كُلِّ شَيْءٍ قَدِيرٌ.

> *If you do not go forth, He will punish you with a painful punishment, and replace you with another people, and you will not hurt Him in the least, and God has power over all things.*[193]

How could we believe in the immaculateness of the companions when the prophetic tradition clearly states,

يَرِدُ عَلَيَّ يَوْمَ القِيَامَةِ رَهْطٌ مِنْ أَصْحَابِي، فَيُحَلَّئُونَ عَنِ الحَوْضِ، فَأَقُولُ: أَيْ رَبِّ! أَصْحَابِي، فَيَقُولُ: إِنَّكَ لَا عِلْمَ لَكَ بِمَا أَحْدَثُوا بَعْدَكَ، إِنَّهُمُ ارْتَدُّوا بَعْدَكَ عَلَى أَدْبَارِهِمُ القَهْقَرَى.

> *On the Day of Resurrection, a group of my companions will come to me but they will be repelled from the Pool [of Paradise]. I will say, 'O' Lord! My companions!' He will say:*

> *You have no knowledge of what they did after you. They turned on*

---

[193] The Noble Quran, 9:38-39.

their heels.[194]

How can we deem the companions to be immaculate when some of them stood face to face with the Prophet (sa) and said,

> *"The Prophet (sa) is delusional, or he is afflicted with pain. God's Book is sufficient for us!"*

There, the companions split into two groups, one of which confronted the Prophet (sa) and disregarded his request!

How can we judge the companions to be immaculate when they confronted the Prophet (sa) about the Treaty of *Ḥudaybiyah*?

The Prophet (sa) responded,

إِنِّي رَسولُ اللَّهِ، ولَنْ يُضَيِّعَنِي اللَّهُ أبَدًا.

> *I am the Messenger of God and God will never forsake me.*[195]

The Prophet's (sa) response was not sufficient for some, so they went to other companions and posed the same question, only to receive the same response![196]

How can the companions be immaculate when they rejected the command of the Prophet (sa) to join *Jaysh Usāmah*[197]? The Prophet (sa) was deeply hurt by their insubordination. It is narrated that he reprimanded those companions that neglected to heed to his orders in joining the ranks of Usāmah. He spoke to them directly and questioned them explicitly as follows,

ما مقالة بلغتني عن بعضكم في تأميري أسامة ولئن طعنتم في تأميري أسامة فقد طعنتم في

---

[194] Ṣaḥīḥ al-Bukhārī, 7:265.

[195] Ṣaḥīḥ Muslim, 3441.

[196] Ibid.

[197] Jaysh Usāmah (the army of Usāmah ibn Zayd) was the last army or brigade prepared by the order of Prophet Muhammad (sa) to battle against the Romans. Because the army was led by Usama b. Zayd it became known as Jaysh Usama.

تأميري أبيه من قبله وأيمّ الله انه كان خليقا بالإمارة وان ابنه بعده لخليق بها.

> *What is this I have heard some of you say about my appointment of Usāmah? If you criticize my appointment of Usāmah then you have criticized my appointment of his father before. By God, he was worthy of leadership and his son is worthy of leadership after him.*[198]

The significance of this army, led by Usama ibn Zayd, extends beyond its military preparations, as it played a crucial role in fulfilling several vital objectives set forth by the Prophet (sa).

The name "Jaysh Usama" is derived from its leader, Usama ibn Zayd, who was a highly respected companion of Prophet Muhammad (sa). This army was meticulously organized and equipped, ready to engage in battle against the Romans. However, a noteworthy aspect of Jaysh Usāmah's history is that it did not embark on its mission to confront the Roman forces during the lifetime of the Prophet (sa).

The delay in launching this campaign was not due to any reluctance or hesitation on the part of Usama or his soldiers. Instead, it stemmed from the fact that several senior companions of Prophet Muhammad (sa) chose to defy his direct command to send troops for this particular expedition. This act of insubordination, in which some influential figures declined to participate in the campaign, raised questions about the character of those individuals. The Prophet (sa) even cursed those who did not join Usāmah's brigade.[199]

It is essential to recognize that the Prophet Muhammad's (sa) decision to assemble Jaysh Usāmah held profound wisdom and implications beyond its military objectives. This directive was intricately linked to the question of succession and the clear path for his designated successor, Imam Ali (a), to assume leadership after his passing.

The delay in sending the army allowed the Prophet (sa) to address

---

[198] Ibn Sa'd, *al-Ṭabaqāt*, 2:136.

[199] Al-Milal wa'l-Niḥal, 1:14.

important matters related to his succession. By demonstrating his unwavering support for Usama ibn Zayd, despite opposition from some senior companions, Prophet Muhammad (sa) emphasized the principle of meritocracy and the importance of individual qualities in leadership rather than age or social status.

In this context, the assembly of Jaysh Usāmah served as a poignant testament to the Prophet's (sa) confidence in Imam Ali (a) and his ability to lead the Muslim community after him. It reinforced the idea that leadership should be based on merit and piety rather than seniority or lineage.

In essence, Jaysh Usāmah, holds a pivotal place in Islamic history. It not only represented the last military expedition organized by the Prophet (sa) but also carried profound implications for the leadership and succession within the Muslim community, highlighting the importance of merit and individual qualities in guiding the Prophet's nation.

The Community

As members of diverse Shia communities residing in various parts of the world, what valuable advice can you offer for fostering unity and cooperation within our respective communities, given that we all coexist and interact with one another?

As individuals, we reside within the fabric of our distinct Shia communities, dispersed across various regions of the world. Our diversity is a testament to the universality of our faith, and in this tapestry, there are valuable lessons and advice that can benefit us all.

First and foremost, let us strive to be individuals who radiate positive energy within our communities. Rather than mere consumers or beneficiaries, we must aspire to be givers, contributors, and active participants in the betterment of our shared faith and society. This echoes the timeless wisdom of our beloved Imam (a), who encouraged us with his words:

كُونُوا دُعاةً لِلنّاسِ بِغَيرِ ألسِنَتِكُم!

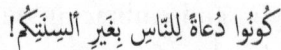

Be callers [unto the path of God] for the people without [using] your

tongues![200]

This profound guidance reminds us that our actions, behaviors, and characters can be potent forms of invitation to our faith. Let our conduct be a testament to the beauty and virtues of our beliefs, and let our lives serve as living examples of the principles we hold dear.

In practical terms, this means embodying the teachings of the Ahl al-Bayt (a) in our daily lives. It means showing compassion, kindness, and empathy to those around us, regardless of their background or beliefs. It means being honest, just, and upright in our dealings with others, reflecting the ethical standards set by our Imams (a).

Moreover, as diverse Shia communities scattered across the globe, we should be mindful of the unique challenges and opportunities that come with our geographical and cultural differences. While our backgrounds may vary, our faith unites us, and this unity should be our strength.

Let us foster a spirit of inclusivity and acceptance within our communities, embracing the rich tapestry of cultures, traditions, and backgrounds that make up our global Shia family. Instead of allowing our differences to divide us, let them enrich our collective experience, providing us with diverse perspectives and insights that can enhance our understanding of Islam.

Furthermore, let us actively engage in dialogue and cooperation with other communities and faiths, promoting interfaith harmony and understanding. As Shia communities dispersed throughout the world, we have a shared responsibility to be ambassadors of our faith through our actions and character. By following the teachings of the Ahl al-Bayt (a) and embracing our diversity, we foster unity and contribute to a brighter future for our communities and the world at large.

---

[200] Al-ʿĀmilī, *Wasāʾil al-Shīʿah*, 1:76.

Could we delve into a more detailed discussion regarding the concept of "al-amr bi al-ma'roof w al-nahee 'an al-munkar"[201] (enjoining good and forbidding evil)?

These two obligations, often coupled as one, are essential duties in Islamic tradition. One of the most important foundations of an Islamic lifestyle, sanctioned through Islamic law, is to enjoin good and forbid evil. The emphasis on these two principles are explained in detail in the Noble Quran and the Sunnah.

From the Noble Quran, read God Almighty's words in the following verse.

كُنتُمْ خَيْرَ أُمَّةٍ أُخْرِجَتْ لِلنَّاسِ تَأْمُرُونَ بِالْمَعْرُوفِ وتَنْهَوْنَ عَنِ الْمُنْكَرِ وتُؤْمِنُونَ بِاللَّهِ

You are the best nation [ever] brought forth for mankind: you bid what is right and forbid what is wrong and have faith in God.[202]

This verse attributes the distinction of being the best nation to three defining traits: enjoining good, forbidding evil, and unwavering faith in God Almighty. The coupling of these virtues underscores their paramount importance.

God draws parallels between enjoining good and forbidding evil and having faith in Him. He judges the Muslim nation as the best nation

---

[201] Two of the ten obligatory practices within ritual law in Shia Islam (also known as *furoo' al-deen or the branches of religion*) are *amr bil ma'ruf* (enjoining good) and *nahi 'an al-munkar* (forbidding evil). These, along with eight others, form the core of religious practice. They include daily prayers (*salah*), fasting during Ramadan (*sawm*), giving to the needy (*zakah*), the pilgrimage to Mecca (*hajj*), striving for God's cause (*jihad*), a 20 percent religious tax on profits, (*khums*), disassociating from the adversaries of the Prophet and Ahl al-Bayt (*tabarra*), and showing love and loyalty to the Prophet and Ahl al-Bayt (*tawallee*). Together, these aspects guide Shia Muslims in their daily lives, promoting faith, worship, charity, ethical behavior, and community unity.

[202] The Noble Quran, 3:110.

brought forth for people because of the three qualities above.

Furthermore, the Quran reinforces the gravity of this duty through verses such as:

لُعِنَ الَّذِينَ كَفَرُوا مِنْ بَنِي إِسْرائِيلَ عَلى لِسانِ داوُدَ وعِيسَى ابْنِ مَرْيَمَ ذلِكَ بِما عَصَوْا وكانُوا يَعْتَدُونَ

The faithless among the Children of Israel were cursed on the tongue of David and Jesus, son of Mary, because they would disobey and they used to commit transgression.

كانُوا لا يَتَناهَوْنَ عَنْ مُنكَرٍ فَعَلُوهُ لَبِئْسَ ما كانُوا يَفْعَلُونَ

They would not forbid one another from the wrongs that they committed. Surely, evil is what they had been doing.[203]

The mention of being cursed here for neglecting the duty of forbidding evil further underscores the great importance of this duty in the Muslim paradigm. As for the honorable Sunnah, the hadiths that can be cited are many. Among them is the narration of *Muhammad ibn ʿArafah*. He said,

سمعت أبا الحسن عليه السّلام يقول: لَتَأْمُرُنَّ بِالْمَعْرُوفِ، ولَتَنْهُنَّ عَنِ الْمُنْكَرِ، أَوْ لَيُسْتَعْمَلَنَّ عَلَيْكُمْ شِرَارُكُمْ، فَيَدْعُو خِيَارُكُمْ فَلَا يُسْتَجَابُ لَهُمْ.

I heard Abu al-Ḥasan [Imam al-Riḍā] (a) say, 'You must enjoin good and forbid evil. Else, the most evil of you will be used against you, and the best among you will call but they will not be answered.'[204]

In another narration, the Prophet (sa) said,

---

[203] The Noble Quran, 5:78-79.

[204] Al-ʿĀmilī, *Wasāʾil al-Shīʿah*, 11:394.

لا يزال النّاس بخيْر مَا أَمَرُوا بِالمَعْرُوفِ وَنَهوا عَنِ المُنْكَر وَتَعاوَنوا عَلى البرّ، فإذا لَمْ يَفْعَلُوا ذلك نُزِعَتْ منهُم البَرَكَات وَسُلِّطَ بعضُهم على بَعْض وَلم يَكُن لهُم نَاصِر في الأَرْضِ وَلَا في السَّمَاء.

People are still well as long as they enjoin good and forbid evil and cooperate in righteousness. If they do not do that, blessings will be taken away from them and some of them will be empowered over others, and they [i.e., the people] will have no supporter on earth or in heaven.[205]

In another narration, the Prophet (sa) said,

إِذَا أُمَّتِي تَوَاكَلَتِ الأَمْرَ بِالْمَعْرُوفِ والنَّهْيَ عَنِ الْمُنْكَرِ، فَلْيَأْذَنُوا بِوِقَاعٍ مِنَ اللهِ.

If my ummah neglects enjoining what is good and forbidding what is evil, then let them be informed of a fall from God.[206]

The verses that urge the enjoining of good and forbidding of evil are in two forms. Some of them are clearly stated and unequivocal on the subject, such as the two previous verses. Other verses are not necessarily explicit, but instead implicitly touch on the subject.

Perhaps the second form can be illustrated by the following verse:

يَا أَيُّهَا الَّذِينَ آمَنُوا قُوا أَنفُسَكُمْ وَأَهْلِيكُمْ نَارًا وَقُودُهَا النَّاسُ وَالْحِجَارَةُ

O' you who have faith! Save yourselves and your families from a Fire whose fuel will be people and stones.[207]

Another set of inspiring verses from the Noble Quran tell us,

---

205 Al-Ṭūsī, *Tahdhīb al-Aḥkām*, 6:181.

206 Al-ʿĀmilī, *Wasāʾil al-Shīʿah*, 11:394.

207 The Noble Quran, 66:6.

وَالْعَصْرِ

By Time!

إِنَّ الْإِنْسَانَ لَفِي خُسْرٍ

Man is indeed in loss,

إِلَّا الَّذِينَ آمَنُوا وَعَمِلُوا الصَّالِحَاتِ وَتَوَاصَوْا بِالْحَقِّ وَتَوَاصَوْا بِالصَّبْرِ

except those who have faith and do righteous deeds, and enjoin one another to [follow] the truth, and enjoin one another to patience.[208]

The first verse clearly indicates that a special responsibility lies on the head of household towards the members of their family. Their duty is to protect their loved ones from committing what necessitates the punishment of Hell. This can only be achieved by enjoining good and forbidding evil. The second verse addresses the virtue of enjoining truth and patience. The verse provides another expression for enjoining good and forbidding evil.

The noble verses related to the issue of enjoining good and forbidding evil are many. The specific verses we are mentioning should be sufficient for the current discussion, as they contain specific noteworthy points.

God also says,

لَيْسُوا سَوَاءً مِنْ أَهْلِ الْكِتَابِ أُمَّةٌ قَائِمَةٌ يَتْلُونَ آيَاتِ اللَّهِ آنَاءَ اللَّيْلِ وَهُمْ يَسْجُدُونَ * يُؤْمِنُونَ بِاللَّهِ وَالْيَوْمِ الْآخِرِ وَيَأْمُرُونَ بِالْمَعْرُوفِ وَ يَنْهَوْنَ عَنِ الْمُنْكَرِ وَ يُسَارِعُونَ فِي الْخَيْرَاتِ وَ أُولَئِكَ مِنَ الصَّالِحِينَ

Yet they are not all alike. Among the People of the

---

[208] The Noble Quran, 103:1-3.

> Book is an upright nation; they recite God's signs in the watches of the night and prostrate. They have faith in God and the Last Day and bid what is right and forbid what is wrong, and they are active in [performing] good deeds. Those are among the righteous.[209]

The indication here suggests the ummah that abides by this duty is a righteous one. A righteous nation must abide by the duty to enjoin good and forbid evil.

God also says,

الَّذِينَ يَتَّبِعُونَ الرَّسُولَ النَّبِيَّ الْأُمِّيَّ الَّذِي يَجِدُونَهُ مَكْتُوباً عِنْدَهُمْ فِي التَّوْرَاةِ وَالْإِنْجِيلِ يَأْمُرُهُمْ بِالْمَعْرُوفِ وَيَنْهَاهُمْ عَنِ الْمُنْكَرِ

> Those who follow the Apostle, the untaught prophet, whose mention they find written with them in the Torah and the Evangel, who bids them to do what is right and forbids them from what is wrong.[210]

The Prophet (sa) made this a lifestyle of his. Throughout his life he enjoined what was good and forbade what was evil. He practiced what he preached and set the example for his people.

The next verse further illustrates this duty as an attribute of the faithful. God says,

وَالْمُؤْمِنُونَ وَالْمُؤْمِنَاتُ بَعْضُهُمْ أَوْلِيَاءُ بَعْضٍ يَأْمُرُونَ بِالْمَعْرُوفِ وَيَنْهَوْنَ عَنِ الْمُنْكَرِ وَيُقِيمُونَ الصَّلَاةَ وَيُؤْتُونَ الزَّكَاةَ وَيُطِيعُونَ اللَّهَ وَرَسُولَهُ أُولَٰئِكَ سَيَرْحَمُهُمُ اللَّهُ

> But the faithful, men and women, are comrades of

---

[209] The Noble Quran, 3:113-14.
[210] The Noble Quran, 7:157.

one another: they bid what is right and forbid what is wrong and maintain the prayer, give the zakat, and obey God and His Apostle. It is they to whom God will soon grant His mercy.[211]

The verse shows that this is a characteristic of the believing men and women by which they attain divine mercy. The mercy of God is connected to this practice and lifestyle, which should be manifested by the faithful.

Similarly, God says,

التَّائِبُونَ الْعابِدُونَ الْحامِدُونَ السَّائِحُونَ الرَّاكِعُونَ السَّاجِدُونَ الْآمِرُونَ
بِالْمَعْرُوفِ وَالنَّاهُونَ عَنِ الْمُنْكَرِ وَالْحافِظُونَ لِحُدُودِ اللَّهِ وَبَشِّرِ الْمُؤْمِنِينَ

[The faithful are] penitent, devout, celebrators of God's praise, wayfarers, who bow [and] prostrate [in prayer], bid what is right and forbid what is wrong, and keep God's bounds—and give good news to the faithful.[212]

God also says,

الَّذِينَ إِنْ مَكَّنَّاهُمْ فِي الْأَرْضِ أَقامُوا الصَّلاةَ وآتَوُا الزَّكاةَ وأَمَرُوا بِالْمَعْرُوفِ
وَنَهَوْا عَنِ الْمُنْكَرِ

Those who, if We granted them power in the land, will maintain the prayer, give the zakat, bid what is right and forbid what is wrong.[213]

This again emphasizes the task of enjoining good and forbidding evil, elevating it to the level of establishing prayer and paying zakat. God

---

[211] The Noble Quran, 9:71.

[212] The Noble Quran, 9:112.

[213] The Noble Quran, 22:41.

warns the believers against neglecting this duty, especially when they are given power and authority.

In the Noble Quran, God shares with us of the wisdoms of *Luqman*[214] and his advice to his son. Luqman tells his son in part,

يا بُنَيَّ أَقِمِ الصَّلاةَ وَأْمُرْ بِالْمَعْرُوفِ وَانْهَ عَنِ الْمُنْكَرِ وَاصْبِرْ عَلى ما أَصابَكَ إِنَّ ذٰلِكَ مِنْ عَزْمِ الْأُمُورِ

O' my son! Maintain the prayer and bid what is right and forbid what is wrong and be patient through whatever may befall you. That is indeed the steadiest of courses.[215]

This verse underscores that the duty of promoting virtue and preventing vice is not exclusive to Islam but has been emphasized in previous civilizations as well. These are a few examples of explicit verses illustrating this principle.

The Muslim Community

God Almighty prescribed this duty as a collective obligation on all Muslims. He says,

---

[214] Luqman, a notable figure mentioned in the Quran, is renowned for his wisdom, counsel, and moral parables, with an entire sura named after him (Chapter 31: Surat Luqman). His teachings encompassed monotheism, humility in interactions with people, a dignified demeanor, moderation in lifestyle, qualities of a virtuous companion, and the ability to derive lessons from impolite behavior. In Quran 31:13-19, Luqman's counsel is eloquently expressed. He imparts invaluable advice to his son, emphasizing the importance of monotheism, prayer, enjoining good, forbidding evil, patience in the face of adversity, humility, graceful conduct, moderation, and speaking softly. In the seminal hadith compilation, *Bihar al-Anwar*, 17th century Shia scholar *Allama al-Majlisi* (1627 – 1699 CE) dedicates a chapter to Luqman's wills and wise sayings, further highlighting the enduring wisdom and moral guidance attributed to this venerable figure in Islamic tradition.

[215] The Noble Quran, 31:17.

وَلْتَكُنْ مِنْكُمْ أُمَّةٌ يَدْعُونَ إِلَى الْخَيْرِ وَيَأْمُرُونَ بِالْمَعْرُوفِ وَيَنْهَوْنَ عَنِ الْمُنْكَرِ
وَأُولَئِكَ هُمُ الْمُفْلِحُونَ

There must be a nation among you summoning to the good, bidding what is right, and forbidding what is wrong. It is they who are the felicitous.[216]

This verse highlights the concept of enjoining good and forbidding evil in a subtle yet profound manner. It emphasizes the role of a righteous community within the broader Islamic ummah. It suggests that among the Muslim community, there should always be a group of individuals who actively promote goodness, encourage righteous actions, and discourage sinful behavior. These individuals are described as the "felicitous" or "successful."

This verse underscores the dual nature of the Muslim community. On one hand, it portrays the community as a unified entity, likening it to a single body where believers should care for and support one another. The analogy reflects the sense of unity, cooperation, and mutual responsibility that should prevail among Muslims. The hadith of Imam al-Ṣādiq (a) further exemplifies this concept, emphasizing the interconnectedness of believers and their collective responsibility.

الْمؤْمِنُونَ فِي تَبَارِّهِمْ وَتَرَاحُمِهِمْ وَتَعَاطُفِهِمْ- كَمَثَلِ الْجَسَدِ إِذَا اشْتَكَى تَدَاعَى لَهُ سَائِرُهُ بِالسَّهَرِ
وَالْحُمَّى.

The believers, in their kindness, mercy and sympathy, are like the body. When [one part] complains, the rest responds to it with sleeplessness and fever.[217]

The Messenger of God (sa) also said,

الْمُؤْمِن للمؤمنِ كالبُنْيانِ يشدُّ بَعضُهُ بعضًا.

---

[216] The Noble Quran, 3:104.

[217] Al-Majlisī, *Biḥār al-Anwār*, 71:274.

> *A believer to a believer is like a building, one part of which supports the other.*[218]

On the other hand, Islam recognizes the individuality of its members, particularly in matters of personal religious obligations, such as prayer. Each individual is accountable for their own actions, and no one can bear the burden of another's disobedience.

Enjoining good and forbidding evil serves as the essential link between these two perspectives. It acts as the protective wall safeguarding the Muslim community from division and deviation. By actively promoting righteousness and discouraging sinful behavior, believers contribute to the well-being and unity of the ummah.

In essence, this verse underscores that enjoining good and forbidding evil is not just a personal duty but a collective responsibility within the Muslim community. It is a means to maintain the harmonious functioning of the ummah, ensuring that individuals work together to uphold the principles of Islam and guide one another on the path of righteousness. Through this duty, the Muslim community remains a united and spiritually thriving entity, adhering to the values and principles of their faith.

A linguistic question arises concerning this verse: What role does the grammatical particle 'min' play in the word 'minkum'?

The particle 'min' can serve as a determiner, imparting the meaning of "some of you." Alternatively, it may be employed for emphasis, resulting in the meaning of "be a nation."

In the case of the latter interpretation, the intent is to exaggerate and underscore the significance of the matter at hand. It emphasizes that the Islamic community, as a whole, must transform into a nation dedicated

---

[218] Al-Hindī, *Kanz al-ʿUmmāl*, 1:141.

to enjoining good and forbidding evil.

It is essential to clarify that the duties of enjoining good and forbidding evil are universal obligations for all members of the Muslim community. They do not apply selectively to certain individuals but rather encompass every individual. There is no evidence to suggest otherwise, particularly as the verses do not specify a particular group. This point is crucial in comprehending the verse.

Arguably, the most appropriate interpretation is that the grammatical particle 'min' functions is a determiner and not in conflict with the general obligation of enjoining good and forbidding evil. Consequently, this duty can be understood as a dual obligation. It is a duty that falls upon each individual independently, and it is also a collective obligation for the entire group.

In every community, there must exist a segment of individuals who investigate such matters and carry out the responsibilities of enjoining good and forbidding evil while adhering to the appropriate legal methods required by their societies. This role is entrusted to a group, since it is not feasible for every individual to bear this burden independently, as it would lead to chaos. This, however, does not negate the fact that the obligation lies on every individual independently, especially when they are capable of fulfilling this duty on their own.

Is there a contradiction between the texts obligating enjoining good and forbidding evil and between the following verse:

يا أَيُّهَا الَّذِينَ آمَنُوا عَلَيْكُمْ أَنْفُسَكُمْ لا يَضُرُّكُمْ مَنْ ضَلَّ إِذَا اهْتَدَيْتُمْ

O you who have faith! Take care of your own souls. He who strays cannot hurt you if you are guided.[219]

[219] The Noble Quran, 5:105.

At first glance, this verse may suggest that individuals are only responsible for reforming themselves and not obligated to guide or reform others. If that were the case, it might seem that there is no place for enjoining others to do what is right and forbidding them from what is wrong. How can we reconcile this apparent contradiction?

The verse in question can be understood in one of two ways:

Firstly, the verse may serve as a form of consolation. In this interpretation, it conveys that if you sincerely engage in enjoining good and forbidding evil, but others do not heed your advice or guidance, then you should not be disheartened or distressed. You are not obligated to guide those who do not seek guidance. In this context, consider God's words in the following verse,

فَلَعَلَّكَ بَاخِعٌ نَفْسَكَ عَلَى آثَارِهِمْ إِنْ لَمْ يُؤْمِنُوا بِهَذَا الْحَدِيثِ أَسَفاً

You are liable to imperil your life out of grief for their sake, if they should not believe this discourse.[220]

This can be understood to mean that you might grieve over their rejection of your guidance, but you are not required to jeopardize your own well-being out of sorrow for their choices.

Secondly, the verse can be interpreted as a reminder that the misguidance of others should not lead you away from the path of guidance and righteousness. It emphasizes that even when others may stray or engage in wrongdoing, you should maintain your commitment to the right path and not be swayed by their misguided behavior. In this sense, the verse underscores the importance of personal responsibility and steadfastness in adhering to one's own faith and principles, regardless of the actions of others.

---

[220] The Noble Quran, 18:6.

There is no inherent contradiction between the obligation to enjoin good and forbid evil and the verse mentioned above. The verse serves as a reminder that individuals should prioritize their own spiritual well-being and not be disheartened by the choices of those who may not follow their guidance. It does not negate the importance of enjoining good and forbidding evil but rather provides guidance on how to approach situations where others may not heed such advice.

Jurists have described the duty of enjoining good and forbidding evil in three stages: rejection with the heart, then with the tongue, then with the hand. They also say that one should not move to the next stage if the previous one suffices. Can you shed some light on this issue?

It is worth noting that the division into these stages is a construct that has apparently been developed over time, as there are no primary texts within Islamic scripture that explicitly delineate these stages as is. However, it is crucial to explore the rationale behind this gradation and the importance of not progressing to the next stage if the previous one is sufficient.

The fundamental reason for this division, despite the absence of explicit Quranic or Hadith references, lies in the intrinsic connection between faith and the rejection of evil. Faith inherently entails a rejection of evil at the heart level; they are intertwined and inseparable. This is precisely why the first stage, the rejection in one's heart, is considered a fundamental requirement of faith. In essence, faith and the internal rejection of evil cannot be disentangled.

The subsequent two stages—verbal admonition and physical intervention—find their basis in the primary texts of Islam. They become obligatory in accordance with the general evidence affirming the obligation of enjoining good and forbidding evil. In fact, even the first stage, the internal rejection, can be understood as obligatory when we consider that it must be manifested through expressions of disapproval or discomfort. It is insufficient merely to feel distress upon witnessing evil; it must be outwardly expressed in some form.

Thus, it is firmly established that all three stages of enjoining good and forbidding evil are obligatory, as supported by the overarching evidence from Islamic teachings. However, the question arises concerning the wisdom behind this gradation and the prohibition of moving from one stage to the next prematurely.

This rationale can be illuminated through two distinct approaches:

A careful examination of Islamic texts on this subject reveals that the overarching purpose is to promote goodness and diminish evil in society. If the objective can be achieved through the lowest stage, the mere rejection in one's heart, then it is not deemed rational to escalate to the more severe stages. This aligns with the Quranic principle,

ادْعُ إِلَىٰ سَبِيلِ رَبِّكَ بِالْحِكْمَةِ وَالْمَوْعِظَةِ الْحَسَنَةِ

Invite to the way of your Lord with wisdom and good advice.[221]

The wise and effective call to righteousness naturally follows a graded approach.

Moreover, this principle underscores the necessity of gradation within each of the three stages themselves, assuming that all three stages are applicable in a given situation. In other words, even within verbal admonition or physical intervention, a gradual and measured approach is essential, adapting to the circumstances and the individuals involved.

Therefore, while the division of enjoining good and forbidding evil into three stages is not explicitly detailed in primary Islamic texts, it is firmly established through the general evidence within the religion. This division is both rational and practical, serving the overarching goal of promoting righteousness and reducing evil in society while

---

[221] The Noble Quran, 16:125.

emphasizing the importance of a gradual and measured approach in fulfilling this duty.

Individual Liberties

Critics of Islam often contend that the religion restricts human freedom by advocating the concept of enjoining good and forbidding evil. They argue that this notion infringes upon individuals' autonomy and deprives them of their freedom to act as they choose. How would one respond to such a claim?

To address this concern, it is essential to understand the Islamic perspective on human freedom and choice. In Islam, it is firmly believed that God Almighty created humankind with free will and the ability to make choices. This capacity for choice allows individuals to navigate the path of righteousness or to venture down the path of wrongdoing. However, it is crucial to recognize that God has also imposed certain obligations and prohibitions upon humanity.

God does not accept the exercise of human freedom in a manner that contradicts His guidance and commandments. The essence of human freedom, therefore, must align with the parameters of choice that God has granted to His creation. This divine framework ensures that freedom operates within the bounds of moral and ethical guidelines. As God Almighty emphasizes in the Quran,

إِنَّا هَدَيْنَاهُ السَّبِيلَ إِمَّا شَاكِرًا وَإِمَّا كَفُورًا

Indeed, We have guided him to the way, be he grateful or ungrateful.[222]

This verse underscores that God has bestowed upon humankind the guidance to discern between right and wrong, but individuals are still

[222] The Noble Quran,76:3.

free to choose whether to follow that guidance or not.

It is crucial to clarify that the claim that individuals possess the freedom to make choices, even if those choices involve disobedience to God's guidance or neglecting divinely prescribed duties, is not acceptable within the Islamic framework. The freedom granted by God is not boundless; it is inherently tied to moral responsibility and accountability.

In essence, Islam acknowledges and upholds the concept of human freedom and choice, but within the context of divine guidance and moral responsibility. This perspective ensures that individuals exercise their freedom while adhering to the principles of righteousness and avoiding actions that contravene God's commandments. Ultimately, true freedom in Islam is not the freedom to disobey God but the freedom to choose the path of virtue and righteousness.

Some individuals would object and argue that the practice of enjoining good and forbidding evil can exacerbate divisions among people and undermine harmony and coexistence. They contend that close bonds of brotherhood can deteriorate when one person admonishes another for their wrongdoing, citing real-life examples to support their claim. How can we reconcile this potential contradiction?

It is essential to address this issue by recognizing that the perception of negative consequences often stems from an incorrect understanding, namely the belief that a person has absolute freedom to act as they please. However, this premise is fundamentally flawed. In the context of Islam, freedom exists within the confines of what is legitimate and permissible. When this fundamental principle is understood, there is no valid basis for the supposed rifts and discord that critics fear.

Negative outcomes in the practice of enjoining good and forbidding evil typically result from either this misunderstanding or from employing violence in the process, contrary to the Quranic injunction:

ادْعُ إِلَىٰ سَبِيلِ رَبِّكَ بِالْحِكْمَةِ وَالْمَوْعِظَةِ الْحَسَنَةِ

Invite to the way of your Lord with wisdom and good advice.[223]

This verse underscores the importance of wisdom and gentle persuasion in the approach to enjoining good and discouraging evil.

Moreover, Islamic jurisprudence provides a set of conditions that must be met for the obligation of enjoining good and forbidding evil to be applicable. These conditions are extensively discussed and elaborated upon in the books of jurisprudence and Islamic legal scholarship. It is essential to review these conditions to ensure that the practice aligns with the established principles of Islamic jurisprudence.

While concerns regarding the potential negative consequences of enjoining good and forbidding evil are valid, it is crucial to address them by emphasizing the correct understanding of human freedom within the framework of Islam's legitimate boundaries.

Additionally, adopting a wise and non-violent approach in the spirit of the Quranic guidance can help mitigate the risk of discord and division while upholding the essential duty of enjoining good and forbidding evil. Finally, a careful examination of the conditions set forth by Islamic jurisprudence ensures that this practice is carried out in accordance with the principles of the faith.

---

[223] The Noble Quran, 16:125.

The Family

Adorning Oneself with Virtue

God Almighty says in the Noble Quran,

يَا أَيُّهَا الَّذِينَ آمَنُوا قُوا أَنفُسَكُمْ وَأَهْلِيكُمْ نَارًا وَقُودُهَا النَّاسُ وَالْحِجَارَةُ

O' you who have faith! Save yourselves and your families from a Fire whose fuel will be people and stones.[224]

The verse seems to lay the responsibility of enjoining good and forbidding evil at the shoulders of the head of the household.

This sacred verse underscores the necessity of promoting righteousness and preventing wrongdoing within one's immediate family circle. Every Muslim is not only responsible for their community but also has a specific obligation to safeguard and guide their family members, protecting them from deviating from the path of virtue. Consequently, the righteousness of the head of the household is not merely a personal obligation but also impacts the moral direction of the entire family unit.

The principle of being a virtuous role model is a universal one,

---

[224] The Noble Quran, 66:6.

applicable to various social structures. Scholars are expected to set an example for their students and society. Rulers and statesmen should embody moral excellence for their citizens, while teachers must inspire their students through their conduct.

In relevant discourse, the seminal work *Jawāhir al-Kalām*[225] touches on this subject in the following excerpt:

> *One of the greatest examples of enjoining good and forbidding evil, especially for a clergyman, is that he wears the garment of good, both in what is obligatory and what is recommended. He must remove the garment of evil, both in what is forbidden and what is abhorred. He must adorn himself with noble morals and purify himself from vices. This will lead others to do good and refrain from evil.*

In essence, individuals must adorn themselves with virtue, as articulated by the author of Jawāhir al-Kalām, who emphasized that enjoining good and forbidding evil, especially for clergy, requires donning the mantle of goodness, both in fulfilling obligatory and recommended acts, while shunning evil, whether forbidden or detestable. This virtuous demeanor serves as a beacon, inspiring others to follow the path of righteousness and abstain from wrongdoing.

It is crucial to recognize that the higher a person's status within society or among their peers, the more reprehensible any misconduct on their part becomes. This principle is illustrated in how God Almighty addressed the wives of the Prophet Muhammad (sa). God emphasizes

---

[225] Jawāhir al-kalām fī Sharḥ Sharāʾiʿ al-Islām, commonly referred to as Jawāhir al-Kalām, is a significant work in jurisprudence (*fiqh*) authored by Muhammad Hasan al-Najafi (d. 1850), also known as *Sahib Jawahir*, which means the author of Jawahir. He was a student of prominent scholars such as Sayyid Muhammad Jawad 'Amili and Shaykh Ja'far Kashif al-Ghita. This book serves as an extensive commentary on *Shara'i' al-Islam*, originally authored by the eminent scholar al-Muhaqqiq al-Hilli (d. 676/1277). Jawāhir al-Kalām is highly regarded for its comprehensive analysis, offering valuable insights into the viewpoints and arguments of past jurists. Researchers and scholars find it particularly valuable for its meticulous examination of Islamic jurisprudential matters.

that those who commit indecent acts will face severe consequences, while those who remain obedient to God and His Messenger and act righteously will be rewarded abundantly.

يَا نِسَاءَ النَّبِيِّ مَن يَأْتِ مِنكُنَّ بِفَاحِشَةٍ مُبَيِّنَةٍ يُضَاعَفْ لَهَا الْعَذَابُ ضِعْفَيْنِ وَكَانَ ذَلِكَ عَلَى اللَّهِ يَسِيراً

> O wives of the Prophet! Whoever of you commits a gross indecency, her punishment shall be doubled, and that is easy for God.

وَمَن يَقْنُتْ مِنكُنَّ لِلَّهِ وَرَسُولِهِ وَتَعْمَلْ صَالِحاً نُؤْتِهَا أَجْرَهَا مَرَّتَيْنِ وَأَعْتَدْنَا لَهَا رِزْقاً كَرِيماً

> But whoever of you is obedient to God and His Apostle and acts righteously, We shall give her a twofold reward, and We will have in store for her a noble provision.[226]

This underscores the importance of individuals, particularly those in influential positions, upholding the highest moral standards to guide and inspire others effectively.

Bid What is Right

In another verse, God Almighty says,

خُذِ الْعَفْوَ وَأْمُرْ بِالْعُرْفِ وَأَعْرِضْ عَنِ الْجَاهِلِينَ

> Adopt [a policy of] excusing [the faults of people], bid what is right, and turn away from the ignorant.[227]

---

[226] The Noble Quran, 33:30-31.
[227] The Noble Quran, 7:199.

God uses the Arabic word *ʿurf* here. What does this mean?

This verse alludes to three basic issues to be considered by every believer throughout their life.

The most appropriate way to understand the first command,[228] in accordance with the context of the verse, is that we are urged to pardon others. If we are wronged or transgressed against, we should pardon, excuse, and forgive.

Naturally, if this is the intended meaning, then it must be understood as a recommended ethical task and a noble trait to be sought by believers.

The second segment of the verse uses the Arabic word *ʿurf*. Etymologically, this word is derived from the root *ʿaraf*, which means to know or recognize. ʿUrf thus refers to everything that is recognized by humankind as good. As such, the verse indicates the obligation of enjoining good and forbidding evil. Now, the verse is addressed to the Prophet (sa), however, we must understand it in context of the following verse,

لَّقَدْ كَانَ لَكُمْ فِي رَسُولِ اللَّهِ أُسْوَةٌ حَسَنَةٌ

There is certainly a good exemplar for you in the Apostle of God.[229]

Collectively, these verses underscore that the duty to promote goodness is an obligation binding upon all believers. Lastly, God says that the ignorant do not deserve anything but turning away. The Noble Quran states,

---

[228] Another meaning mentioned in the books of *tafsir* (exegesis) is that *ʿafū* was a type of alms obligated before, and later replaced by, the obligation of zakat. See: al-Ṭurayḥī, *Majmaʿ al-Baḥrayn*, 1:299.

[229] The Noble Quran, 33:21.

وإذا خاطَبَهُمُ الْجاهِلُونَ قالُوا سَلاماً

When the ignorant address them, say, 'Peace!'[230]

In summary, the noble verse in its second segment (which was the subject of this question) indicates the obligation of enjoining good. This serves as a reminder of the moral and ethical responsibilities that believers bear in their interactions with others and in contributing to a virtuous society.

Call with Wisdom

In another verse, God urges us to call onto His path with wisdom. He says,

ادْعُ إِلَىٰ سَبِيلِ رَبِّكَ بِالْحِكْمَةِ وَالْمَوْعِظَةِ الْحَسَنَةِ

Invite to the way of your Lord with wisdom and good advice.[231]

Does this verse indicate the duty of enjoining good and forbidding evil as well?

Indeed, as mentioned earlier in the discussion, this noble verse emphasizes the obligation to call people to the path of God and highlights two essential elements in this call: wisdom and good advice. Consequently, it is reasonable to deduce that the obligation of enjoining good and forbidding evil can be inferred from this verse, as it constitutes a specific instance of inviting others to God's path. Given that the call to God's path is obligatory, as indicated by the apparent meaning of the verse, enjoining good also carries the weight of obligation as a means to fulfill this duty effectively.

---

[230] The Noble Quran, 25:63.

[231] The Noble Quran, 16:125.

Furthermore, the verse subtly hints at the importance of gradation in the stages of enjoining good and forbidding evil. If it is possible to deter individuals from wrongdoing through a simple display of disapproval or displeasure, then that approach is the wisest and most effective. If merely showing displeasure proves inadequate, the wise course of action involves verbal admonition. However, if verbal advice fails to yield the desired results, wisdom dictates that one should consider taking any appropriate action that effectively dissuades individuals from wrongdoing.

In essence, this Quranic verse not only underscores the duty of inviting others to God's path but also implies the necessity of employing wisdom and good advice, alongside gradation in efforts to enjoin good and forbid evil. It serves as a comprehensive guide for believers on how to fulfill their moral and ethical responsibilities in promoting righteousness within society.

Of course, this Quranic verse offers valuable teachings that extend beyond the duty of inviting others to God's path. It emphasizes the importance of conducting this call with wisdom and good advice, encouraging believers to use sound judgment and a genuine desire to guide others towards righteousness. Additionally, the verse underscores the need for a gradual approach when enjoining good and forbidding evil, suggesting that harsh methods should only be employed if gentler approaches prove ineffective.

Moreover, the verse sets a high moral standard for believers in their interactions with others. It highlights the significance of maintaining good manners, speaking kindly, and treating people with respect. Even when declining requests for assistance or confronting wrongdoing, believers are encouraged to do so with gentleness and compassion. The principle of repelling evil with what is best is reinforced, emphasizing that responding to wrongdoing with acts of kindness is both morally superior and more likely to lead to reconciliation. God says,

وَإِمَّا تُعْرِضَنَّ عَنْهُمُ ابْتِغَاءَ رَحْمَةٍ مِّن رَّبِّكَ تَرْجُوهَا فَقُل لَّهُمْ قَوْلًا مَّيْسُورًا

If you must hold off from [assisting] them [for now], seeking your Lord's mercy which you expect [in the future], speak to them gentle words.[232]

ولا تَسْتَوِي الْحَسَنَةُ وَلَا السَّيِّئَةُ ادْفَعْ بِالَّتِي هِيَ أَحْسَنُ فَإِذَا الَّذِي بَيْنَكَ وَبَيْنَهُ عَدَاوَةٌ كَأَنَّهُ وَلِيٌّ حَمِيمٌ

Good and evil [conduct] are not equal. Repel [evil] with what is best. [If you do so,] he between whom and you was enmity, will then be as though he were a sympathetic friend.[233]

Furthermore, the verse discourages retaliation and escalation of conflicts, promoting self-restraint and a commitment to responding to hostility with patience and virtue. These teachings align with broader Islamic ethical principles, emphasizing compassion, patience, and maintaining the moral high ground in interactions with others. They guide believers in their efforts to enjoin good and forbid evil, fostering an environment of harmony, understanding, and virtuous conduct within society.

Numerous noble traditions further emphasize these ethical principles, reminding believers of their responsibilities in promoting goodness and kindness to all, regardless of deservingness, thereby contributing to the cultivation of a virtuous and harmonious community. The following are examples of such traditions:

اصْنَعِ الْمَعْرُوفَ إِلَى مَنْ هُوَ أَهْلُهُ، وإِلَى مَنْ لَيْسَ مِنْ أَهْلِهِ، فَإِنْ لَمْ يَكُنْ هُوَ أَهْلَهُ فَكُنْ أَنْتَ مِنْ أَهْلِهِ.

---

[232] The Noble Quran, 17:28.

[233] The Noble Quran, 41:34.

Do good to those who are worthy and to those who are not worthy. Surely, if they are not worthy [of receiving good], then you are worthy [of doing it].[234]

أَيُّمَا مُؤْمِنٍ أَوْصَلَ إِلَى أَخِيهِ الْمُؤْمِنِ مَعْرُوفاً، فَقَدْ أَوْصَلَ ذَلِكَ إِلَى رَسُولِ اللهِ (ص).

If a believer does something good for his believing brother, then he has done good for the Messenger of God (sa).[235]

The Family's Role Model

You spoke previously about the family and the responsibility of the head of the household. This topic is very important for our communities across the world. Is it possible to expand on the topic?

Indeed, the role of the head of the household in ensuring the well-being and spiritual guidance of their family members is of paramount importance in our communities worldwide. Expanding on this topic further, we find that the responsibilities of the head of the household extend beyond providing the basic necessities of life, such as shelter, sustenance, and clothing.

The head of the household is entrusted with a profound duty, which is to safeguard their family from straying off the righteous path and transgressing against the commandments of God. This responsibility encompasses various dimensions. First and foremost, a man is responsible for upholding the modesty and dignity of family. This entails creating an environment within the family that fosters decency, respect, and the protection of their honor and virtue.

Additionally, the head of the household plays a crucial role in ensuring that the family members diligently perform their religious obligations,

---

[234] Al-ʿĀmilī, *Wasāʾil al-Shīʿah*, 11:528.

[235] Ibid, 11:530.

including daily prayers, fasting during the prescribed times, and fulfilling other religious duties. They are not only responsible for their own religious observance but are also tasked with guiding and facilitating the practice of faith for their loved ones.

As previously discussed, the concept of enjoining good and forbidding evil applies to every individual within the Muslim community, emphasizing collective responsibility for one another's actions. However, the head of the family bears a higher degree of responsibility in this regard. They are entrusted with the duty of shielding their family members from any deviations that may lead them towards sinful behavior or disobedience to God's commandments. This includes protecting them from engaging in actions that could potentially lead them to the fires of Hell.

This is indicated by the words of God Almighty,

يَا أَيُّهَا الَّذِينَ آمَنُوا قُوا أَنفُسَكُمْ وَأَهْلِيكُمْ نَارًا وَقُودُهَا النَّاسُ وَالْحِجَارَةُ عَلَيْهَا
مَلَائِكَةٌ غِلَاظٌ شِدَادٌ لَّا يَعْصُونَ اللَّهَ مَا أَمَرَهُمْ وَيَفْعَلُونَ مَا يُؤْمَرُونَ

O you who have faith! Save yourselves and your families from a Fire whose fuel will be people and stones, over which are [assigned] severe and mighty angels, who do not disobey whatever God commands them and carry out what they are commanded.[236]

In essence, the head of the household assumes a multifaceted role as both a provider of physical necessities and a guardian of spiritual well-being. They must create an environment where faith, righteousness, and moral values thrive, instilling these virtues within their family members. By doing so, they not only fulfill their obligations as head of the household but also contribute significantly to the spiritual growth and moral development of their family and, by extension, the broader

---

[236] The Noble Quran, 66:6.

Muslim community.

Consider the following verse. God says,

يا أَيُّهَا الَّذِينَ آمَنُوا لِيَسْتَأْذِنْكُمُ الَّذِينَ مَلَكَتْ أَيْمانُكُمْ وَ الَّذِينَ لَمْ يَبْلُغُوا الْحُلُمَ
مِنْكُمْ ثَلاثَ مَرَّاتٍ مِنْ قَبْلِ صَلاةِ الْفَجْرِ وَ حِينَ تَضَعُونَ ثِيابَكُمْ مِنَ الظَّهِيرَةِ
وَمِنْ بَعْدِ صَلاةِ الْعِشاءِ ثَلاثُ عَوْراتٍ لَكُمْ لَيْسَ عَلَيْكُمْ وَلا عَلَيْهِمْ جُناحٌ
بَعْدَهُنَّ طَوَّافُونَ عَلَيْكُمْ بَعْضُكُمْ عَلى بَعْضٍ كَذلِكَ يُبَيِّنُ اللَّهُ لَكُمُ الْآياتِ وَاللَّهُ
عَلِيمٌ حَكِيمٌ* وَإِذا بَلَغَ الْأَطْفالُ مِنْكُمُ الْحُلُمَ فَلْيَسْتَأْذِنُوا كَما اسْتَأْذَنَ الَّذِينَ مِنْ
قَبْلِهِمْ كَذلِكَ يُبَيِّنُ اللَّهُ لَكُمْ آياتِهِ وَاللَّهُ عَلِيمٌ حَكِيمٌ

O you who have faith!

Your slaves and any of you who have not yet reached puberty should seek your permission three times: before the dawn prayer, and when you put off your garments at noon, and after the night prayer.

These are three times of privacy for you. Apart from these, it is not sinful of you or them to frequent one another [freely]. Thus does God clarify the signs for you, and God is all-knowing, all-wise.

When your children reach puberty, let them always ask permission [] just as those [who grew up] before them asked permission. Thus does God clarify His signs for you, and God is all-knowing, all-wise.[237]

There are many examples of how the head of a family should set the example and lead the family on the path of guidance. For example, they should ensure that their family members are performing their obligatory prayers.

The verse above is referring to another example, which is that the head

---

[237] The Noble Quran, 24:59.

of the family must instruct his family members to seek permission and knock the door if they want to enter a private area at the times when he is usually alone with his wife. The noble verse specifies three times when this usually happens – early morning, midafternoon, and evening – but this should not be understood as an exclusive list. Rather, the command is to set a zone of privacy whenever the couple wishes to be intimate.

This generalization is understood from the verse itself. It says, "These are three times of privacy for you." If there are other times of privacy, then permission is required then as well.

It is worth pointing out that protecting one's family from deviation and the fire of hell can be achieved through multiple means. Guidance and verbal advice are one way of achieving this goal. Practically demonstrating and embodying righteousness is another. A father who controls his tongue, does not lie, does not backbite, and only speaks kind words will see that reflected in his family. A person who does the opposite will see it reflected in his family as well.

Hence, we can say that the sin committed by the head of the family is recorded against him twice; once because it is a sin, and another because it is setting the wrong example for his children. A father's sin is a failure to protect his family from the fire. This can be understood from God's words,

يَا نِسَاءَ النَّبِيِّ مَنْ يَأْتِ مِنْكُنَّ بِفَاحِشَةٍ مُبَيِّنَةٍ يُضَاعَفْ لَهَا الْعَذَابُ ضِعْفَيْنِ وَكَانَ ذَلِكَ عَلَى اللَّهِ يَسِيراً

O wives of the Prophet! Whoever of you commits a gross indecency, her punishment shall be doubled, and that is easy for God.

وَمَنْ يَقْنُتْ مِنْكُنَّ لِلَّهِ وَرَسُولِهِ وَتَعْمَلْ صَالِحاً نُؤْتِهَا أَجْرَهَا مَرَّتَيْنِ وَأَعْتَدْنَا لَهَا رِزْقاً كَرِيماً

But whoever of you is obedient to God and His

> ***Apostle and acts righteously, We shall give her a twofold reward, and We will have in store for her a noble provision.***[238]

A sin committed by one of the wives of the Prophet (sa) would have a disastrous effect on society. Thus, the reward for their good deeds is multiplied, and the punishment for any of their misdeeds is also multiplied. This is not simply because they are the wives of the Prophet (sa). Rather, it comes with every high rank and station that a person holds in society.

This is a profound lesson for everyone who has an elevated and respected position in their community. They are not like the rest of the people. A good deed from a person of high social status, be it a man or a woman, is doubled. A misdeed is also doubled.

Why is this the case? There could be several reasons.

It could be because the elevation of status requires that, so the increase in magnitude for good and bad deeds is the tax of the position itself.

It could be because the degree of knowledge among those with a high status is greater than that of others, and reward and punishment revolve around the degree of knowledge.

It could be because a good deed from people of high status encourages the rest of the community to do the same. It becomes an incentive for righteousness and a motivation towards it, which necessitates a compound reward. On the other hand, the misdeeds of a person of high status encourage the rest of the community to act in a similar way. It becomes an impetuous for further misdeeds, so its punishment is multiplied.

It could be because a good deed strengthens the position and raises its status, while a misdeed undermines the position and lowers its status. This is because the individual holding this status and position has two

---

[238] The Noble Quran, 33:30-31.

dimensions: a personal dimension and a social dimension. Their actions reflect not only themselves, but also the position they represent. For example, the actions of a clergyman reflect not only on himself, but also on what his religious garb represents. Similarly, the actions of a judge reflect on the integrity and credibility of the judicial system.

It could be some combination of these things, not just one of them.

A Profound Lesson

The totality of the verses gives us profound lessons for men and women of high status. These verses emphasize the great rewards and consequences that accompany the actions of people in society.

A virtuous woman is covered by two laws:

وإنْ كُنْتُنَّ تُرِدْنَ اللهَ ورَسُولَهُ والدَّارَ الآخِرَةَ فَإنَّ اللهَ أعَدَّ لِلْمُحْسِناتِ مِنكُنَّ أجْراً عَظِيماً

But if you desire God and His Apostle and the abode of the Hereafter, then God has indeed prepared a great reward for the virtuous among you.[239]

ومَنْ يَقْنُتْ مِنكُنَّ لِلَّهِ ورَسُولِهِ وتَعْمَلْ صالِحاً نُؤْتِها أجْرَها مَرَّتَيْنِ وَأعْتَدْنا لَها رِزْقاً كَرِيماً

But whoever of you is obedient to God and His Apostle and acts righteously, We shall give her a twofold reward, and We will have in store for her a noble provision.[240]

On the contrary, a wicked woman is covered by two other laws:

---

[239] The Noble Quran, 33:29.

[240] The Noble Quran, 33:31.

> يَا أَيُّهَا النَّبِيُّ قُل لِّأَزْوَاجِكَ إِن كُنتُنَّ تُرِدْنَ الْحَيَاةَ الدُّنْيَا وَزِينَتَهَا فَتَعَالَيْنَ أُمَتِّعْكُنَّ وَأُسَرِّحْكُنَّ سَرَاحاً جَمِيلًا
>
> *O' Prophet! Say to your wives, 'If you desire the life of the world and its glitter, come, I will provide for you and release you in a graceful manner.*[241]

> يَا نِسَاءَ النَّبِيِّ مَن يَأْتِ مِنكُنَّ بِفَاحِشَةٍ مُبَيِّنَةٍ يُضَاعَفْ لَهَا الْعَذَابُ ضِعْفَيْنِ وَكَانَ ذَلِكَ عَلَى اللَّهِ يَسِيراً
>
> *O' wives of the Prophet! Whoever of you commits a gross indecency, her punishment shall be doubled, and that is easy for God.*[242]

While these verses specifically mention women, it is essential to understand that they convey universal principles applicable to all members of humankind, irrespective of gender. The Quranic laws and principles emphasize that righteousness, virtue, and obedience to God's guidance are commendable traits for individuals, regardless of their societal standing. Conversely, indulging in worldly desires and moral transgressions carries consequences, emphasizing the universality of moral responsibility.

In essence, these Quranic laws and teachings serve as a reminder that virtue, righteousness, and moral conduct should be pursued and celebrated by all individuals, regardless of their social status or gender. Ultimately, it is the alignment with God's guidance and the commitment to good deeds that bring forth rewards and blessings, while deviations from this path bear consequences. These principles underscore the universality and timeless relevance of moral accountability and spiritual growth for all of humanity.

---

[241] The Noble Quran, 33:28.

[242] The Noble Quran, 33:30.

Spiritual Growth

I would like to express my gratitude once more for your time and insightful responses. Your contributions are highly valued, as they serve to further elucidate the principles of the Shia Muslim faith, offering invaluable clarity on essential aspects.

May I humbly seek your counsel on the path to spiritual guidance? How can one establish a deeper connection with the Divine? Where would you suggest one commence this sacred journey?

I begin with introspection and remind myself before extending guidance to others. Each one of us must center their attention on the soul, an entity that God Almighty reverently acknowledges in His Noble Book. This soul is of such paramount importance that God Himself swears by its creation, as stated in the following verses:

بِسْمِ اللَّهِ الرَّحْمَٰنِ الرَّحِيمِ

وَالشَّمْسِ وَضُحَاهَا ﴿١﴾ وَالْقَمَرِ إِذَا تَلَاهَا ﴿٢﴾ وَالنَّهَارِ إِذَا جَلَّاهَا ﴿٣﴾
وَاللَّيْلِ إِذَا يَغْشَاهَا ﴿٤﴾ وَالسَّمَاءِ وَمَا بَنَاهَا ﴿٥﴾ وَالْأَرْضِ وَمَا طَحَاهَا
﴿٦﴾ وَنَفْسٍ وَمَا سَوَّاهَا ﴿٧﴾ فَأَلْهَمَهَا فُجُورَهَا وَتَقْوَاهَا ﴿٨﴾ قد أَفْلَحَ
مَن زَكَّاهَا ﴿٩﴾ وَقَدْ خَابَ مَن دَسَّاهَا

In the Name of God, the All-beneficent, the All-merciful.

By the sun and her forenoon splendor, by the moon when he follows her, by the day when it reveals her, by the night when it covers her, by the sky and Him who built it, by the earth and Him who spread it, by the soul and Him who fashioned it, and inspired it with [discernment between] its virtues and vices: one who purifies it is felicitous, and one who betrays it fails.[243]

Yes, indeed, God swears by the celestial bodies, the passage of time, the vastness of the heavens and the earth, and then He solemnly swears by the human soul. He underscores how He guides and inspires this soul towards piety or impiousness.

Subsequently, God then shows us the important result. He says,

One who purifies it is felicitous, and one who betrays it fails. Felicity and ultimate success lies in purifying one's soul!

The key to ultimate success and true felicity lies in the purification of one's own soul! Upon delving further into the Quran's verses, we discover a more detailed guideline in Surat al-Mu'minun. Here, God elucidates the means by which an individual can achieve this felicity and

---

[243] The Noble Quran, 91:1-10.

success. He emphasizes,

قَدْ أَفْلَحَ الْمُؤْمِنُونَ

Certainly, the faithful have attained felicity

الَّذِينَ هُمْ فِي صَلاتِهِمْ خاشِعُونَ

—those who are humble in their prayers.[244]

Hence, the initial step on the path to success for a believer is to approach God with humility and devotion in prayer.

Begin at the Foundation

Embarking on a solid foundation of faith and practice, Imam al-Ṣādiq (a) imparted invaluable guidance regarding the essence of prayer. He emphasized the importance of not only fulfilling the obligation of prayer but ensuring its acceptance by God Almighty. His teachings can profoundly impact our approach to worship. In this regard, Imam al-Ṣādiq (a) said,

إِذَا صَلَّيْتَ صَلَاةً فَرِيضَةً فَصَلِّهَا لِوَقْتِهَا، صَلَاةَ مُوَدِّعٍ يَخَافُ أَنْ لَا يَعُودَ إِلَيْهَا أَبَداً، ثُمَّ اصْرِفْ بَصَرَكَ إِلَى مَوْضِعِ سُجُودِكَ، فَلَوْ تَعْلَمُ مَنْ عَنْ يَمِينِكَ وشِمَالِكَ لَأَحْسَنْتَ صَلَاتَكَ، وَاعْلَمْ أَنَّكَ بَيْنَ يَدَيْ مَنْ يَرَاكَ وَلَا تَرَاهُ.

When you pray an obligatory prayer, pray it as if it were your farewell and that you will never be able to perform it ever again. Then turn your eyes to the place of your prostration. If you knew who stood to your right and left, you would have surely perfected your prayer. Know that you stand before Him who sees you, while you

[244] The Noble Quran, 23:1-2.

cannot see Him.[245]

When performing an obligatory prayer, Imam al-Ṣādiq (a) encourages us to invest ourselves in it as if it were our final act of devotion, a prayer of farewell, and we would never have the opportunity to perform it again. This perspective invokes a heightened sense of sincerity and devotion in our prayers. Additionally, he advises us to focus our attention on the place of prostration, for within this realm of humbling ourselves before God, our devotion can flourish.

It is essential to clarify that the concept of acceptance by God is distinct from the mere validity of prayer. Validity ensures that the obligation is fulfilled, requiring no repetition or makeup. Acceptance, however, signifies a higher state achievable only by the God-fearing. As affirmed in the Quran,

إِنَّمَا يَتَقَبَّلُ اللَّهُ مِنَ الْمُتَّقِينَ

God accepts only from the Godwary.[246]

Those who attain this elevated status discover that not only their prayers but also their other deeds find acceptance.

Conversely, a rejected prayer may lead to the rejection of one's other deeds. Hence, it becomes crucial for the believer to recognize that their spiritual journey begins with the prayer. A tradition states:

أَوَّلُ مَا يُحَاسَبُ بِهِ الْعَبْدُ الصَّلَاةُ، فَإِنْ قُبِلَتْ قُبِلَ سَائِرُ عَمَلِهِ، وإذَا رُدَّتْ رُدَّ عَلَيْهِ سَائِرُ عَمَلِهِ.

The first thing for which a servant [of God] is held accountable is prayer. If it is accepted, all of his other deeds are accepted. If it is rejected, all of his other deeds are rejected.[247]

Moreover, the acceptance of a single prayer can shield an individual

---

[245] Al-ʿĀmilī, *Wasāʾil al-Shīʿah*, 3:22.

[246] The Noble Quran, 5:27.

[247] Al-ʿĀmilī, *Wasāʾil al-Shīʿah*, 3:22.

from divine punishment. Another tradition states:

مَنْ قَبِلَ اللهُ مِنْهُ صَلَاةً وَاحِدَةً لَمْ يُعَذِّبْهُ، وَمَنْ قَبِلَ مِنْهُ حَسَنَةً لَمْ يُعَذِّبْهُ.

Whomsoever God accepts one prayer from shall not be punished by Him. Whomsoever God accepts a single good deed from shall not be punished by Him.[248]

Even if a single prayer was accepted, the individual will not be punished! However, it is imperative to underscore that not every prayer is accepted. The condition for acceptance is profound sincerity and wholehearted devotion. A tradition underscores this, stating that God may raise half, a third, a fourth, or a fifth of a person's prayer. What ascends to God is what was approached with a pure heart. Thus, recommended prayers (nāfilah) were ordained to supplement any deficiencies found in obligatory prayers. One tradition says:

إِنَّ الْعَبْدَ لَيُرْفَعُ لَهُ مِنْ صَلَاتِهِ نِصْفُهَا، أَوْ ثُلُثُهَا أَوْ رُبُعُهَا أَوْ خُمُسُهَا، فَمَا يُرْفَعُ لَهُ إِلَّا مَا أَقْبَلَ عَلَيْهِ مِنْهَا بِقَلْبِهِ، وَإِنَّمَا أَمَرْنَا بِالنَّافِلَةِ لِيَتِمَّ لَهُمْ بِهَا مَا نَقَصُوا مِنَ الْفَرِيضَةِ.

A servant may have only half, a third, a fourth, or a fifth of his prayer raised [to the heavens and be accepted]. What is raised is only that which was approached wholeheartedly. Indeed, God commanded us to perform nāfilah (recommended prayers) so that He may use it to supplement what they miss in the obligatory prayers.[249]

To maintain this connection with God, it is incumbent upon believers to perform their prayers at their prescribed times without neglect. Neglecting the five daily prayers can embolden Satan, leading to involvement in grave sins. Therefore, safeguarding these prayers serves as a barrier against spiritual deviation. As the tradition says:

لَا يَزَالُ الشَّيْطَانُ ذَعِراً مِنَ الْمُؤْمِنِ، مَا حَافَظَ عَلَى الصَّلَوَاتِ الْخَمْسِ لِوَقْتِهِنَّ، فَإِذَا ضَيَّعَهُنَّ

---

248 Al-ʿĀmilī, *Wasāʾil al-Shīʿah*, 3:22.

249 Al-ʿĀmilī, *Wasāʾil al-Shīʿah*, 3:52.

تَجَرَّأَ عَلَيْهِ فَأَدْخَلَهُ فِي الْعَظَائِمِ.

Satan remains afraid of a believer so long as the believer maintains the five prayers in their [proper] times. If the believer squanders them [the prayers], Satan will grow bold and draw him into the Great Sins.[250]

Imam al-Ṣādiq (a) imparts profound wisdom regarding prayer, urging us to approach it with utmost sincerity and devotion, as our connection with God begins here. The notion of acceptance by God transcends mere validity and leads to the acceptance of all our deeds, underscoring the significance of nurturing our spiritual connection through prayer and safeguarding it from neglect.

Maintaining Prayer

The concept of maintaining prayer encompasses multiple dimensions, each carrying its own significance, some being obligatory, while others are highly recommended but not obligatory.

Firstly, maintaining prayer implies not deliberately failing to perform the obligatory prayers. In this sense, it is a binding duty for every believer to ensure that they do not neglect their prescribed prayers. This fundamental aspect of maintaining prayer constitutes an obligation upon every individual.

Secondly, it signifies not delaying the prayer beyond the commencement of its prescribed time - what is commonly known as waqt al-faḍīlah. Although this aspect is highly recommended and not obligatory, its importance should not be underestimated. Delaying the prayer beyond beginning of its appointed time can be perceived as taking the obligation of prayer lightly, which is a grave offense in the eyes of God.

---

[250] Al-ʿĀmilī, *Wasāʾil al-Shīʿah*, 3:18.

The Prophet Muhammad (sa) emphasized the seriousness of taking one's prayers lightly by stating that those who do so will not receive his intercession and will not have the privilege of communing at the Pool of Paradise with him. The tradition states:

لَا يَنَالُ شَفَاعَتِي مَنِ اسْتَخَفَّ بِصَلَاتِهِ، لَا يَرِدُ عَلَيَّ الْحَوْضَ لَا واللهِ.

One who takes his prayers lightly will not have my intercession. Nay! By God! He will not commune at the Pool [of Paradise] with me![251]

This stern warning underscores the significance of approaching prayer with utmost devotion and sincerity.

Believers are admonished to perform their prayers with energy and enthusiasm, distinguishing themselves from hypocrites who may not neglect prayer outright but perform it with laziness and indifference. God Almighty cautions against approaching prayer while intoxicated, not just in the literal sense of substance abuse but also in terms of spiritual alertness. Laziness, sleepiness, or any factor that weakens one's engagement in prayer is considered a form of intoxication of the soul, undermining the essence of prayer. God Almighty says:

يا أَيُّهَا الَّذِينَ آمَنُوا لا تَقْرَبُوا الصَّلاةَ وأَنْتُمْ سُكارى

O' you who have faith! Do not approach prayer when you are intoxicated.[252]

This is further elucidated in a narration by Zurārah, attributed to Imam al-Bāqir (a). He said,

لا تَقُم إِلى الصَّلاةِ مُتَكَاسِلاً وَلا مُتَنَاعِساً وَلا مُتَثَاقِلاً فِإنَّها مِن خلَلِ النِّفَاق فانَّ اللهَ نَهى المؤمنين اَنْ يَقُومُوا إِلَى الصَّلَاةِ وَهُمْ سُكَارَى، يَعْنِي مِنَ النَّوم.

Do not stand up for prayer lazily, sleepily, or sluggishly. Indeed, these

---

[251] Al-ʿĀmilī, *Wasāʾil al-Shīʿah*, 3:17.

[252] The Noble Quran, 4:43.

are the trappings of hypocrisy. God forbade the believers to stand up for prayer while intoxicated, meaning while [intoxicated by] sleep.[253]

Maintaining prayer is a multifaceted commitment that encompasses both the fulfillment of obligatory prayers and the enthusiastic performance of prayers within their prescribed times. Neglecting this duty or approaching prayer with indifference undermines the sincerity and devotion required for a believer's spiritual journey. Therefore, believers are encouraged to approach their prayers with vigor, ensuring they are not counted among those who take this sacred act lightly.

Supplication

We know that many of the teachings that help us to draw closer to God Almighty are found in the supplications that the Ahl al-Bayt taught us.

What supplications do you advise us to read, so that we can build and nurture our character?

Supplications hold a special place in our tradition, encompassing a wide range of prayers and visitations. Interestingly, these supplications can have different impacts on readers, shaped by their personal circumstances and preferences.

Take, for instance, someone who delves into the depths of *al-Ziyārah al-Jāmiʿah*[254]. This profound supplication unveils the elevated status of the

---

[253] Al-ʿAyyāshī, *Tafsīr al-ʿAyyāshī*, 1:268.

[254] Al-Ziyārah al-Jāmiʿah is a comprehensive Ziyarah, or prayer of visitation, of the Imams of Ahl al-Bayt. These visitations are highly important in Shia piety as they teach adherents of the faith on how to communicate with and through the Imams. Allama al-Majlisi (1627 – 1699 CE) regards this particular form of Ziyarah as the most sublime and comprehensive in terms of its textual substance, chain of authority, eloquence, and clarity. In his commentary on *Men-la-Yahduruhul-Faqih* (10th century seminal work of Shaykh al-Saduq, and one of the Four Books of Twelver Shia Islam) Allama al-Majlisi's father, the First Majlisi, also affirmed that this Ziyarah is the most excellent and perfect form, noting that when he visited the shrines of the Holy Imams (a), he would exclusively recite this particular Ziyarah.

Imams, offering a profound opportunity for character development and spiritual growth. For those who resonate with it, it becomes an excellent means of connecting with their faith.

On the other hand, some individuals have a deep affinity for *Duʿāʾ Kumayl*[255] a supplication often recited on Friday eves (Thursday nights). Its beautifully crafted words and profound meanings resonate deeply with them, providing a unique spiritual experience. Shia across the world recite this particular supplication and it is often a vehicle of communal spirituality.

There are also those who find solace in other supplications and visitations. *Ziyārat al-Nāḥiyah* [256] , for example, holds immense significance and importance for many. Others are captivated by the supplications found in *al-Ṣaḥīfah al-Sajjādiyyah*[257] which are equally enriching and spiritually uplifting.

In essence, the journey of seeking a connection with God Almighty is highly personal. Each individual may find their own path and resonance

---

[255] Du'a Kumayl is a profound supplication in Shia Islam attributed to Imam Ali (a) and named after his companion Kumayl ibn Ziyad. Imam Ali (a) taught him Du'a Kumayl, a prayer that seeks God's forgiveness, guidance, and mercy. It emphasizes repentance, humility, and acknowledgment of one's sins. Du'a Kumayl is recited by Shia Muslims, especially on Thursday nights, to draw closer to God and attain spiritual purification.

[256] Ziyārat al-Nāḥiyah is a significant Ziyārat for Imam al-Husayn (a), shared from the lens of Imam al-Mahdi (a) and transmitted through one of his deputies. This Ziyārat vividly describes the events of Ashura and the suffering of Imam al-Husayn (a). The text of Ziyārat al-Nahiya can be found in early collections such as *al-Mazar al-Kabir* by Muhammad Ibn Ja'far al-Mash'hadi and *al-Mazar* by Shaykh al-Mufid, mentioned in Bihar al-Anwar, Volume 98. Ziyārat al- Nāḥiyah is spiritually rich and carries divine recognition, religious knowledge, and historical truths tracing its origins from the Ahl al-Bayt.

[257] The title al-Ṣaḥīfah al-Sajjādiyyah translates simply to "The Book of al-Sajjad," – attributed to the fourth Imam of the Shia, Imam Ali ibn Husayn al-Sajjad (659 – 713 CE). This book has been referred to by various honorary titles, including "Sister of the Qur'an," "Gospel of Ahl al-Bayt," and "Psalms of the House of Muhammad." Imam al-Sajjad (a) compiled his supplications and imparted them to his children, particularly Imam al-Baqir (a). Over time, the text became widely known among Shia communities. Hadith scholars affirm the text's *mutawatir* (successive) status, signifying that it has been widely recognized and transmitted through numerous reliable chains of narration.

with a particular supplication. The key is to hold fast to what draws them closer to the Divine, for in the realm of spirituality, there are multiple avenues to deepen one's faith and understanding.

Supplication and Self-Purification

How can we benefit from supplication in nurturing and purifying the soul?

God Almighty says,

وَقَالَ رَبُّكُمُ ادْعُونِي أَسْتَجِبْ لَكُمْ إِنَّ الَّذِينَ يَسْتَكْبِرُونَ عَنْ عِبَادَتِي سَيَدْخُلُونَ جَهَنَّمَ دَاخِرِينَ

> *Your Lord has said, 'Call Me, and I will hear you!' Indeed those who are disdainful of My worship will enter hell in utter humiliation.*[258]

وَإِذَا سَأَلَكَ عِبَادِي عَنِّي فَإِنِّي قَرِيبٌ أُجِيبُ دَعْوَةَ الدَّاعِ إِذَا دَعَانِ فَلْيَسْتَجِيبُوا لِي وَلْيُؤْمِنُوا بِي لَعَلَّهُمْ يَرْشُدُونَ

> *When My servants ask you about Me, [tell them that] I am indeed nearmost. I answer the supplicant's call when he calls Me. So let them respond to Me, and let them have faith in Me, so that they may fare rightly.*[259]

إِنَّهُمْ كَانُوا يُسَارِعُونَ فِي الْخَيْرَاتِ وَيَدْعُونَنَا رَغَبًا وَرَهَبًا وَكَانُوا لَنَا خَاشِعِينَ

> *Indeed, they were active in [performing] good works, and they would supplicate Us with eagerness and awe*

---

[258] The Noble Quran, 40:60.
[259] The Noble Quran, 2:186.

*and were humble before Us.*²⁶⁰

قُلْ مَنْ يُنَجِّيكُمْ مِنْ ظُلُمَاتِ الْبَرِّ وَالْبَحْرِ تَدْعُونَهُ تَضَرُّعاً وَخُفْيَةً لَئِنْ أَنْجَانَا مِنْ هَذِهِ لَنَكُونَنَّ مِنَ الشَّاكِرِينَ

*Say, 'Who delivers you from the darkness of land and sea, [when] You invoke Him suppliantly and secretly: "If He delivers us from this, we will surely be among the grateful"?'*²⁶¹

ادْعُوا رَبَّكُمْ تَضَرُّعاً وَخُفْيَةً إِنَّهُ لَا يُحِبُّ الْمُعْتَدِينَ

Supplicate your Lord, beseechingly and secretly. Indeed, He does not like the transgressors.

وَلَا تُفْسِدُوا فِي الْأَرْضِ بَعْدَ إِصْلَاحِهَا وَادْعُوهُ خَوْفاً وَطَمَعاً إِنَّ رَحْمَتَ اللَّهِ قَرِيبٌ مِنَ الْمُحْسِنِينَ

*And do not cause corruption on the earth after its restoration, and supplicate Him with fear and hope: indeed, God's mercy is close to the virtuous.*²⁶²

تَتَجَافَى جُنُوبُهُمْ عَنِ الْمَضَاجِعِ يَدْعُونَ رَبَّهُمْ خَوْفاً وَطَمَعاً وَمِمَّا رَزَقْنَاهُمْ يُنْفِقُونَ

*Their sides vacate their beds to supplicate their Lord in fear and hope, and they spend out of what We have provided them.*²⁶³

The verses encouraging supplication in the Quran are certainly not limited to the ones mentioned earlier, but these can be considered

---

[260] The Noble Quran, 21:90.

[261] The Noble Quran, 6:63.

[262] The Noble Quran, 7:55-56.

[263] The Noble Quran, 32:16.

among the most significant. From these verses, we can draw several important lessons and insights:

One, supplication is an act of worship and a means of closeness to the Almighty. First and foremost, these verses emphasize that supplication is an act of worship similar to other acts of devotion such as prayer, fasting, and almsgiving. Just as we are obliged to engage in these forms of worship, we are also urged to supplicate to God. To arrogantly refuse or neglect supplication is considered a grave omission, and it is a path to humiliation in the hereafter.

Two, supplication must be completed with humility and reverence. The manner in which we engage in supplication is crucial. It should be done with a profound sense of humility and complete reverence toward God. Recognizing His greatness and our own insignificance, we approach Him with utmost humility in our hearts and words.

Three, privacy and closeness with God is essential. Unlike public proclamations or loud declarations, supplication is a private and intimate conversation between the supplicant and their Creator. There is no need for loudness, as God is closer to us than our own jugular vein. Thus, supplication can be a quiet, heartfelt dialogue with the Divine.

Four, there should be a balance between hope and fear. In our supplication, it is essential to maintain a delicate balance between hope and fear. A believer hopes and trusts that their petitions will be answered by the Most Merciful, but they also maintain an element of fear, acknowledging their own shortcomings and the possibility that their requests may not be granted. This balance reflects a deep sense of trust in God's wisdom and divine plan.

Moreover, these Quranic verses highlight the significance of supplication as a fundamental aspect of worship. They underscore the need for humility, privacy, and the harmonious interplay between hope and fear in our supplications. Ultimately, the act of supplication is a means of drawing closer to God, seeking His guidance, and acknowledging our profound dependence on Him in our journey of faith.

Close to the Good Doers

God's mercy is close to the doers of good. It is necessary to hope that every supplication is answered. However, the obstacles and unknown wisdom that necessitate not answering also affect the possibility of an answer. Thus, the believer must supplicate with fear and uncertainty of whether their prayers will be answered.

Just as the Noble Quran emphasized the issue of supplication, the Sunnah did not neglect it either. Muyassar ibn ʿAbdu'l-ʿAzīz[264] on the authority of Imam al-Ṣādiq (a) narrates that the Imam said,

يا ميسّر ادع ولا تقُل انَّ الأمْرَ قَدْ فُرِغَ مِنه انَّ عنْدَ الله عزَّ وَجَلّ مِنزِلَة لَا تُنَال إلّا بِمَسْألة. وَلَوْ انَّ عَبْداً سَدَّ فَاه وَلمْ يَسْأل لَم يُعْطَ شَيْئاً فَسَلْ تُعْطَ يَا ميسّر، انه لَيْسَ مِنْ بَابٍ يُقْرَعُ إلّا يُوشَكُ انْ يُفْتَح لِصَاحِبه.

Pray, O' Muyassar.

Do not say, 'The case is closed.' Indeed, there is a station with God that cannot be reached except through pleading [to Him].

If a servant were to shut his mouth and not ask, he would not be given. So, ask and you will be given, Muyassar!

Indeed, every door that's knocked will soon be opened.[265]

The blessings of God Almighty upon His servants are innumerable. Among them is the opening of the door of supplication and answering their prayers. This is a means through which the servant can achieve what he wants and desires without the need to knock on people's doors.

---

[264] Muyassir Ibn 'Abdul 'Aziz is renowned as one of the esteemed companions of Imam Muhammad al-Baqir (a) and Imam Ja'far al-Sadiq (a). His character and contributions have earned him high praise in the field of 'Ilmul Rijal (the science of narrators' biographies).

[265] Al-Kulaynī, *al-Kāfī*, 2:466.

As the Imam teaches us to say in the Supplication of Abū Ḥamzah,

وإنَّ الرّاحِلَ إلَيكَ قَريبُ المَسافَةِ وأنَّكَ لا تَحتَجِبُ عَن خَلقِكَ إلّا أن تَحجِبَهُمُ الأَعمالُ دونَكَ.

He who travels towards You will find the distance to be short. You do not conceal Yourself from Your creatures unless their misdeeds stand between them and You.

وَالْحَمْدُ للهِ الَّذي أُناديهِ كُلَّما شِئْتُ لِحاجَتي، وَأَخْلُو بِهِ حَيْثُ شِئْتُ، لِسِرّي بِغَيْرِ شَفيع فَيَقْضى لي حاجَتي.

All praise be to God, Whom I call whenever I need something and Whom I secretly converse with for my secret [needs] without need for an intercessor.

He thus grants my need.[266]

Supplication is the means that creates tranquility in the soul of the believer whenever something worries them. The believer finds by their side a reliable means to remove all ailments and hardships.

سيِّدِي عَبْدُكَ بِبابِكَ أَقامَتْهُ الخَصاصَةُ بَيْنَ يَدَيْكَ، يَقْرَعُ بابَ إِحْسانِكَ بِدُعائِهِ، فَلا تُعْرِضْ بِوَجْهِكَ الكَرِيمِ عَنّي.

O' my master, Your servant is driven to stand at your door due his neediness before You, and he knocks at the door of your favors with his supplications, so do not turn You generous face away from me.[267]

My God, I ask You, by the right of Muhammad (sa) and the family of Muhammad (a), my need. If You fulfill this need for me, whatever You withhold will not harm me. But if You withhold it, whatever You give me will not benefit me.

I ask you to free me from the shackles of hellfire!

---

[266] Imam al-Sajjād, Supplication of Abū Ḥamzah.

[267] Ibid.

Mourning Rituals

There are some who are critical of the rituals of mourning for Imam Ḥusayn (a). Others may attack these rituals unintentionally because of their lack of awareness.

What is your advice and opinion on this issue?

God Almighty says in His Noble Book,

وَمَنْ يُعَظِّمْ شَعائِرَ اللّٰهِ فَإِنَّهَا مِنْ تَقْوَى الْقُلُوبِ

And whoever venerates the sacraments of God—indeed that arises from the Godwariness of hearts. [268]

One of the greatest examples of this verse is the veneration and practice of the rituals of mourning for Imam Ḥusayn (a). A *sha'īrah* (sacrament) is any sign or practice that leads towards God Almighty and obedience to Him. Accordingly, the noble verse urges veneration and practice of everything that leads to God and necessitates drawing near to Him and obeying Him.

This principle is so obvious and necessary that no Muslim can question it. Can anyone question the importance of practices which connect

---

[268] The Noble Quran, 22:32.

human beings to God and guide them to Him?

Now, the question becomes:

- What happens when we doubt whether this principle applies to a specific practice?
- What if we doubt, for example, the desirability of visiting Imam al-Riḍā (a), walking on foot?
- What if we doubt the desirability of wearing black for Imam Ḥusayn (a)?
- All these are practices that venerate the Ahl al-Bayt. Do they still fall under the principle outlined by the verse?

To say that they fall under this principle, we must first prove that they are "sacraments of God" and rituals which connect us to our Creator. The verse itself does not prove that to us. Only if they are "sacraments", then they must be practiced.

This is like the command, "Help the poor." The command does not tell us who the poor person is, only to help them if that label applies to them.

Legislative Directives

The jurists say that the label of "sacraments" is *ʿunwān tawqīfī* – that it cannot be applied except through directives from the divine legislator. There must be some evidence taken from the Quran or the Sunnah to apply this label.

Of course, one should not doubt that any ritual which venerates the Ahl al-Bayt (a) is a divine sacrament and desirable action.

How?

God Almighty instructs us to respect and honor every believer, and this is expressly urged in the Noble Quran and the Sunnah. Respecting and honoring the Ahl al-Bayt (a) is the highest example of that, as they are the masters and the greatest of all believers.

Moreover, venerating the Ahl al-Bayt (a) is a clear example of showing affection to them, which is something we are commanded to do. God tells the Prophet (sa),

قُلْ لا أَسْئَلُكُمْ عَلَيْهِ أَجْراً إِلَّا الْمَوَدَّةَ فِي الْقُرْبى

Say, 'I do not ask you any reward for it except the love of [my] relatives.'[269]

These rituals are also a clear example of bringing life to their memory and cause. Imam al-Bāqir (a) said in an authentic narration,

رَحِمَ اللهُ مَنْ أَحيَى أَمْرَنَا.

May God have mercy on one who brings life to our remembrance. [270]

Wearing black

In essence, the act of wearing black attire and engaging in these rituals serves as a profound expression of our love and devotion to the family of the Prophet Muhammad (sa). These practices transcend mere traditions; they are a living embodiment of our commitment to preserving the memory and legacy of the Prophet's beloved kin. It is a testament to our unwavering loyalty to the principles laid out in the Shari'a, grounded in the sacred verses and traditions that guide us.

As we undertake these rituals, let us do so with a deep understanding of their significance and purpose. They are not empty gestures, but powerful means to rekindle the flame of love and reverence for Imam Husayn (a) and his noble companions. It is through these acts of remembrance that we seek to keep their noble cause alive in our hearts and minds.

---

[269] The Noble Quran, 42:23.

[270] Al-ʿĀmilī, *Wasāʾil al-Shīʿah*, 10:459.

May God shower His blessings upon every believer who wholeheartedly engages in these rituals, for their commitment to this sacred tradition is an act of devotion that resonates with the essence of Islam. May God, in His infinite mercy, grant us the honor of standing alongside Imam Husayn (a) on the Day of Judgment, as we bear witness to our unwavering love and allegiance to his cause.

It is indeed true that during the first ten days of the Month of Muharram, every believer, from the East to the West, feels a deep connection with Imam Husayn (a). However, the Imam (a) desires something more profound from us. He yearns for a lasting and unwavering connection that extends beyond the confines of these sacred days.

Imam Husayn (a) beckons us to forge a spiritual bond that transcends time and place—a connection that serves as a bridge between us and the Almighty. He desires us to remain tethered to our Creator throughout the year, drawing strength and guidance from the sacred teachings of the Ahl al-Bayt. This connection is not merely a fleeting sentiment but a lifelong commitment to upholding the values and principles exemplified by Imam Husayn (a) and, ultimately, to remain linked with the spiritual legacy of our beloved Twelfth Imam (a).

In nurturing this profound connection, we not only honor the sacrifice of Imam Husayn (a) but also fulfill his aspiration of guiding us towards a deeper relationship with God Almighty. It is a journey of the heart and soul, one that unites us with the luminous path illuminated by the Ahl al-Bayt, ensuring that their legacy continues to shine as a beacon of light in our lives.

Career Choices

In our contemporary society, characterized by its dynamism and inclusivity, individuals from diverse backgrounds and with varying beliefs have the opportunity to actively engage and collaborate in nation-building efforts. This holds true even in the face of differing ideologies, guiding principles, approaches, and legal frameworks.

For Twelver Shia Muslims, the question arises as to whether they can play a role in the governance structures of their respective countries. Is it permissible for them to assume government positions, and if so, what guidance can be offered to those considering such roles?

Over the course of history, Shia Muslims have endured numerous trials and tribulations, spanning from the era of the Commander of the Faithful, Imam Ali (a), to the present day. Throughout this journey, Shia communities have often faced isolation and discrimination solely due to their faith and unwavering love for the family of the Prophet Muhammad (sa).

In today's interconnected world, Shia Muslims find themselves in a unique position to actively participate in the nation-building process alongside the diverse segments of society. As Shia communities have become a global presence, their engagement in the wider society has become not only possible but also essential.

However, it is crucial to recognize that such participation comes with its own set of limits and controls, guided by both religious principles and civic responsibilities. These boundaries serve as a framework for Twelver Shia Muslims as they navigate their roles in government positions within their respective countries.

Here we delve into the principles and guidelines that Twelver Shia Muslims should consider when contemplating involvement in governmental roles and the responsibilities that come with it.

Intellectual, Ethical, and Philosophical Limits

Participation in one's society and government is a complex matter, and Shia individuals must navigate it with a keen awareness of intellectual, ethical, and philosophical boundaries. These boundaries are not only informed by religious principles but also by the broader principles of fiqh. However, it is essential to underscore that there is a paramount consideration that should guide our actions, not only in this context but in all aspects of life: the preservation of faith, religion, and the safeguarding of blood and honor.

Living in diverse societies, we often find ourselves coexisting with people who do not share our religious beliefs or moral values. In such an environment, the protection of our religious identity and doctrinal tenets is of utmost importance. We must ensure that our participation in any activity, especially in government roles, does not compromise our intellectual integrity or threaten our core beliefs.

If engaging in a particular activity, including government positions, poses a genuine risk of undermining our faith or leading us astray from our doctrinal foundations, then it is imperative for us to exercise caution and refrain from such involvement. In these situations, the preservation of one's religious identity and moral principles should take precedence.

The guiding principle here is clear: our faith and adherence to our religious tenets must remain steadfast, and we should not allow our participation in any sphere, be it political or otherwise, to jeopardize the integrity of our beliefs. By upholding this fundamental principle, Shia individuals can engage in their respective societies while remaining true to their faith and values.

What if there is a necessity?

Indeed, circumstances may arise where a genuine necessity compels an individual to engage in activities that they would typically avoid. However, the determination of such necessity lies with the individual, as they are in the best position to assess their unique situation. This evaluation should be undertaken conscientiously, guided by the principles (*al-qawāʿid*) of fiqh and a deep understanding of one's faith.

Recognizing and justifying the presence of necessity or the absence of undue burden is a responsibility that falls squarely on the individual's shoulders. It demands careful consideration of the potential harm or adverse consequences that may result from abstaining versus participating in a particular activity. This evaluation should be conducted in a manner that aligns with the ethical and moral compass of Shia Islam.

The individual's assessment of necessity should be grounded in a profound understanding of their faith's principles and teachings. It is not a decision to be taken lightly, and individuals should seek guidance from qualified religious scholars or authorities when faced with such complex choices. By adhering to the principles of fiqh and seeking appropriate counsel, Shia Muslims can navigate situations of necessity while upholding the integrity of their religious convictions.

Principles (*al-Qawāʿid*) of Fiqh

You mentioned the term 'principles (*al-qawāʿid*) of fiqh.' This may derail us shortly from the current topic, but is it possible to shed some light on this term?

In the process of deduction of jurisprudential rulings, jurists try to encapsulate the rules that they come upon into principles.

What is a principle *(al-qaʿida)*?

It is a foundational proposition that can be built upon, like the foundation of a house.

In every science and discipline, there is a set of principles that help the specialist to reach the desired result. They help them in the process of taking what they know to identify, diagnose, and make judgements about something that is unknown. In that sense, these principles act like a middle term in the process of deduction (to borrow some terminology from the study of logic).

We have many principles in the discipline of *uṣūl al-fiqh*[271] that have been revised and refined. I am not exaggerating when I say that studying the principles of fiqh are no less important than studying the principles of uṣūl. Take the following set of questions:

- What happens if an individual forgets to recite Surat al-Fātiḥah in their prayer? What if they forget to recite the second surah?
- What if they pray without wuḍūʾ?
- What if they follow an imam in congregational prayers who does not meet the requisite preconditions?

In answering all these questions, one can turn to the principle of fiqh

[271] The principles of fiqh are an important part of the discipline of fiqh studied in the Islamic seminaries. These principles are studied and applied by scholars, and many of them are not meant to be applied outside the scope of scholarly application of the disciplines of fiqh and uṣūl. The discussion here is meant to give the reader a glimpse of the inner workings and complexity of the process of juristic deduction.

which states:

A prayer is not to be repeated except for defect[272] *in purity, time, direction, rukū ʿ, or sujūd.*

Whenever there is a defect in one of these five things, the prayer must be repeated. If an error falls outside these five categories, it may be excused.

So, what if the person forgets to recite Surat al-Fātiḥah?

They do not need to repeat their prayer, as recitation is not one of the five categories listed in the principle. What if they pray behind an imam who does not meet the conditions? Again, there is no need to repeat because that is not one of the five categories.

What if they unintentionally pray without wuḍūʾ?

Then their prayer is invalid since purity is listed as one of the above categories and must be repeated.

This is one example of a principle of fiqh. There are many other principles that are no less important.

Are these rules generally researched by scholars? Are there books authored on this subject?

Jurists did not pay as much attention to the principles of fiqh as they gave the principles of uṣūl. They dedicated a special course of study for the principle of uṣūl, and they authored books on this subject. The discipline of uṣūl developed gradually and with the passage of time, until it reached its apex in our present time. On the other hand, principles of fiqh did not receive the same treatment. It is not singled out in research as an independent discipline. Instead, it is discussed discursively in the study of uṣūl, in fiqh, or on some special occasion.

For example, the principle of 'no-harm' was discussed by Shaykh al-

---

[272] The principle is addressing unintentional defects. If there is an intentional mistake made in prayer, then it must be repeated, regardless of whether it falls within these five categories or not.

Anṣārī his book on uṣūl titled *al-Rasāʾil.* As a book of uṣūl, it had a dedicated chapter on the principle of *barāʾah* – a principle of uṣūl that basically states all actions are permissible unless there is evidence to the contrary. At the end of that discussion, he concluded that the principle of barāʾah only applies when the jurist expends his efforts in researching the relevant evidence, and not finding any evidence that would lead to a contrary conclusion. Otherwise, before a thorough examination of the evidence, the principle cannot be applied. There, he addressed the opinion of al-Fāḍil al-Tūnī, who said that one of the conditions for applying the principle of barāʾah is that it does not contradict the principle of no-harm. Shaykh al-Anṣārī then proceeded to discuss the principle of no-harm and its application in that scenario. After completing that discussion, he found it appropriate to discuss the principle of no-harm more broadly and independently.

Following that, scholars continued to discuss the principle of no-harm in the same way.

Thus, the principle of no-harm – which is a principle of fiqh – was studied in the discipline of uṣūl. It was not studied as part of fiqh, nor was it studied independently or in a specific course of study set for similar principles.

The same is true of some other principles of fiqh. Others still are studied discursively in the discipline of fiqh.

Perhaps the first scholar to dedicate a book to think about the principles of fiqh independently was al-Shahīd al-Awwal, Muhammad ibn Jamāl al-Dīn Makkī al-ʿĀmilī, in his book *al-Qawāʿid wa'l-Fawāʾid.* However, the book was not dedicated to the principles of fiqh alone. It discussed many other principles, including those of linguistics, literature, theology, and uṣūl.

In any case, the book studied principles of fiqh only rarely. When it did, its discussions were in the mode of the current period. It did not discuss the evidence for the principle, nor its different discussions or uses.

Is this true even in contemporary times?

Recently there have been some good attempts in this field. Among them, I want to especially mention the following books: *al-Qawāʿid al-Fiqhiyyah* by Sayyid al-Bujnurdī, *al-Qawāʿid al-Fiqhiyyah* by Shaykh al-Shīrāzī, and *Miʾat Qāʿidah* by Sayyid al-Muṣṭafawī.

Of course, the middle period between the era of al-Shahīd al-Awwal and recent times included some other written and printed works.

They include:

- ʿAwāʾid al-Ayyām fī Bayān Qawāʿid al-Aḥkām, by Mawlā Aḥmad al-Narāqī.
- Muhimmāt Masāʾil al-Ḥalāl wa'l-Ḥarām by Shaykh al-Narāqī. This book is not comprehensive, as it studies about ten principles while discussing other issues as well.
- Some manuscripts include those mentioned by Shaykh Āgā Buzurk referred to in al-Dharīʿah. These include the treatise of Sayyid Muhammad Mahdī al-Qazwīnī, the treatise of Mawlā Muhammad Jaʿfar al-Astrābādī, and others.

Is it possible to point out, even briefly, the difference between the principles *al-qawāʿid* of fiqh and the principles *al-qawāʿid* of uṣūl?

We mentioned this in some of our textbooks. In short, several differences may be presented, some of which may be subject to discussion. We leave those discussions to specialized research, so we will not prolong the discussion here. In any case, below are some of the differences in this regard.

Firstly, a principle of fiqh is a rule that includes a general legal rule through which one may obtain specific legal rulings that are examples of the general rule. On the other hand, a principle of uṣūl is a rule that implies a general rule about deriving comprehensive legal rulings distinct from that general rule.

For example, the principle of purity, which is a principle of fiqh, states that everything that is suspected of being impure is judged to be pure, unless there is viable reason to believe otherwise.

This is a general legal rule. If we apply it, we will not get other rules that differ in their content. Rather, applying it results in judgements that are examples of the general rule, but are narrower. When we apply it on a piece of clothing which is suspected of impurity, we judge that the clothes should be considered pure. This is an application of the general rule, only to a narrower and more specific scope.

This contrasts with the principle of accepting singular traditions which are deemed trustworthy, which is a principle of uṣūl. Let us assume that there is a trustworthy tradition that states, 'If grape juice is boiled, it becomes ḥarām.' By applying the principle, we accept the tradition and rule that grape juice becomes ḥarām when boiled. The principle and the rule which was derived using it are very different in terms of content.

So, the principle of fiqh is a general legal ruling that can be applied to specific circumstances that are examples of that general rule. In contrast, the principle of uṣūl allows us to derive legal rulings that are distinct from that general rule.

In other words, a principle of fiqh is applied to specific examples in the real world, while a principle of uṣūl is used in the process of deducing religious rulings.

Secondly, a principle of fiqh offers us, through its application, specific rulings. In contrast, a principle of uṣūl allows us to derive a comprehensive ruling. By applying the principle of purity, we conclude that this water is pure or that food is pure. On the other hand, by applying the principle of authoritativeness of a singular tradition, we can conclude that grape juice is ḥarām if it is boiled; not that this juice or that juice is ḥarām, specifically.

The principle of fiqh is to be applied by any individual in their daily lives. The mujtahid presents his followers with the general rule, the principle of purity, for example. The layperson can use this principle to deem that this thing or that are pure in cases of doubt. Thus, it is the role of the individual to apply this principle in their daily lives. There is no need to refer back to a jurist on every particular issue. Of course, it could be objected that some principles of fiqh cannot be readily applied by the layperson.

As for a principle of uṣūl, its application is the role and duty of the specialized jurist in the process of deriving religious rules. When it comes to the principle of authoritativeness of a singular tradition, it is the role of the mujtahid to investigate the corpus of ḥadīth and make judgements about what is trustworthy and what is not.

What is the difference between a principle of fiqh and a fiqh ruling?

The difference is that the subject of the latter is specific, unlike the subject of the former which is general.

For example, our saying "prayer is obligatory" and "drinking alcohol is forbidden" is a jurisprudential issue. The first is specific to the subject of prayer, and the second is specific to the subject of drinking alcohol.

This is in contrast to saying, "everything for you is pure until you know that it is impure." This is a principle of fiqh, as its topic is general and comprehensive. It has no specific subject and can be applied to many areas.

To summarize, principles of fiqh are like principles of uṣūl in one way, and they are distinct in another way. The point of convergence is that both have a comprehensiveness that can be applied to more than one issue. The point of divergence is that a principle of uṣūl allows a jurist to derive legal rules that differ from it. On the other hand, a principle of fiqh is applied to make judgments that are not dissimilar from the general rule, only more specific. Is there a specific number of principles of fiqh?

That is a good summary, indeed. As we have discussed, the principle of fiqh is a general legal ruling which has a broad and comprehensive set of applications and examples. Such principles cannot be limited to a specific number. There are numerous principles that can be gleamed from the works of our scholars. Examples include the following precepts:

- The claimant has the burden of proof, and the denier has the burden of oath-making.
- Debts due to God are more deserving of being paid than debts due to people.
- Possession indicates a presumption of ownership.
- Every condition in a contract is enforceable, unless it contradicts the Book of God or the ends of the contract.
- There is no liability for the good-doer.

And there are many more. In general, the principles of fiqh can be divided into two parts: some are specific to a subject of fiqh, and some are general to more than one subject.

An example of the first is the principle that prayer should not be repeated except for one of five defects, as it is specific to the subject of prayer. The principle presuming purity is specific to the subject of purity. The principle of "what is guaranteed as valid is guaranteed as invalid, and vice versa," is specific to transactions.

An example of the second is the principle of no-harm and principle of no undue hardship. Such principles apply across different subject areas.

Permissibility of Political Engagement

Let us go back to the original conversation.

- Will an individual's participation in the political process lead them to committing a forbidden act?
- Or will their work lead to promoting things that are forbidden?
- Will it cause intentional harm?

These and other matters should be for the experts and community leaders to determine in detail. They can make the appropriate decision, which changes with the change of time and place.

But there is an important issue that we must address!

When an individual assumes a specific political or government position and mission, they have decided for themselves that they are qualified for it. If they believe in the religion of Islam and school of the Ahl al-Bayt (a), they must internalize their words and translate their teachings into action.

For example, the Commander of the Faithful, Ali ibn Abī Ṭālib (a), wrote to his son, Imam al-Ḥasan (a),

إِنَّمَا لَكَ مِنْ دُنْيَاكَ مَا أَصْلَحْتَ بِهِ مَثْوَاكَ، وإِنْ كُنْتَ جَازِعاً عَلَى مَا تَفَلَّتَ مِنْ يَدَيْكَ، فَاجْزَعْ عَلَى كُلِّ مَا لَمْ يَصِلْ إِلَيْكَ.

> *You should have from this world only that with which you can adorn your permanent abode.*
>
> *If you cry over what has gone out of your hands, then also cry for what has not at all come to you.*[273]

Keep this important piece of advice in mind. Remember that these are the words of the Commander of the Faithful (a) compiled by al-Sharīf Al-Raḍī[274] in the book *Nahj al-Balāghah*[275]. Every word in this book is a reminder, admonishment, and advice for us to think about and preach.

---

[273] Al-Raḍī, *Nahj al-Balāghah*, Letter 31.

[274] Sharīf Al-Raḍī (970 – 1015 CE) was a Twelver Shia scholar and hadith compiler. He is most notably known for his seminal work of Nahj al-Balāghah, a compilation of sermons, letters and sayings of Imam Ali (a). He was born and died in the city of Baghdad, Iraq under Abbasid dynasty rule.

[275] Nahj al-Balāghah, meaning "The Peak of Eloquence," is a renowned collection of the words of Imam Ali (a). It was compiled by the renowned 10th/11th century scholar Sharif al-Radi. The compilation is divided into three sections: sermons, letters, and short sayings. These texts are admired for their eloquence, wisdom, and moral guidance, covering various topics such as theology, governance, morality, and social justice. Nahj al-Balāghah has had a significant impact on Islamic literature, theology, ethics, and is revered for its timeless wisdom and guidance.

The purpose of these words is to remind us.

Some of us do not benefit from advice until we experience the negative repercussions of our actions. We get burned by the reality of life to see the truth and change.

That is why Imam Ali (a) said,

وَلَا تَكُونَنَّ مِمَّنْ لَا تَنْفَعُهُ الْعِظَةُ إِلَّا إِذَا بَالَغْتَ فِي إِيلَامِهِ، فَإِنَّ الْعَاقِلَ يَتَّعِظُ بِالْآدَابِ، وَالْبَهَائِمَ لَا تَتَّعِظُ إِلَّا بِالضَّرْبِ.

> *Do not be like those whom preaching does not benefit unless you inflict pain on them, because the wise take instruction from teaching while beasts learn only from beating.*[276]

Here, the Imam (a) is telling us that people are of two types:

- Some learn and take heed at the slightest warning. They pay attention to what is wrong and quickly seek change and reform.
- Others do not learn unless they see and experience the consequences of their actions. The Imam (a) advises us to learn from the advice and experiences of others. There is no need to wait until calamity strikes.

The Imam (a) said,

إِنَّمَا لَكَ مِنْ دُنْيَاكَ مَا أَصْلَحْتَ بِهِ مَثْوَاكَ...

> *You should have from this world only that with which you can adorn your permanent abode.*

A person may seek position, prestige, and power. They may try everything to reach those ranks. But for how long? To what end? Remember that each of us will end up in the same place.

What will we take from the material things of this world?

Nothing but the shroud we are buried in!

---

[276] Ibid, Letter 31.

Wealth, Children, and Deeds

A person must remember to hold steadfast to whatever will benefit them in their final resting place! Otherwise, this entire will is nothing but dust in the wind.

In a beautiful narration, the Commander of the Faithful (a), said,

إنَّ ابنَ آدَم إذا كانَ في آخر يومٍ مِنْ أيَامِ الدُّنْيَا وَأَول يَوْمٍ مِن أيَّامِ الآخِرة مثّل لَهُ مَاله وَوَلده وَعَمله، فيلتفتُ إلى مالِه فيقول: وَالله إنِّي كُنْتُ عَلَيْكَ حَرِيصاً شَحِيحاً فَمَالِي عِنْدَك؟

فيقول: خُذْ مِنّي كَفَنك،

When the son of Adam is in their last day in his world and their first day of the hereafter, his wealth, children, and deeds are embodied for him.

He will turn to his wealth and say,

'By God, I used to be protective of you and stingy. What do you owe me?'

It would reply,

'Take from me only your burial shroud.'

فيلتفت إلى وُلْدِه فيقُولُ: والله إنِّي كُنْتُ لَكُمْ مُحِبّاً وإنّي كُنْتُ عَلَيْكُم مُحامِياً فَمَاذا لي عِنْدَكُم؟

فيقولُون: نُؤَدِيكَ إلَى حُفْرَتِكَ نُوَارِيكَ فِيهَا،

He will then turn to his children and say,

'By God, I used to love you and I was your protector. What do you owe me?'

They would say,

'We will escort you to your hole and bury you in it.'

فيلتفتُ إلَى عَمَلِهِ فيقولُ: وَالله إنِّي كُنْتُ فِيكَ لَزَاهِدَا وَانْ كُنْتَ عَلَيّ لَثَقِيلا فَمَاذَا عِنْدِك؟

فيقولُ: أَنَا قَرِينُكَ في قَبرِكَ وَيَومَ نَشْرِكَ حَتّى أُعْرَض أَنَا وَأَنْتَ عَلى رَبّك،

He will turn to his deeds and say,

'By God, I used to pay little heed to you, and you seemed cumbersome to me. What do you have?'

It will say,

'I am your companion in your grave and on the day, you are resurrected until we are both presented to your Lord.'

فإِنْ كانَ لله وَليّا أَتَاه أَطْيَبُ النّاسِ رِيحاً وَأَحسَنهم مَنْظَراً وَأَحْسَنَهُم رِيَاشَاً

فقالَ: أَبْشِر بِرَوْح وَرَيْحَان وَجَنّةِ نَعِيم وَمَقْدَمُك خَيْرُ مَقْدِمٍ،

فيقولُ له: مَنْ أَنْت ؟

If [the person] was a friend of God, it [the embodiment of his deeds] would come to him as the most fragrant, greatest looking, and best adorned people.

It would say,

'Take glad tidings of ease, abundance, and a garden of bliss. Your entry [into paradise] shall be the best entry.'

He will say,

'Who are you?'

فيقول: أنَا عَملُكَ الصّالح ارْتَحَلَ من الدُّنيا إلى الجَنّةِ.

It will respond,

'I am your good deeds. Leave this world and proceeded to heaven.'

وإنه ليَعْرِف غَاسِله وينَاشِد حامِله أنْ يُعَجّله فإذَا أُدْخِلَ قبرَه أتَاهُ ملكا القبر يجُرّان أشعارَهما ويخدان الأرضَ بأقدامِها، أصواتُهما كالرعدِ القاصِف وأبصارُهما كالبرقِ الخاطِف فيقولان له: من ربُّك ؟ وما دينُك ؟ ومن نبيُّك ؟

Surely, he will know the one who will wash him. He will beseech the one who carries him [to the grave], telling him to make haste.

When he enters his grave, the two angels of the grave will come with the hair trailing, dragging their feet on the ground. Their voices will be like clapping thunder, and their eyes like blinding lightning.

They will ask him,

'Who is your Lord?

What is your religion?

Who is your prophet?'

فيقولُ: الله ربي وديني الاسلام، ونبيي محمد (صلى الله عليه وآله)،

فيقولان له: ثَبّتَكَ اللهُ فيما تُحِبُّ وَتَرْضَى، وَهُوَ قول الله عز وجل:

He will say,

'God is my Lord. Islam is my religion. Muhammad (sa) is my prophet.'

They will say to him,

'May God fortify you in whatever you wish and please.'

This is God Almighty's words,

يُثَبِّتُ ٱللَّهُ ٱلَّذِينَ ءَامَنُوا۟ بِٱلْقَوْلِ ٱلثَّابِتِ فِى ٱلْحَيَوٰةِ ٱلدُّنْيَا وَفِى ٱلْـَٔاخِرَةِ

'God fortifies those who have faith with a constant creed in the life of this world and in the Hereafter.'[277]

ثم يفسحان لَهُ في قَبرِهِ مَدّ بَصَرِهِ ثُمّ يَفْتَحانِ لَهُ بَاباً إلى الجَنَّةِ، ثم يقولان له: نَمْ قَرِيرَ العَيْنِ، نَوم الشابّ النَاعِمِ، فإنّ اللهَ عَزّ وَجَلّ يَقول:

[277] The Noble Quran, 14:27.

They will expand his grave for him past what his eyes could see. Then, they will open for him a door to paradise. They will say,

'Sleep soundly, like a young man. Surely, God Almighty says,

أَصْحَٰبُ ٱلْجَنَّةِ يَوْمَئِذٍ خَيْرٌ مُّسْتَقَرًّا وَأَحْسَنُ مَقِيلًا

"On that day the inhabitants of paradise will be in the best abode and an excellent resting place.[278]"'

وإن كان لربّه عَدُوّا فإنّه يَأتِيه أقْبَح مِن خلقَ الله زَيّا وَرُؤيا وَأنتنه رِيحاً فيقول لهُ:

أبشر بنزل من حميم وتصلية بجحيم، وإنه ليعرِف غاسِله وَينَاشِد حملته أن يحبسوه...

If he were an enemy of his Lord, he will be visited by the vilest of God's creation in dress, looks, and fragrance. It will say to him,

'Take [ill] tidings of a treat of boiling water and entry into hell.'

Surely, he will know the one who will wash him. He will beseech the one who carries him [to the grave], telling him to keep him [from being buried].

فإذا أُدْخِلَ القَبر أَتَاهُ ممتحنا القبرِ فَألقَيَا عَنْه أكفانه ثُمّ يقُولان له: مَنْ رَبّك وَمَا دينك؟ وَمَنْ نبيك؟ فيقول: لا أدري!

When he enters the grave, he will be visited by the two examiners of the grave. They will rip off his shroud and say,

'Who is your Lord?

What is your religion?

Who is your prophet?'

He will respond, 'I do not know.'

فيقولان: لا دَرَيت وَلا هديت، فَيضْرِبَان يَافُوخَه بمرزبة مَعَهُما ضَرْبَة مَا خَلَقَ الله عزّ وجلّ مِن

---

[278] The Noble Quran, 25:24.

دابة إلا وَتَذْعُرُ لَهَا مَا خَلا الثَّقَلَيْنِ ثم يُفْتَحَانِ لهُ باباً إلى النّار، ثم يقولان له: نم بشرِّ حال.

They will say,

'You did not know, nor were you guided!'

Then will they strike his skull with a great hammer.

The strike [is so horrible that] every creature of God Almighty is fearful of it, save for humankind and jinn-kind. They will open a door to hell and say,

'Sleep in the worst state.'

فيهِ مِن الضيقِ مثلَ مَا فيهِ القنا مِن الرّمحِ حَتّى أنّ دماغَه ليخرُجَ مِن بَيْنِ ظفرِهِ ولحمِهِ ويسلّط الله عليه حيّاة الأرضِ وعقاربها وَهَوامَّها فتنْهَشه حَتّى يبعثَه اللهُ مِنْ قبرِه وإنه لَيَتَمَنّى قيامَ السّاعةِ فيمَا هو فيهِ مِن الشّرِ.

He will be squeezed [tremendously], so that it seems that his brain is squeezed out of his fingertips. God will send the snakes, scorpions, and insects of the earth to devour him. It will be so until God resurrects him from his grave. All the while, he would wish the resurrection would come soon because of the evil he lives in.[279]

- What does the Imam (a) want to say?
- When a person wants to take any position, do they stop and think?
- Do they wonder?
- Will this undermine their hereafter?
- Will they be able to serve others through the position?

The Imam (a) gave us a clear standard. If this work does not benefit you in your resting place, then there is no good in it. He said,

إنَّمَا لَكَ مِنْ دُنْيَاكَ مَا أَصْلَحْتَ بِهِ مَثْوَاكَ...

---

[279] Al-Kulaynī, al-Kāfī, tradition #4708.

> *You should have from this world only that with which you can adorn your permanent abode.*

The important thing is that your work should serve your Hereafter!

This is the important work in this world. It is exactly what the Imam (a) did when he assumed the caliphate. He refused to sell his religion for any worldly benefit.

In one sermon, the Imam (a) mentions what he did when his brother ʿAqīl asked him for money from the treasury. The Imam (a) said,

واللهِ لَقَدْ رَأَيْتُ عَقِيلًا وَقَدْ أَمْلَقَ حَتَّى اسْتَمَاحَنِي مِنْ بُرِّكُمْ صَاعاً، وَرَأَيْتُ صِبْيَانَهُ شُعْثَ الشُّعُورِ، غُبْرَ الْأَلْوَانِ مِنْ فَقْرِهِمْ، كَأَنَّمَا سُوِّدَتْ وُجُوهُهُمْ بِالْعِظْلِمِ،

> *By God, I certainly saw [my brother] ʿAqīl fallen in destitution and he asked me a ṣāʿ [about three kilograms in weight] out of your [share of] wheat.*
>
> *I also saw his children with disheveled hair and a dusty countenance due to starvation, as though their faces had been painted with indigo.*

وَعَاوَدَنِي مُؤَكِّداً، وَكَرَّرَ عَلَيَّ الْقَوْلَ مُرَدِّداً، فَأَصْغَيْتُ إِلَيْهِ سَمْعِي، فَظَنَّ أَنِّي أَبِيعُهُ دِينِي، وَأَتَّبِعُ قِيَادَهُ مُفَارِقاً طَرِيقَتِي، فَأَحْمَيْتُ لَهُ حَدِيدَةً، ثُمَّ أَدْنَيْتُهَا مِنْ جِسْمِهِ لِيَعْتَبِرَ بِهَا، فَضَجَّ ضَجِيجَ ذِي دَنَفٍ مِنْ أَلَمِهَا، وَكَادَ أَنْ يَحْتَرِقَ مِنْ مِيسَمِهَا،

> *He came to me several times and repeated his request to me again and again.*
>
> *I heard him, and he thought I would sell my faith to him and follow his tread leaving my own way.*
>
> *I heated a piece of iron and took it near his body so that he might take a lesson from it.*
>
> *He cried as a person in protracted illness cries with pain and he was about to get burnt with its branding.*

فَقُلْتُ لَهُ: ثَكِلَتْكَ الثَّوَاكِلُ يَا عَقِيلُ! أَتَئِنُّ مِنْ حَدِيدَةٍ أَحْمَاهَا إِنْسَانُهَا لِلَعِبِهِ، وَتَجُرُّنِي إِلَى نَارٍ

سَجَرَهَا جَبَّارُهَا لِغَضَبِه! أَتَئِنُّ مِنَ الأَذَى ولَا أَئِنُّ مِنْ لَظَى ؟!

Then I said to him,

'May mourning women mourn you, O' ʿAqīl.

Do you cry on account of this [hot] iron which has been made by a man for fun while you are driving me towards the fire which God, the Powerful, has prepared for His wrath?

Should you cry from pain, but I should not cry from [fear of] the flames [of hellfire]?'

وأَعْجَبُ مِنْ ذَلِكَ طَارِقٌ طَرَقَنَا بِمَلْفُوفَةٍ فِي وِعَائِهَا، ومَعْجُونَةٍ شَنِئْتُهَا، كَأَنَّمَا عُجِنَتْ بِرِيقِ حَيَّةٍ أَوْ قَيْئِهَا، فَقُلْتُ: أَصِلَةٌ أَمْ زَكَاةٌ، أَمْ صَدَقَةٌ؟ فَذَلِكَ مُحَرَّمٌ عَلَيْنَا أَهْلَ الْبَيْتِ! فَقَالَ: لَا ذَا ولَا ذَاكَ، ولَكِنَّهَا هَدِيَّةٌ.

A stranger incident than this is that a man came to us in the night with a closed flask full of honey paste, but I disliked it as though it was the saliva of a serpent or its vomit.

I asked him whether it was a reward, zakat, or charity.

All these are forbidden to us members of the Prophet's (sa) family. He said it was neither this nor that but a present.

فَقُلْتُ هَبِلَتْكَ الْهَبُولُ! أَعَنْ دِينِ اللَّه أَتَيْتَنِي لِتَخْدَعَنِي؟ أَمُخْتَبِطٌ أَنْتَ أَمْ ذُو جِنَّةٍ، أَمْ تَهْجُرُ؟ واللَّه لَوْ أُعْطِيتُ الأَقَالِيمَ السَّبْعَةَ بِمَا تَحْتَ أَفْلَاكِهَا، عَلَى أَنْ أَعْصِيَ اللَّه فِي نَمْلَةٍ أَسْلُبُهَا جُلْبَ شَعِيرَةٍ مَا فَعَلْتُه،

I said,

'May grieving mothers grieve for you!

Have you come to deviate me from the religion of God?

Are you mad, possessed, or delusional?'

'By God, even if I am given all the domains of the seven (stars) with all that exists under the skies in order that I may disobey God to the

extent of snatching one grain of barley from an ant I would not do it.

وإِنَّ دُنْيَاكُمْ عِنْدِي لأَهْوَنُ مِنْ وَرَقَةٍ فِي فَمِ جَرَادَةٍ تَقْضَمُهَا. مَا لِعَلِيٍّ ولِنَعِيمٍ يَفْنَى، ولَذَّةٍ لَا تَبْقَى! نَعُوذُ بِاللهِ مِنْ سُبَاتِ الْعَقْلِ، وقُبْحِ الزَّلَلِ. وبِه نَسْتَعِينُ.

For me your world is lighter than the leaf in the mouth of a locust that is chewing it.

What has Ali to do with bounties that will pass away and pleasures that will not last?

We seek the protection of God from the slip of wisdom and the evils of mistakes, and from Him we seek succor.[280]

Grieving for What Passed

Again, the Imam (a) said,

إِنَّمَا لَكَ مِنْ دُنْيَاكَ مَا أَصْلَحْتَ بِه مَثْوَاكَ، وإِنْ كُنْتَ جَازِعاً عَلَى مَا تَفَلَّتَ مِنْ يَدَيْكَ، فَاجْزَعْ عَلَى كُلِّ مَا لَمْ يَصِلْ إِلَيْكَ.

You should have from this world only that with which you can adorn your permanent abode.

If you cry over what has gone out of your hands, then also cry for what has not at all come to you.[281]

Is anxiety a solution? Should I panic and stress over everything?

No, that is not a solution. It would only multiply your problems.

The Commander of the Faithful (a) visited al-Ashʿath ibn Qays to pay condolences for the passing of his brother ʿAbdu'l-Raḥmān. The Imam (a) said to al-Ashʿath,

[280] Al-Raḍī, *Nahj al-Balāghah*, Sermon 223.

[281] Al-Raḍī, *Nahj al-Balāghah*, Letter 31.

إن جزعت فحقّ الرحم أتَيْت، وَإنْ صَبْرت فحقّ الله أدَّيْت، عَلى أنّك إنْ صَبَرت جَرَى عَلَيْك القضَاء وَأَنْتَ مَحْمُود، وَإنْ جَزَعْتَ جَرَى عَلَيْك القَضَاء وَأَنْت مَذْمُوم

If you are to despair, then you have fulfilled the right of kinship. If you are patient, then you have fulfilled the right of God.

Yet, if you are patient, then [God's] judgement will be done and you will be praised [and rewarded by God].

If you despair, then [God's] judgement will be done and you will be blamed [and punished by God].

Al-Ash'ath said, "We belong to God and to Him we shall return."

The Imam (a) said,

أتَدْرِي مَا تَأْويلها؟

Do you know what it means?

Al-Ash'ath said, "No, but you are the greatest and deepest in knowledge [so please teach me]."

The Imam (a) said,

أمّا قَوْلك (إنّا لله) فَإقرارٌ بِالمُلك، وَأمّا قَوْلك (وإنّا إليهِ رَاجِعُون) فإقرار بالهلاك.

As for your saying, 'We belong to God,' it is submission to His ownership [over you].

As for your saying, 'To Him we shall return,' it is submission to death [as an inevitability].[282]

Do not forget that God Almighty says,

---

[282] Al-Burūjurdī, *Jāmi' Aḥādīth al-Shī'ah*, 3:494.

وَلَنَبْلُوَنَّكُم بِشَيْءٍ مِّنَ الْخَوْفِ وَالْجُوعِ وَنَقْصٍ مِّنَ الْأَمْوَالِ وَالْأَنفُسِ وَالثَّمَرَاتِ وَبَشِّرِ الصَّابِرِينَ

We will surely test you with a measure of fear and hunger and a loss of wealth, lives, and fruits; and give good news to the patient—

الَّذِينَ إِذَا أَصَابَتْهُم مُّصِيبَةٌ قَالُوا إِنَّا لِلَّهِ وَإِنَّا إِلَيْهِ رَاجِعُونَ

those who, when an affliction visits them, say, 'Indeed we belong to God and to Him do we indeed return.'

أُولَٰئِكَ عَلَيْهِمْ صَلَوَاتٌ مِّن رَّبِّهِمْ وَرَحْمَةٌ وَأُولَٰئِكَ هُمُ الْمُهْتَدُونَ

It is they who receive the blessings of their Lord and [His] mercy, and it is they who are the [rightly] guided.[283]

Fear, hunger, loss of wealth, and death of loved ones… God reminds us and says,

> "Give good news to the patient."

Those who are patient have a sign, and it is if a calamity befalls them, they say,

> "We belong to God and to Him we shall return."

Protection from Tribulation

Ask God Almighty! Confess to Him!

We have all failed when faced with these trials. Let us beg Him to safeguard us from such tribulations. Pray to Him. Turn to Him.

Some may object to such a supplication, saying that this is not correct

---

[283] The Noble Quran, 2:155-57.

or reasonable!

I say with God, this is surely possible.

There is a chapter in the book of *al-Kāfi*[284] titled, "Those who are protected from tribulation."

In one tradition, Imam al-Bāqir (a) said,

إنّ لله عزّ وجلّ ضَنَائِنٌ يَضُنّ بِهم عَنِ البَلَاء فَيُحْيِيهم فِي عَافِيَة ويرزُقُهم في عافيةٍ وَيُمِيتُهم في عافِيَة وَيَبْعَثُهم فِي عَافيه وَيُسْكِنُهم الجنّة في عَافِيَة.

God Almighty has wards which he safeguards from tribulation. He allows them to live soundly, He blesses them soundly, and makes them die soundly.

He will resurrect them soundly and allow them to live in paradise soundly.[285]

Imam al-Ṣādiq (a) also said,

إنّ الله عزّ وجلّ خلق خلقاً ضنّ بهم عن البَلَاء خَلَقهم في عَافِية، وَأَحْيَاهُم في عافِية، وَأَمَاتَهُم في عافِية، وَأَدْخَلَهُم الجنّة في عَافِيَة.

God Almighty created some creatures which He safeguards from tribulation.

He created them soundly, allowed them to live soundly, made them die soundly, and allowed them to enter paradise soundly.[286]

---

[284] Kitab al-Kāfi is an extensive collection of hadiths within Twelver Shia Islam, meticulously compiled by Shaykh Muhammad ibn Ya'qub al-Kulayni, or Shaykh al-Kulayni for short. Its contents are thoughtfully organized into three distinct sections: Uṣūl al-Kāfi, matters of epistemology, theology, history, ethics, supplication, and the interpretation of the Qur'ān; Furū' al-Kāfi, dedicated to practical and legal issues; and Rawdat (or Rauda) al-Kāfi, a repository of miscellaneous traditions that includes lengthy letters and speeches handed down which delves into from the revered Imāms. This comprehensive compilation consists of 16,199 narrations, making it an invaluable resource for scholars and practitioners of the faith.

[285] Al-Kulaynī, *al-Kāfi*, 2:462.

[286] Ibid.

He also said,

إنّ لله عزّ وجلّ ضنائنٌ من خَلقِه يغذوهُم بنِعْمَتِه، وَيَحْبُوهُم بعافِيتِه، وَيُدْخِلهم الجنّة بِرَحْمَتِه، تمُرُّ بهم البَلَايَا وَالفتن لا تَضُرُّهُم شَيْئاً.

> *God Almighty has wards from amongst His creatures which He maintains with His blessings, favors with wellness from Him, and allows them to enter paradise by His mercy.*
>
> *Tribulations and strife pass over them without harming them in the least.*[287]

I ask God Almighty to protect us from every tribulation in this world and the hereafter!

[287] Ibid.

The Twelfth Imam (a)

Some people question the origin of the idea of the Twelfth Imam (a) and his existence.

Is it possible to shed light on this idea?

This question can be broken into two potential questions about the Imam (a).

- First, there are those who question the idea in its entirety. A person may say that Imam al-Mahdī (a) was not born and will not be born. They refuse the idea that he will appear at the end of time, and that the world will be reformed at his hands.
- Second, there are those who accept the idea of Imam al-Mahdī (a) in general. However, they claim that he was not born yet and will be born towards the end-times. So, while the idea of a promised savior is true, a person with the title of Imam al-Mahdī (a) has not been realized yet.

Let us take the first type of skepticism, i.e., skepticism about the idea of a promised savior in its entirety. In response, we say that Muslims are virtually unanimous in agreement on the idea's validity.

Shia and Sunnis unanimously agree that at the end of time a man will appear at whose blessed hands the world will be reformed. This has been indicated by many verses and narrations.

Verses Regarding al-Mahdī (a)

There are five or six verses that present the idea of al-Mahdī (a) explicitly. These verses do not need interpretation by the Ahl al-Bayt (a), as they are apparent by themselves. This includes God's words,

يُرِيدُونَ لِيُطْفِئُوا نُورَ اللَّهِ بِأَفْوَاهِهِمْ وَاللَّهُ مُتِمُّ نُورِهِ وَلَوْ كَرِهَ الْكَافِرُونَ

They desire to put out the light of God with their mouths, but God will perfect His light though the faithless should be averse.[288]

The light of God is Islam, and God perfects His light!

This is a message from God Almighty that His light will be perfected and spread over the entirety of the earth. This has not been achieved yet.

Of course, it is not possible that God Almighty would say anything that is contrary to reality. The spread of His light must be achieved one day. It is not possible to achieve it except at the hands of this reformer: the Imam (a). This verse is apparent within itself, without the need for a narration to interpret it.

God also says,

وَلَقَدْ كَتَبْنَا فِي الزَّبُورِ مِن بَعْدِ الذِّكْرِ أَنَّ الْأَرْضَ يَرِثُهَا عِبَادِيَ الصَّالِحُونَ

Certainly We wrote in the Psalms, after the Torah: 'Indeed My righteous servants shall inherit the earth.'[289]

The reference to the earth here means the entirety of the planet. To this day, the entirety of the earth has not been inherited by God's righteous servants. This must be achieved at some point in the future. It is not possible to achieve this except at the hands of Imam al-Mahdī (a).

---

[288] The Noble Quran, 61:8.

[289] The Noble Quran, 21:105.

These two verses confirm the idea of al-Mahdī (a).

However, these verses do not confirm that this person was born and is present now. The two verses indicate that this dream and promise will come true one day. Sure, the earth will be inherited by God's righteous servants, but it is still possible that the Imam is not born yet and will be born in the future.

Such verses do not prove the birth of Imam al-Mahdī (a), and that he is in a state of *ghaybah* (occultation).

Narrations Regarding al-Mahdī (a)

There are numerous narrations about the promised savior, and that al-Mahdī will fulfill this promise at the end of time. Even if we disregard the narrations which speak specifically about his birth, there are many others that confirm the idea generally. These narrations are accepted by Twelver Shia as well as Muslims of all other sects.

In fact, Muslim scholars of all sects have authored books in which they compiled narrations on the subject. These narrations confirm the emergence of a person at the end of time in the name of al-Mahdī (a). I have personally seen more than thirty books from scholars of other schools of thought on this issue.

For example, the Prophet (sa) is narrated to have said,

لا تَذْهَبُ الدُّنْيَا، حَتَّى يَمْلِكَ الْعَرَبَ رَجُلٌ مِنْ أَهْلِ بَيْتِي، يُوَاطِئُ اسْمُهُ اسْمِي.

> *The world will not cease until Arabs are led by a man from my household whose name shall be my name.*[290]

Another tradition states,

لا تقومُ السّاعَةُ حَتَى تملأ الأرضُ ظُلْماً وَجوراً وَعدوَاناً ثُمّ يَخْرُجُ مِنْ آهلِ بَيْتِي مَنْ يَمْلَأهَا قِسْطَاً

---

[290] Ibn Ḥanbal, *Musnad Aḥmad*, 1:377, tradition #3563.

وَعَدْلاً كَمَا مُلِئَتْ ظُلْماً وَجوراً.

The [Final] Hour will not be until the earth is filled with oppression, transgression, and aggression.

Then, a member of my household will emerge who will fill it with equity and justice just as it was filled with oppression and transgression.[291]

There are many other narrations in this vein.

These narrations have been accepted by scholars from other schools as well. That includes Ibn Taymiyyah and Ibn Ḥajar, who accepted these narrations, as well as this idea in general. In more recent times, ʿAbd al-ʿAzīz ibn Bāz has accepted them as well. He stated in an article that this idea is correct, and the narrations regarding it are true and undeniable.

Therefore, Muslims in general have accepted the idea of al-Mahdī (a), in accordance with the verses and narrations on the topic.

If there is anyone who denies the idea, then they are very rare. Examples include Ibn Khaldun and Abū Zuhrah. Muhammad Rashīd Riḍā in his book *Tafsīr al-Manār* says, "The narrations are weak." Of course, simply claiming that narrations are weak is insufficient to disprove a concept unanimously agreed upon by Muslims and supported by a great deal of evidence.

In any case, the general idea of al-Mahdī (a), and that he will realize the divine promise for the end of times, is accepted by most Muslims with very rare exceptions.

---

[291] Ibid, 3:36, tradition #10920.

Imam al-Mahdī (a) and the Seminary

What is the proposed mechanism for strengthening the relationship between the seminary and the Awaited Imam (a)?

If all of the believers have a degree of attachment and relationship to the Awaited Imam (a), then that degree must be stronger in us – in the students and professors of the seminary. We believe that we are his representatives in some sense. We believe that we are the 'narrators of the traditions of Ahl al-Bayt (a)' whom he had instructed his followers to refer to during his occultation. That is why we live the idea of Imam al-Mahdī (a) more keenly and throughout our lives.

All the believers acknowledge the sublime stations of their Imam (a). We, in the seminary, believe that one of those sublime stations for him is the station of oversight over all of our actions and behaviors.

All the believers live in a state of intense longing to meet and talk with the blessed Imam (a). We in the seminary are more eager.

Who does not yearn to see that radiant light?

But, longing alone does not achieve this goal. It must be accompanied by honest work and good behavior. Taking a step towards God with our actions brings us closer to seeing that shining sun.

All believers need the supplication of the Imam (a). We are in greater need of it. Our intellectual and religious path needs guidance and support. The best way to obtain that is through the supplications of our Imam (a). However, we will lose the benefit of those supplications if we stray away from the path of righteousness and Godwariness.

We must all direct our efforts to ward off misconceptions that arise about our Twelfth Imam (a) and his occultation. These misconceptions have been around since the beginning of the era of occultation. Early scholars like al-Ṣadūq[292], al-Mufīd[293], and al-Ṭūsī[294] authored books answering such misconceptions.

Today, we must bear the burdens of this mission. We must preserve the trust and deliver it to future generations safely, as it was delivered safely to us. If we want success in our lives, we must not forget to pray for the safety of our Imam (a) and for the hastening of his reemergence. We must chant with our tongues and our hearts every Friday – no, every day – raising our hands in supplication:

أَيْنَ السَّبَبُ الْمُتَّصِلُ بَيْنَ الأَرْضِ وَالسَّماءِ ؟

أَيْنَ صاحِبُ يَوْمِ الْفَتْحِ وَناشِرُ رايَةِ الْهُدى ؟

أَيْنَ مُؤَلِّفُ شَمْلِ الصَّلاحِ وَالرِّضا ؟

---

292 Shaykh al-Ṣadūq, also known as Sheikh Abu Ja'far Muhammad ibn Babawayh al-Qummi, was a prominent Shia Islamic scholar of the 10th century. He was born in Qom, Iran, and studied in Baghdad under renowned Shia scholars. His notable works include "Kitab al-Khisal," which focuses on ethical and theological teachings, and "Man La Yahduruhu al-Faqih," a compilation of hadith on Islamic jurisprudence. Shaykh al-Saduq played a vital role in preserving and transmitting Shia traditions during a challenging period for the Shia community, and his works continue to be respected in Shia scholarship today.

293 Shaykh al-Mufid was a renowned 10th century Shia Islamic scholar born in Kufa, Iraq. He made significant contributions to various fields of Islamic knowledge, including theology, jurisprudence, and hadith studies. He studied under prominent Shia scholars and authored important works such as "Kitab al-Irshad" and "Kitab al-Jami." Shaykh al-Mufid played a crucial role in shaping Twelver Shia theology and jurisprudence, defending and propagating Shia beliefs during a challenging period for Shia Muslims. His contributions have had a lasting impact on Shia Islamic scholarship.

294 Shaykh al-Tusi, also known as *Sheikh al-Ta'ifah* (translates to the Head of the School of Thought), was a prominent Twelver Shia scholar born in 995 CE in Tus, Iran. One of his major accomplishments was establishing the Hawza of Najaf in Iraq which has survived over a millennium. Shaykh al-Tusi authored important works on theology, jurisprudence, ethics, and compiled collections of hadiths, such as "*Al-Tahdhib*" and "*Al-Istibsar*," which remain essential references for Shia scholars. He defended and promoted Twelver Shia beliefs through debates and writings, earning the title "Sheikh al-Ta'ifah." His contributions had a lasting impact on Twelver Shia Islam, and he passed away in 1067 CE in Najaf, leaving behind a significant scholarly legacy.

أَيْنَ الطَّالِبُ بِذُحُولِ الأَنْبِياءِ وَأَبْناءِ الأَنْبِياءِ؟

Where is the means that is connected between the earth and the heavens?

Where is the patron of the Day of Victory and the carrier of the standard of guidance?

Where is the one reunifying the dispersed parts of uprightness and contentment?

Where is the one demanding vengeance for the Prophets and their sons?[295]

We must send salutations to him and recite his visitation:

السَّلامُ عَلَيْكَ حِينَ تَقُومُ السَّلامُ عَلَيْكَ حِيْنَ تَقْعُدُ السَّلامُ عَلَيْكَ حِينَ تَقْرَأُ وَتُبَيِّنُ السَّلامُ عَلَيْكَ حِينَ تُصَلِّيَ وَتَقْنُتُ السَّلامُ عَلَيْكَ حِينَ تَرْكَعُ وَتَسْجُدُ

Peace be upon you whenever you stand.

Peace be upon you whenever you sit.

Peace be upon you whenever you recite and elucidate.

Peace be upon you whenever you offer prayer and supplicate. Peace be upon you whenever you genuflect and prostrate.

السَّلامُ عَلَيْكَ حِينَ تُهَلِّلُ وَتُكَبِّرُ السَّلامُ عَلَيْكَ حِينَ تَحْمَدُ وَتَسْتَغْفِرُ السَّلامُ عَلَيْكَ حِينَ تُصْبِحُ وَتُمْسِي السَّلامُ عَلَيْكَ فِي اللَّيْلِ إِذا يَغْشى وَالنَّهارِ إِذا تَجَلّى

Peace be upon you whenever you profess God's unicity and profess His All-greatness.

Peace be upon you whenever you praise God and implore His forgiveness.

Peace be upon you whenever you begin and end your day.

---

[295] Du'ā' al-Nudbah.

> *Peace be upon you in the night when it draws a veil and the day when it shines in brightness.*[296]

We must hold seminars and forums to talk about the Imam's (a) blessed existence and everything related to it. We must teach people about this, and in turn, we will grow closer to him.

The Death of the Age of Ignorance

The Prophet (sa) said, "Whoever dies without knowing the Imam of his time dies the death of the Age of Ignorance."

This clearly indicates that there is a living Imam for every era. Otherwise, God would not command us to know him. However, some people ask for evidence of the existence and birth of the Imam (a). Others ask about the wisdom behind having an Imam who is absent and inaccessible.

How can we respond to these questions?

Here we recall the saying of the Imams (a), who described the benefit achieved by the presence of the Awaited Imam (a) as the benefits of the sun behind the clouds. Even if a cloud prevents the sun from being seen, it is not devoid of benefit. No one can deny that.

There is a wealth of narrations mentioned in the books of hadith which confirm the Imam's (a) presence. The narrations also state if the Imam (a) is removed from the earth, it would implode with everything on it. His presence is peace and safety for the earth. The Prophet (sa) said,

النُّجُومُ أَمَانٌ لِأَهْلِ السَّمَاءِ وأَهْلُ بَيْتِي أَمَانٌ لِأُمَّتِي.

> *The stars are a safety to the denizens of the heavens, and my*

---

[296] Ziyārat Āl Yāsīn.

household are a safety for the people of the earth.[297]

This statement has roots in the Noble Quran. God Almighty says,

وَمَا كَانَ اللَّهُ لِيُعَذِّبَهُمْ وَأَنتَ فِيهِمْ وَمَا كَانَ اللَّهُ مُعَذِّبَهُمْ وَهُمْ يَسْتَغْفِرُونَ

But God will not punish them while you are in their midst, nor will God punish them while they plead for forgiveness.[298]

The presence of the Prophet (sa) prevents humanity from being punished and tormented. Just as this is the case in the presence of the Prophet (sa), it is also the case for his progeny. They are a haven against divine wrath and torment.

Our Behavior and Knowing the Imam

How does believing in Imam al-Mahdī (a) affect our behavior?

That is in the concept of *intiẓār al-faraj*, or 'waiting for relief.' The concept of waiting refers to actual preparation through serious and righteous work. It is preparing the appropriate atmosphere for the reappearance of our Imam (a). That includes paying charity on his behalf and praying for him. As we read in the well-known supplication:

اللّهُمَّ عَرِّفْنِي نَفْسَكَ فَإِنَّكَ إِنْ لَمْ تُعَرِّفْنِي نَفْسَكَ لَمْ أَعْرِفْ رَسُولَكَ، اللّهُمَّ عَرِّفْنِي رَسُولَكَ فَإِنَّكَ إِنْ لَمْ تُعَرِّفْنِي رَسُولَكَ لَمْ أَعْرِفْ حُجَّتَكَ،

O' God, allow me to know You, for if You do not allow me to know You, I shall not know Your Prophet (sa).

O' God, allow me to know Your Prophet (sa), for if You do not allow

[297] Al-Majlisī, *Biḥār al-Anwār*, 27:309.

[298] The Noble Quran, 8:33.

me to know Your Prophet (sa), I shall not know Your proof [the Imam of the Time].

اللَّهُمَّ عَرِّفْنِي حُجَّتَكَ فَإِنَّكَ إِنْ لَمْ تُعَرِّفْنِي حُجَّتَكَ ضَلَلْتُ عَنْ دِينِي، اللَّهُمَّ لا تُمِتْنِي مِيتَةً جاهِلِيَّةً وَلا تُزِغْ قَلْبِي بَعْدَ إِذْ هَدَيْتَنِي.

O' God, allow me to know Your proof, for if You do not allow me to know Your proof, I shall be misguided away from my religion.

O' God do not allow me to die the death of the Age of Ignorance, and do not make my heart sway after You have guided me.[299]

We should pray for him at the beginning of every morning. Imam al-Ṣādiq (a) taught the following supplication for the time of occultation:

اللَّهُمَّ كُنْ لِوَلِيِّكَ الْحُجَّةِ بْنِ الْحَسَنِ صَلَواتُكَ عَلَيْهِ وَعَلى آبائِهِ فِي هذِهِ السَّاعَةِ وَفِي كُلِّ ساعَةٍ وَلِيّاً وَحافِظاً وَقائِداً وَناصِراً وَدَلِيلاً وَعَيْناً حَتَّى تُسْكِنَهُ أَرْضَكَ طَوْعاً وَتُمَتِّعَهُ فِيها طَوِيلاً.

O' God, be for Your representative, the Hujjah [proof], son of al-Ḥasan, Your blessings be on him and his forefathers, in this hour and in every hour, a guardian, a protector, a leader, a helper, a proof, and an eye, until You make him live on the earth in obedience [to You] and cause him to live in it for a long time.[300]

Advice for the Followers of the Imam

We thirst for advice that draws us closer to the Imam of our time. Can you share some specific advice with us?

The Commander of the Faithful (a) said,

فَانْظُرُوا أَهْلَ بَيْتِ نَبِيِّكُمْ فَإِنْ لَبَدُوا فَالْبُدُوا، وَإِنِ اسْتَنْصَرُوكُمْ فَانْصُرُوهُمْ، فَلَيُفَرِّجَنَّ اللَّهُ بَغْتَةً بِرَجُلٍ مِنَّا أَهْلَ الْبَيْتِ.

---

[299] Supplication for the time of ghaybah (occultation).

[300] Supplication for the Twelfth Imam (a).

Look towards the household of your Prophet (sa).

If they stay, stay as well.

If they ask for your aid, aid them. Surely, God will bring sudden relief through a man from us, the Ahl al-Bayt.[301]

The case of our Awaited Imam (a) is a test for Muslims and all people. Some denied it entirely, and some accepted it and tried to benefit from it in one way or another. Some claimed to have a special association with the Imam (a), such as being a proxy or designated representative.

Shaykh al-Ṭūsī mentions in his book *al-Ghaybah*[302] a number of those who falsely claimed to represent the Imam (a). Some were even rebuked in signed letters that were sent by the Imam (a) to his Four Ambassadors[303]. Some more recent claimants were able to gather supporters and followers, such as Mirzā Ali Muhammad Riḍā al-Shīrāzī ("*the Báb*").[304]

Regrettably, this trend of false claims has persisted throughout history

---

[301] Al-Majlisī, *Biḥār al-Anwār*, 59:121.

[302] Kitab al-Ghaybah, or "The Book of Occultation", is the title of a book about the occultation of Imam al-Mahdi (a) written by Shaykh al-Tusi. This book is considered among some of the important references in learning about Imam al-Mahdi (a) and his occultation. It has offered the view of Shi'a about Imam al-Mahdi (a) and has answered questions posed about his occultation using evidence-based approaches from the Quran, hadiths and reason.

[303] The Four Ambassadors of Imam Mahdi (also known as the Four Deputies or Four Special Representatives) is significant in Twelver Shia Islam. These four individuals played a crucial role in representing and conveying the messages of Imam Mahdi (a) to the Shia community during his Minor Occultation (874–941 CE), a period when he was not directly accessible to his followers after the martyrdom of his father Imam Hassan al-Askari (846 – 874 CE). They were 'Uthmān ibn Sa'īd al-'Amrī, Muhammad ibn 'Uthmān al-'Amrī, al-Ḥusayn ibn Rūḥ al-Nūbakhtī, and Ali ibn Muhammad al-Samarī.

[304] The Báb, born Ali Muhammad Riḍā al-Shīrāzī, (1819 – 1850 CE) was a figure whose life became intertwined with the emergence of Bábism and the Bahá'í Faith. Born in Shiraz in Qajar Iran, he made a bold assertion in 1844, at the age of 25, by proclaiming himself a messenger of God. Referred to by his followers as "the Báb", a term meaning "Gate" or "Door" in Arabic, he positioned himself as the deputy of the Hidden Imam, challenging established Islamic laws and traditions. His teachings gave rise to a millenarian movement and proposed the establishment of an entirely new religion.

and will likely continue. People will continue to make unfounded assertions, and some individuals will be swayed by these falsehoods. Understanding this historical reality, a true believer should not be taken aback by contemporary occurrences.

For example, one of the followers of the Báb was a woman called Qurrat al-ʿAyn. She was an eloquent preacher, even having followers in the city of Karbala. This matter happened 200 or 300 years ago. She was the niece of Shaykh Muhammad Taqī al-Bāthiqī, one of the scholars of Kermanshah[305]. One day at dawn, while the sheikh was going to pray in the mosque, this woman stood in front of her uncle and gathered her followers to attack. They brutally murdered him at her request.

The Báb did not only claim to be the actual gateway to the Imam, but he proceeded to escalate his assertions. His audacious claims extended to proclaiming prophethood and even compiling his own scripture. Shockingly, he went so far as to assert his divinity, as some have reported.

These historical accounts serve as a poignant reminder and raise critical issues that merit our consideration. Let us address these issues individually.

First: Don't Rush

Do not rush to align with those who claim to be related in one way or another to our Imam (a). God Almighty has given us a intellect, so let us use it. Many claims are made, we must be rational and wise in judging them.

For example, when I was living in the holy city of Qom, Iran, an individual began to make some of these claims. Some people believed him despite their claim that they were wise and learned.

We all love our Twelfth Imam (a), may we be sacrificed for him. But

[305] Kermanshah, is the capital of Kermanshah Province, located 525 kilometers from Tehran in the western part of Iran.

this love does not mean that we should believe anyone that claims to be associated with him. We must use our intellects, with which God Almighty has blessed us with.

Second: Be Careful

Signs of the reappearance of our Imam (a) have been mentioned in various books. You should not rush to apply these signs. Do not say this sign applies to such-and-such. Do not say *al-Sufyānī*[306] is so-and-so, al-Ḥasanī[307] is so-and-so, and that sign means this or that.

This is not the appropriate way to understand and apply those traditions. The seminary teaches us to have accuracy and depth in our approach. We say this might be the interpretation of these signs. However, we cannot be certain. Their true application could be something in the future.

Some narrations mention that at the time of the Imam's (a) reemergence, or shortly before that, people in the west will be able to see those in the east, and vice versa. What does this mean? Someone may come and say that this applies to smartphones and modern telecommunications technologies.

We cannot say for certain whether it is the true interpretation. Instead, we say this is a possible interpretation.

Do not say, "I am sure." A new future technology may come that applies more accurately and clearly. We cannot predict the future!

Did we believe this was possible before? Did we believe a person on one side of the world could see and speak to someone on the other side?

---

306 The term "al-Sufyānī " is associated with Islamic eschatology, primarily in Twelver Shia Islam. It refers to a tyrannical leader who is prophesied to emerge before the return of Imam al-Mahdi (a). The Sufyānī is seen as an oppressive figure associated with chaos and corruption, and his rise is considered a sign of the impending reappearance of Imam al-Mahdi, who will ultimately defeat him and establish justice.

307 The term "al-Hasani" is associated with Islamic eschatology, in Twelver Shia Islam, and is in reference to one of the righteous figures and supporters of Imam al-Mahdi (a).

Again, we cannot apply these signs with certainty. We can only recognize possibilities.

This is the primary principle in these matters.

Third: Be Patient

Do not attempt to predict a time for the reemergence of the Imam (a). Do not say he will appear in the next year or in seven years. Where did you come up with that? Who told you that this is true? Who said that the Imam (a) will definitely appear in the next year? Who said he will appear in a month? Who said he would *not* appear in a month?

This is something that only God Almighty knows.

It is possible that he will emerge tomorrow, in a year, or in 100 years. Those are all possibilities. There is no certainty! Therefore, do not be one of the false predictors and timers. This is not rationally sound and does not have any religious justification.

Fourth: Don't Waste Time

Do not be too preoccupied with the signs and timing of the Imam's (a) reemergence. Islam did not attach much importance to these matters. Focus on scientific issues that entail a more general and comprehensive benefit to humankind. Addressing those issues generally is no problem, but do not be overly preoccupied with them.

Let us remember that our Imam (a) is aware of everything we do. We must do what pleases him and should not hurt him with our actions. Let us educate people about these issues. Trying to interpret signs and predict times is a futile endeavor. Do not waste your time on that. Instead, focus on nurturing your relationship with the Imam (a). Nurture people's relationships with the Twelfth Imam (a). That is a worthy endeavor.

Afterword

A Journey of Faith and Understanding

Our voyage through the pages of this book should be more than an intellectual endeavor; it should be a profoundly transformative experience, marked by and through our deep love and adoration for the Ahl al-Bayt. As we reflect upon the vast wealth of knowledge and wisdom we've encountered, we find ourselves compelled to delve even deeper into the profound lessons we've learned and explore their potential impact on our lives.

Tawhid and the Oneness of God

At the core of Shia Islam lies the profound concept of Tawhid, the belief in the Oneness of God—a belief deeply cherished and articulated by the Ahl al-Bayt. This transcendent monotheism extends its reach beyond religious boundaries, inviting all individuals, regardless of their faith tradition, to contemplate the existence of a Higher Power. The Ahl al-Bayt, through their unwavering devotion to God, remind us that in a world often marred by division and conflict, there exists a unifying force that connects us all.

Moral Virtues and Ethical Living

Our exploration of moral virtues and ethical principles within Shia Islam has illuminated the universal significance of qualities such as honesty, kindness, and integrity—virtues personified by the Ahl al-Bayt. These virtues serve as a shared moral compass for humanity, transcending the confines of religious and cultural differences. By striving to embody these virtues, we align ourselves with the noble examples set by the Ahl al-Bayt, thereby contributing to a world marked by greater harmony and compassion.

Interconnectedness of Faith and Action

The teachings of Shia Islam, as exemplified by the Ahl al-Bayt, underline the inseparable bond between faith and action. Faith, in this context, extends beyond mere belief; it becomes a catalyst for positive change in our world. Whether it manifests through acts of charity, kindness towards others, or the pursuit of justice, the principles we've encountered remind us that our faith should naturally translate into meaningful action—actions that mirror the profound devotion of the Ahl al-Bayt.

Enjoining Good and Forbidding Evil

The duty of enjoining good and forbidding evil, a central theme we've explored, carries far-reaching implications, echoing the unwavering commitment of the Ahl al-Bayt to righteousness. It underscores the shared responsibility we all carry in promoting moral excellence and confronting wrongdoing. As we stand alongside the Ahl al-Bayt in speaking out against injustice and actively striving to enhance our world, we become agents of positive transformation in society.

The Personal Relationship with the Divine

Our journey has placed a spotlight on the deeply personal nature of one's relationship with the Divine, a relationship that the Ahl al-Bayt cherished and nurtured. Our faith helps us harbor the innate capacity for spirituality and a profound connection with God—connections that the Ahl al-Bayt, through their prayers and devotion, have vividly demonstrated. Whether it is through prayers, supplications, or moments of reflection, we are all capable of seeking a deeper understanding of our purpose and our place within the grand tapestry of the universe, inspired by the unwavering faith of the Ahl al-Bayt.

Diversity, Community and Understanding

Among the many remarkable facets of Shia Islam that we've uncovered, the emphasis on community amidst diversity shines particularly bright, guided by the radiant examples set by the Ahl al-Bayt. Within the tapestry of Shia tradition, we discover a rich interplay of cultural, ethnic, and linguistic diversity. Yet, it is the common thread of faith and devotion, nurtured and exemplified by the Ahl al-Bayt, that binds Shia Muslims together, reminding us that diversity need not be a source of division; instead, it can be a wellspring of strength. This community is founded upon shared beliefs and values, bestowed upon us through the profound teachings of the Ahl al-Bayt.

In a world marked by divisions and misunderstandings, our exploration of Shia Islam, guided by the love and respect we hold for the Ahl al-Bayt, beckons us to community and understanding. It serves as a compelling reminder that through the pursuit of knowledge about different faith traditions and engaging in open dialogue, we have the power to bridge gaps and construct pathways to mutual respect and cooperation.

Continuing the Journey

Our voyage through the pages of this book marks the inception of a lifelong quest, one that we embark upon with the love and guidance of the Ahl al-Bayt. The wisdom and insights we've garnered are not meant to stagnate; they are a source of inspiration for continued exploration, learning, and personal growth. The pursuit of knowledge, empathy, and spiritual enrichment is an ongoing process, accessible to all who seek it, fueled by the unwavering love and devotion to the Ahl al-Bayt.

As we conclude this chapter of our exploration, let us carry the invaluable lessons we've learned into our daily lives, inspired by the love and reverence we hold for the Ahl al-Bayt. May we become active agents of positive change, beacons of compassion, and unwavering seekers of truth, all in the radiant spirit of the Ahl al-Bayt.

May this journey stand as a testament to the enduring power of faith, understanding, and the shared quest for a deeper connection with the Divine—a quest that the Ahl al-Bayt have immaculately shown. Let us, in community and tolerance, persist in seeking common ground, nurturing empathy, and collaboratively working towards a world where respect, love, and compassion reign supreme.

The voyage of faith and understanding, guided by our profound love for the Ahl al-Bayt, is an infinite one, and together as a community of faithful seekers, we shall continue to explore its limitless depths.

Select Bibliography

The Noble Quran.

Abī Dawūd, Sulaymān ibn al-Ash'ath. *Sunan Abī Dawūd*. Dār al-Risālah (2009).

Aḥmad al-Najāshī. *Rijāl al-Najāshī*. Qom: Jamā'at al-Mudarrisīn (1416 AH).

Al-'Āmilī, Muḥammad ibn al-Ḥasan. *Wasā'il al-Shī'ah*. Qum: Mu'assasat Ahl al-Bayt, 1414/1993.

Al-'Asqalānī, Aḥmad ibn 'Alī ibn Ḥajar. *Fatḥ al-Bārī*. Dār al-Risālah (2013).

Al-Baghdādī, Abū Bakr. *Tarīkh Baghdād*. Beirut: Dār al-Kutub al-'Ilmiyyah (2004).

Al-Bukhārī, Muhammad ibn Ismā'īl. *Ṣaḥīḥ al-Bukhārī*. Beirut: Dār al-Fikr (1st edition, 1411 AH).

Al-Dārimī, 'Abdu'l-lāh. *Sunan al-Dārimī*. Dār al-Mughnī (2000).

Al-Dhahabī, Muhammad ibn Aḥmad. *Tadhkirat al-Ḥuffāẓ*.

Al-Haytamī, Aḥmad ibn Ḥajar. *Al-Ṣawā'iq al-Muḥriqah*. Maktabat Fayyāḍ (2008).

Al-Kulaynī, Muḥammad ibn Ya'qūb. *Al-Kāfī*, ed. 'Alī-Akbar Ghaffārī, 8 vols. Tehran: Dār al-Kutub al-Islāmiyyah, 1388 Sh/2009.

Al-Majlisī, Muḥammad Bāqir. *Biḥār al-Anwār*. 110 vols. Beirut: Mu'assasat al-Wafā', 1983.

Al-Naysābūrī, Muslim ibn al-Ḥajjāj. *Ṣaḥīḥ Muslim*. Beirut: Dār al-Fikr.

Al-Nīsābūrī, Muhammad ibn 'Abdul-lāh. *Al-Mustadrak*. Beirut: Dār al-Kutub al-'Ilmiyyah (2004).

Al-Qummī, 'Abbās. *Mafātīḥ al-Jinān*. Beirut: Dār al-Aḍwā', 2014.

Al-Raḍī, al-Sharīf Muḥammad ibn al-Ḥusayn. *Nahj al-Balāghah*. Beirut: Dār al-Ma'rifah.

Al-Ṭabarī, Muḥammad ibn Jarīr. *Tārīkh al-Rusul wa 'l-Umam wa 'l-Mulūk [Tārīkh al-Ṭabarī]*, ed. Muḥammad Abū'l-Faḍl Ibrāhīm, 10 vols. Cairo: Dār al-Ma'ārif, 1960.

Al-Tirmidhī, Muhammad ibn 'Īsā. *Al-Jāmi' al-Kabīr [Sunan al-Tirmidhī]*. Beirut: Dār al-Gharb al-Islāmī.

Amīn, Aḥmad. *Fajr al-Islām*. Mu'assasat al-Hindawī (2018).

Ibn Ḥanbal, Aḥmad. *Musnad Aḥmad*. Mu'assasat al-Risālah.

Ibn Sa'd, Muhammad. *Al-Ṭabaqāt al-Kubrā*. Beirut: Dār Ṣādir.

Author Biography

Haidar Bahreluloom

Sayyid Haidar Bahreluloom is a strategist, lecturer, and public intellectual.

His studies under the tutelage of the professors of the Islamic Seminary in the Holy City of Najaf, and his lectures in communities across the globe, have ranged across theology, jurisprudence, philosophy, ethics, and community development.

In addition to serving as an advisor and trustee of The Mainstay Foundation, Sayyid Bahreluloom is a strategy consultant at a research and advisory firm.

www.ingramcontent.com/pod-product-compliance
Lightning Source LLC
Chambersburg PA
CBHW052103280426
43673CB00083B/435/J
* 9 7 8 1 9 4 3 3 9 3 1 5 2 *